Affordable HOUSES

300 Modest Plans for Savvy Homebuyers

HOME PLANNERS, LLC
Wholly owned by Hanley-Wood, LLC
TUCSON, ARIZONA

Published by Home Planners, LLC
Wholly owned by Hanley-Wood, LLC
3275 West Ina Road, Suite 110
Tucson, Arizona 85741

Distribution Center:
29333 Lorie Lane
Wixom, Michigan 48393

Jayne Fenton, *President*
Jennifer Pearce, *Vice President Group Content*
Linda B. Bellamy, *Executive Editor*
Jan Prideaux, *Editor in Chief*
Vicki Frank, *Publications Administrator*
Laura Hurst Brown, *Associate Editor*
Ashleigh E. Stone, *Plans Editor*
Matthew S. Kauffman, *Graphic Designer*
Sara Lisa, *Senior Production Manager*
Brenda McClary, *Production Manager*

Front cover:
Plan HPT790028 by ©1996 Donald A. Gardner Architects, Inc.
See page 29

Back cover and opposite page:
Plan HPT790031 by ©1995 Donald A. Gardner Architects, Inc.
See page 32

Title page:
Plan HPT790303 by ©1995 Donald A. Gardner Architects, Inc.
See page 224

Covers and front matter:
Photographs courtesy of Donald A. Gardner Architects, Inc.

Book design by Matthew S. Kauffman

First Printing, October 2001

10 9 8 7 6 5 4 3 2

Printed in the United States of America

Library of Congress Catalog Card Number: 2001089704

ISBN softcover: 1-881955-93-1

Contents

Photo by ©1993 Donald A. Gardner Architects, Inc., Photo by Riley & Riley Photography, Inc.

Timeless Traditions

This home features large arched windows, round columns, a covered porch and brick veneer siding. The arched window in the clerestory above the entrance provides natural light to the interior. The great room boasts a cathedral ceiling, a fireplace and built-in cabinets and bookshelves. Sliding glass doors lead to the sun room. The L-shaped kitchen serves the dining room, the breakfast area and the great room. The master suite— warmed by a fireplace—uses a private passage to the deck and its spa. Three additional bedrooms—one could serve as a study—are at the other end of the house for privacy.

PLAN HPT790001

Square Footage: 2,663
Bonus Room: 653 square feet
Width: 72'-7"
Depth: 78'-0"

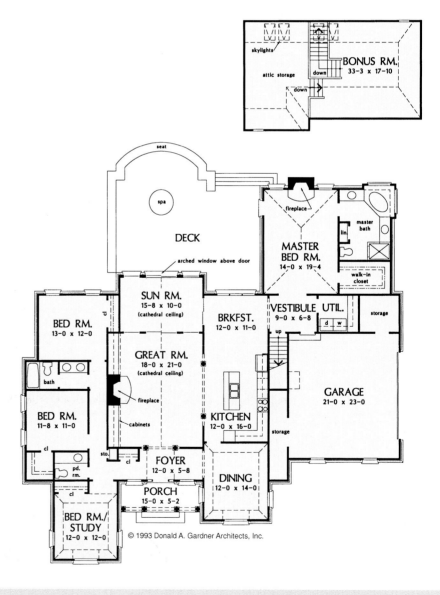

© 1993 Donald A. Gardner Architects, Inc.

A Taste of Europe

With a distinctly European flavor, this home features family living at its best. The foyer opens to a study or living room on the left. The dining room on the right offers large proportions and full windows. The family room remains open to the kitchen and the breakfast room. Here, sunny meals are guaranteed with a bay window overlooking the rear yard. In the master suite, a bayed sitting area, a walk-in closet and a pampering bath are sure to please. Upstairs, two family bedrooms flank a loft.

PLAN HPT790002

First Floor: 1,715 square feet
Second Floor: 620 square feet
Total: 2,335 square feet
Bonus Room: 265 square feet
Width: 58'-6"
Depth: 50'-5"

QUOTE ONE®
Cost to build? See page 246
to order complete cost estimate
to build this house in your area!

This home, as shown in the photograph, may differ from the actual blueprints. For more detailed information, please check the floor plans carefully.

Photo by ©1994 Donald A. Gardner Architects, Inc., Photo by Riley & Riley Photography, Inc.

Warm Welcome

This home is a true Southern original. Inside, the spacious foyer leads directly to a vaulted great room with its handsome fireplace. The dining room features a dramatic ceiling. The kitchen offers both storage and large work areas opening up to the breakfast room. At the rear of the home, you will find the master suite with its garden bath, His and Hers vanities and oversized closet. The second floor provides two additional bedrooms with a shared bath. This home is designed with a walkout basement foundation.

Cost to build? See page 246 to order complete cost estimate to build this house in your area!

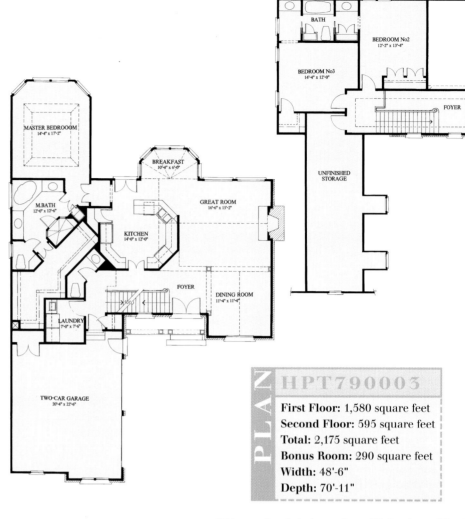

PLAN HPT790003

First Floor: 1,580 square feet
Second Floor: 595 square feet
Total: 2,175 square feet
Bonus Room: 290 square feet
Width: 48'-6"
Depth: 70'-11"

This home, as shown in the photograph, may differ from the actual blueprints. For more detailed information, please check the floor plans carefully.

Photo by Dave Dawson

This home, as shown in the photograph, may differ from the actual blueprints. For more detailed information, please check the floor plans carefully.

Star Struck

This stately brick facade features a columned, covered porch that ushers visitors into the foyer. An expansive great room with a fireplace and access to a covered porch awaits. The centrally located kitchen is within easy reach of the great room, formal dining room and skylit breakfast area. Split-bedroom planning places the master bedroom to the right of the home. Two bedrooms with abundant closet space reside to the left, while an optional bedroom or study with a Palladian window faces the front.

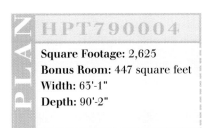

PLAN

HPT790004

Square Footage: 2,625
Bonus Room: 447 square feet
Width: 63'-1"
Depth: 90'-2"

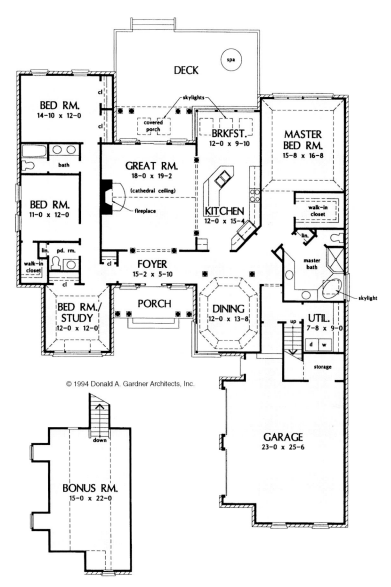

© 1994 Donald A. Gardner Architects, Inc.

Photo by Ron and Donna Kolb, Exposures Unlimited

This home, as shown in the photograph, may differ from the actual blueprints. For more detailed information, please check the floor plans carefully.

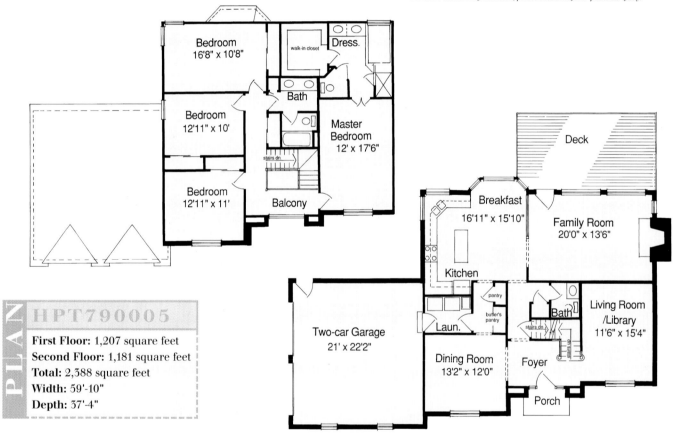

PLAN

HPT790005

First Floor: 1,207 square feet
Second Floor: 1,181 square feet
Total: 2,388 square feet
Width: 59'-10"
Depth: 37'-4"

Second floor labels:
Bedroom 16'8" x 10'8"
walk-in closet
Dress.
Bedroom 12'11" x 10'
Bath
Master Bedroom 12' x 17'6"
stairs dn.
Bedroom 12'11" x 11'
Balcony

First floor labels:
Deck
Breakfast 16'11" x 15'10"
Family Room 20'0" x 13'6"
Kitchen
Living Room /Library 11'6" x 15'4"
pantry
butler's pantry
Bath
Two-car Garage 21' x 22'2"
Laun.
stairs dn.
Dining Room 13'2" x 12'0"
Foyer
Porch

Perfectly Pampered

Homeowners will be perfectly pampered in this luxurious home. Double gables, an exciting arched entry, wood trim and sidelights adorn the exterior, while the interior blends formal spaces with casual living areas. The gourmet island kitchen opens to a brightly-lit breakfast bay overlooking the rear of the home. The spacious master bedroom is enhanced by a private bath with a huge closet. Three additional family bedrooms on the second floor share a full hall bath. A charming balcony overlooks the two-story foyer.

This home, as shown in the photograph, may differ from the actual blueprints. For more detailed information, please check the floor plans carefully.

Photo by Ron and Donna Kolb, Exposures Unlimited

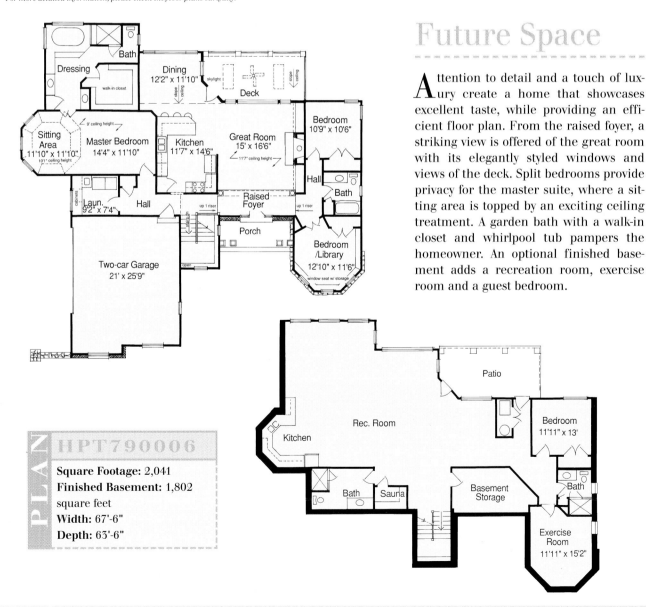

Bath
Dressing
Dining
12'2" x 11'10"
skylight
Deck
storage
ceiling
walk-in closet
Bedroom
10'9" x 10'6"
9' ceiling height
Sitting Area
11'10" x 11'10"
10'1" ceiling height
Master Bedroom
14'4" x 11'10"
Kitchen
11'7" x 14'6"
Great Room
15' x 16'6"
11'7" ceiling height
Hall
Bath
cabinets
Laun.
9'2" x 7'4"
Hall
Raised Foyer
up 1 riser
up 1 riser
open
Porch
Two-car Garage
21' x 25'9"
Bedroom /Library
12'10" x 11'6"
window seat w/ storage

Future Space

Attention to detail and a touch of luxury create a home that showcases excellent taste, while providing an efficient floor plan. From the raised foyer, a striking view is offered of the great room with its elegantly styled windows and views of the deck. Split bedrooms provide privacy for the master suite, where a sitting area is topped by an exciting ceiling treatment. A garden bath with a walk-in closet and whirlpool tub pampers the homeowner. An optional finished basement adds a recreation room, exercise room and a guest bedroom.

Patio
Rec. Room
Bedroom
11'11" x 13'
Kitchen
Bath
Sauna
Basement Storage
Bath
Exercise Room
11'11" x 15'2"

PLAN HPT790006

Square Footage: 2,041
Finished Basement: 1,802 square feet
Width: 67'-6"
Depth: 63'-6"

9

PLAN HPT790007

First Floor: 1,184 square feet
Second Floor: 1,067 square feet
Total: 2,251 square feet
Width: 42'-6"
Depth: 40'-0"

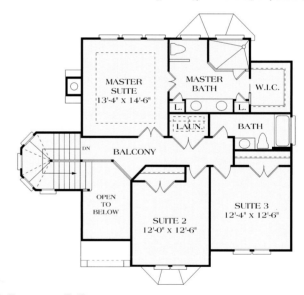

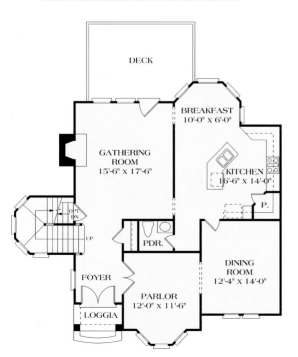

New Norman

An unusual turret at the side of this French cottage creates the look of a castle. A solid arched entrance leads inside to the foyer, which introduces a staircase winding upward through the turret. Straight ahead is the gathering room, with its fireplace and access to the deck. The kitchen and breakfast room form a large open area with a bay window, a work island and a walk-in pantry. The dining room and parlor are at the front of the plan. Upstairs, a balcony hall separates two family bedrooms from the master suite.

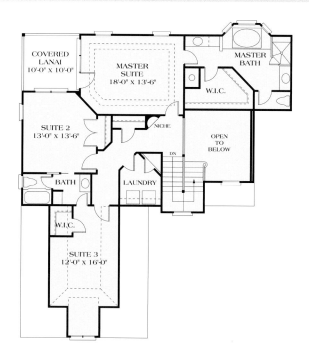

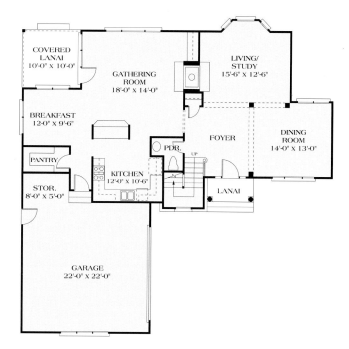

Great For Gathering

A myriad of gables produces an interesting roofline for this contemporary design with European influences. A covered lanai opens to a grand foyer. The living room boasts a bay window and shares a fireplace with the gathering room. The U-shaped kitchen with a walk-in pantry overlooks the rear covered lanai. A luxurious master suite features a cove ceiling in the bedroom, direct access to the lanai, and a private bath with a garden tub in a recessed bay. Two additional large bedrooms and a full bath are also on this floor.

PLAN HPT790008

First Floor: 1,307 square feet
Second Floor: 1,293 square feet
Total: 2,600 square feet
Width: 54'-8"
Depth: 54'-0"

This home, as shown in the photograph, may differ from the actual blueprints. For more detailed information, please check the floor plans carefully.

Photo by Living Concepts Home Planning

11

Photo courtesy of Design Basics, Inc.

This home, as shown in the photograph, may differ from the actual blueprints. For more detailed information, please check the floor plans carefully.

A Twist of Tradition

Dramatic gables and a formal frame shape the exterior of this family design. Formal rooms flank the foyer, while the vaulted family room is warmed by a fireplace. The kitchen is thoughtfully placed between the dining room and casual breakfast nook. The master suite is a pampering retreat with a walk-in closet and private bath with a whirlpool tub. A two-car garage completes the first floor. Upstairs, three additional family bedrooms—all with walk-in closets—share a full bath. Please specify crawl-space, slab or basement foundation when ordering.

PLAN HPT790009

First Floor: 1,568 square feet
Second Floor: 680 square feet
Total: 2,248 square feet
Width: 50'-0"
Depth: 48'-0"

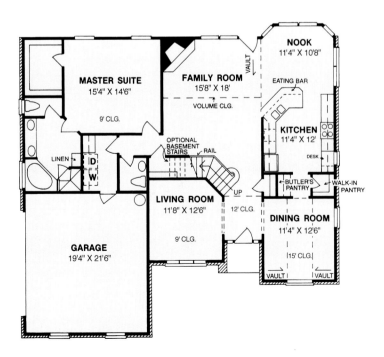

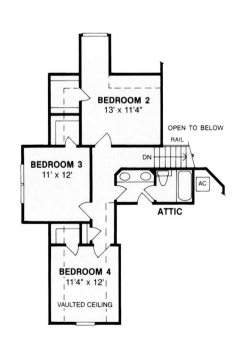

This home, as shown in the photograph, may differ from the actual blueprints. For more detailed information, please check the floor plans carefully.

Photo by Ron and Donna Kolb, Exposures Unlimited

Classic Beauty

An attractive combination of styles creates a lovely exterior for this transitional home. The first floor offers a raised foyer and open great room leading to the dining room with a sloped ceiling. Exposed on two sides, a fireplace warms the formal gathering area. A less formal space is created in the island kitchen and breakfast/hearth room combination. The master bedroom is located on the main floor, featuring a sloped ceiling through the private bath with a large walk-in closet, dressing area, dual vanities and an angled soaking tub.

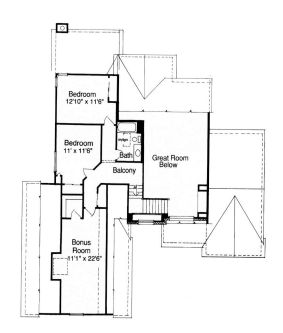

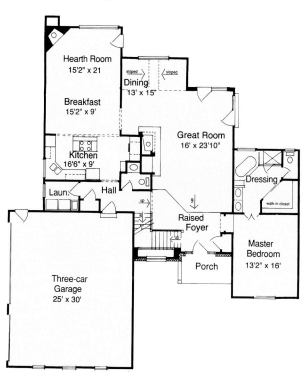

PLAN **IIPT790010**

First Floor: 1,784 square feet
Second Floor: 566 square feet
Total: 2,350 square feet
Bonus Room: 336 square feet
Width: 59'-0"
Depth: 67'-0"

Vibrant Victorian

Multiple gables and different window treatments create an interesting exterior on this plan. A covered porch and Victorian accents create a classical elevation. Double doors to the entry open to a spacious great room and an elegant dining room. In the gourmet kitchen, features include an island snack bar and a large pantry—French doors lead to the breakfast area. Cathedral ceilings in the master suite and dressing area add an exquisite touch. A vaulted ceiling in Bedroom 2 accents a window seat and an arched transom window.

PLAN HPT790011

First Floor: 905 square feet
Second Floor: 863 square feet
Total: 1,768 square feet
Width: 40'-8"
Depth: 46'-0"

WHIRLPOOL

SEAT

Mbr.
13⁰ x 14⁴

CATHEDRAL CEILING

SKYLIGHT

LIN.

DN

Br. 2
10⁰ x 12⁰

Br. 3
11⁰ x 10⁰

10'-0" CLG.

SEAT

Grt. rm.
14⁰ x 18⁴

Bfst.
11⁴ x 10⁰

COVERED PORCH

Kit.
13⁸ x 13⁸

PANT.

LIN.

SNACK BAR

UP

DN

E.

SEAT

Din.
11⁰ x 12⁰

D.

W.

R.

STORAGE

Gar.
20⁰ x 24⁸

COVERED PORCH

Photo courtesy of Design Basics, Inc.

This home, as shown in the photograph, may differ from the actual blueprints.
For more detailed information, please check the floor plans carefully.

Photo by ©1991 Donald A. Gardner Architects, Inc., Photo by Riley & Riley Photography, Inc.

PLAN

HPT790012

First Floor: 1,416 square feet
Second Floor: 445 square feet
Total: 1,861 square feet
Bonus Room: 284 square feet
Width: 58'-3"
Depth: 68'-6"

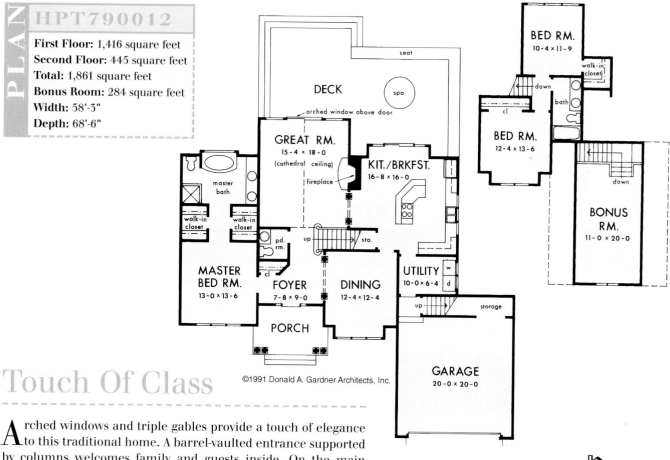

©1991 Donald A. Gardner Architects, Inc.

Touch Of Class

Arched windows and triple gables provide a touch of elegance to this traditional home. A barrel-vaulted entrance supported by columns welcomes family and guests inside. On the main level, the dining room offers round columns at the entrance, while the great room boasts a cathedral ceiling, a fireplace, and an arched window over doors to the deck. The kitchen features an island cooktop and an adjoining breakfast nook for informal dining. The master suite offers twin walk-in closets and a lavish bath that includes a whirlpool tub and a double-basin vanity.

QUOTE ONE®
Cost to build? See page 246
to order complete cost estimate
to build this house in your area!

15

Photo by Andrew D. Lautman

This home, as shown in the photograph, may differ from the actual blueprints. For more detailed information, please check the floor plans carefully.

Period Charm

The most popular feature of the Victorian house has always been its covered porches. The two finely detailed outdoor living spaces found on this home add much to formal and informal entertaining options. However, in addition to its wonderful Victorian facade, this home provides a myriad of interior features that cater to the active, growing family. The second floor provides three family bedrooms and a luxurious master suite with a whirlpool spa and His and Hers walk-in closets.

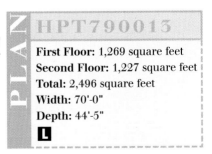

PLAN HPT790013

First Floor: 1,269 square feet
Second Floor: 1,227 square feet
Total: 2,496 square feet
Width: 70'-0"
Depth: 44'-5"

L

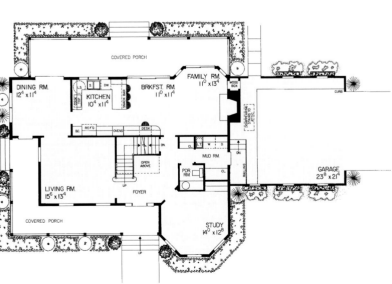

This home, as shown in the photograph, may differ from the actual blueprints. For more detailed information, please check the floor plans carefully.

Photo by Bob Greenspan

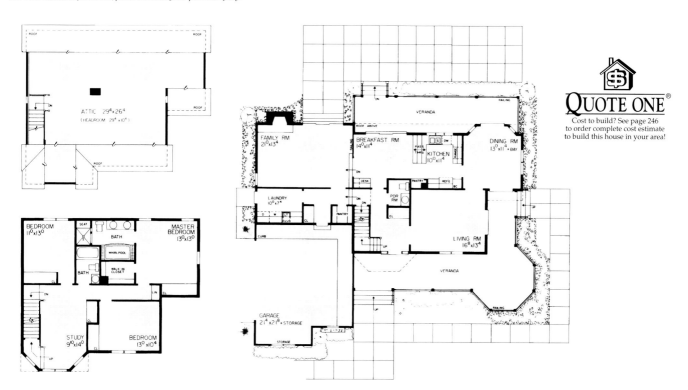

QUOTE ONE®
Cost to build? See page 246
to order complete cost estimate
to build this house in your area!

Family Victorian

PLAN HPT790014

Covered porches, front and back, are a fine preview to the livable nature of this Victorian home. Living areas are defined in a family room with a fireplace, formal living and dining rooms and a kitchen with a breakfast room. An ample laundry room and a garage with storage round out the first floor. Three second-floor bedrooms are joined by a study and two full baths. The master suite provides two closets, as well as a relaxing bath with a tile-rimmed whirlpool tub and a separate shower with a seat.

First Floor: 1,375 square feet
Second Floor: 1,016 square feet
Total: 2,391 square feet
Bonus Room: 303 square feet
Width: 62'-7"
Depth: 54'-0"
L

Photo courtesy of Living Concepts Home Planning

This home, as shown in the photograph, may differ from the actual blueprints. For more detailed information, please check the floor plans carefully.

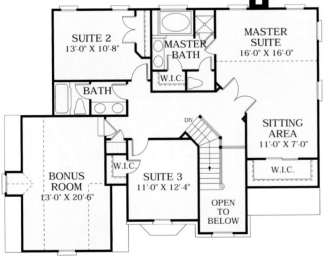

SUITE 2
13'-0" X 10'-8"

MASTER
BATH

MASTER
SUITE
16'-0" X 16'-0"

W.I.C.

BATH

DN.

SITTING
AREA
11'-0" X 7'-0"

W.I.C.

BONUS
ROOM
13'-0" X 20'-6"

W.I.C.

SUITE 3
11'-0" X 12'-4"

OPEN
TO
BELOW

PLAN

HPT790015

First Floor: 1,200 square feet
Second Floor: 1,039 square feet
Total: 2,239 square feet
Bonus Room: 309 square feet
Width: 50'-0"
Depth: 40'-5"

Simply Great

A bay window accents the facade of this handsome, contemporary design. An angled staircase in the foyer leads to the second floor. A formal dining room is to the left of the foyer and the living room is to the right. A large family room features a fireplace and direct access to the rear deck. The U-shaped kitchen provides lots of room for a breakfast nook. The master suite on the second floor offers two walk-in closets and a separate sitting area. Please specify crawlspace or slab foundation when ordering.

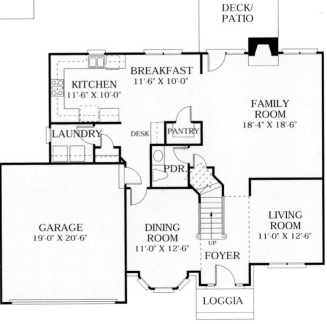

DECK/
PATIO

KITCHEN
11'-6" X 10'-0"

BREAKFAST
11'-6" X 10'-0"

FAMILY
ROOM
18'-4" X 18'-6"

LAUNDRY

DESK

PANTRY

PDR.

GARAGE
19'-0" X 20'-6"

DINING
ROOM
11'-0" X 12'-6"

UP

FOYER

LIVING
ROOM
11'-0" X 12'-6"

LOGGIA

Narrow-Lot Design

Victorian houses are well known for their orientation on narrow building sites. At only 38 feet wide, this home still offers generous style and comfort. Beautiful arched glass panels, skylights and large double-hung windows allow natural light to fill this home, giving a golden glow to oak and maple hardwood floors and trim. From the covered front porch, the foyer leads to the living and dining rooms, with an extended-hearth fireplace and access to both the veranda and screened porch. Sleeping quarters on the second floor include a master suite, plus two family bedrooms.

PLAN

HPT790016

First Floor: 911 square feet
Second Floor: 861 square feet
Total: 1,772 square feet
Bonus Room: 884 square feet
Width: 38'-0"
Depth: 52'-0"

L

QUOTE ONE®

Cost to build? See page 246
to order complete cost estimate
to build this house in your area!

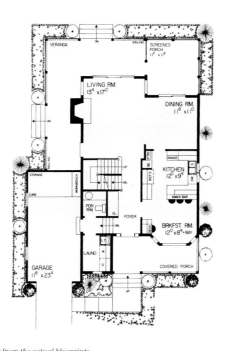

This home, as shown in the photograph, may differ from the actual blueprints.
For more detailed information, please check the floor plans carefully.

Photo by Bob Greenspan

Photo by Andrew Lautman, Lautman Photography

This home, as shown in the photograph, may differ from the actual blueprints. For more detailed information, please check the floor plans carefully.

PLAN HPT790017

First Floor: 1,112 square feet
Second Floor: 881 square feet
Total: 1,993 square feet
Width: 49'-0"
Depth: 54'-4"

D

QUOTE ONE®

Cost to build? See page 246
to order complete cost estimate
to build this house in your area!

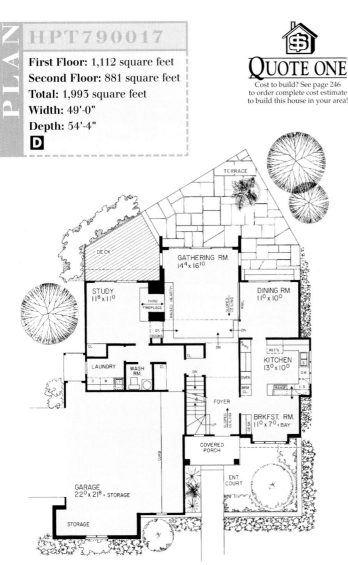

Singular Sensation

This classic American homestead is all dressed up with contemporary character and country spirit. Well-defined rooms, flowing spaces and the latest amenities blend the best of traditional and modern elements. The spacious gathering room offers terrace access and shares a through-fireplace with a secluded study. The kitchen is set between the dining and breakfast rooms. The second-floor master suite shares a balcony hallway, which overlooks the gathering room, with two family bedrooms. Dual vanities, built-in cabinets and shelves, and triple-window views highlight the master bedroom.

This home, as shown in the photograph, may differ from the actual blueprints.
For more detailed information, please check the floor plans carefully.

Photo by Nick Kelsh

QUOTE ONE®
Cost to build? See page 246
to order complete cost estimate
to build this house in your area!

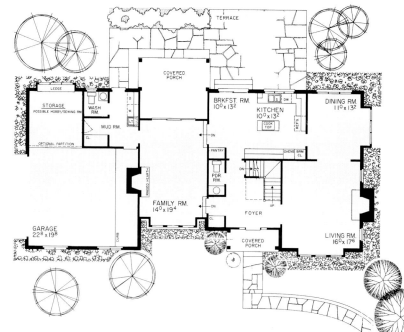

Graceful Tudor

This elegant Tudor house is perfect for the family that wants to move up in living area, style and luxury. As you enter this home, you will find a living room with a fireplace to the right. The adjacent formal dining room easily accesses the kitchen. The open kitchen/breakfast room leads to the rear terrace. Sunken a few steps, the spacious family room is highlighted with a fireplace and access to the rear covered porch. Upstairs, the family will enjoy three bedrooms and a full bath, along with a spacious master suite.

PLAN HPT790018

First Floor: 1,372 square feet
Second Floor: 1,245 square feet
Total: 2,617 square feet
Width: 70'-0"
Depth: 38'-4"

LD

Attractive Farmhouse

A wraparound porch introduces this practical design that's full of amenities. Windows open up the living room on three sides to let in natural light and let you keep an eye on kids playing on the porch. The U-shaped kitchen opens to the bright breakfast room. A spacious dining room and a powder room complete the first floor. The second floor offers the master suite—with a walk-in closet and private bath—and two family bedrooms that share a hall bath. Please specify basement, crawlspace or slab foundation when ordering.

PLAN HPT790019

First Floor: 832 square feet
Second Floor: 789 square feet
Total: 1,621 square feet
Width: 44'-0"
Depth: 32'-0"

This home, as shown in the photograph, may differ from the actual blueprints. For more detailed information, please check the floor plans carefully.

Photo courtesy of The McGuire Group Architects

This home, as shown in the photograph, may differ from the actual blueprints. For more detailed information, please check the floor plans carefully.

Photo by Bob Greenspan ©Alan Mascord Design Associates, Inc.

HPT790020

First Floor: 1,371 square feet
Second Floor: 916 square feet
Total: 2,287 square feet
Width: 43'-0"
Depth: 69'-0"

BR. 3
10/6 X 13/0

FAMILY RM.
BELOW

PLANT SHELF

SOAKING TUB

VAULTED
MASTER
12/0 X 15/0 +

LINEN

DN

BR. 2
12/4 X 11/0

GARAGE
21/4 X 20/0

W D

NOOK
10/6 X 13/0
(9' CLG.)

REF.

10/6 X 13/0

PANTRY BELOW

DESK

FAMILY
15/0 X 16/4 +/-
(9' CLG.)

DINING
12/0 X 10/0
(9' CLG.)

UP

DN

DEN
14/0 X 10/0
(9' CLG.)

FOYER
(9' CLG.)

LIVING
14/0 X 11/0 +/-
(9' CLG.)

American Beauty

S tep up to this magnificent country farmhouse with a stunning wraparound porch and transom. On the first floor, living quarters are equipped for every family, beginning with a living and dining room to the right of the foyer. To the left of the foyer is the den, featuring French doors and a passageway to the family room. The kitchen is complete with a cooktop island, built-in desk and breakfast nook. Upstairs, the master bedroom presents a lavish private bath with dual vanities, a corner whirlpool tub, separate shower and vast walk-in closet.

Photo by Andrew Lautman, Lautman Photography

This home, as shown in the photograph, may differ from the actual blueprints. For more detailed information, please check the floor plans carefully.

Family Favorite

Come home to country tradition every time you enter this charming home. The appeal of the exterior is wrapped up in a myriad of features—they include interesting rooflines, a delightful window treatment and a covered front porch. The comfort of the interior is represented by a long list of convenient living features. The formal area consists of a living room with a fireplace and a dining room. The family room offers a raised-hearth fireplace, a wood box and a beamed ceiling. Three bedrooms, a lounge and two baths are found upstairs.

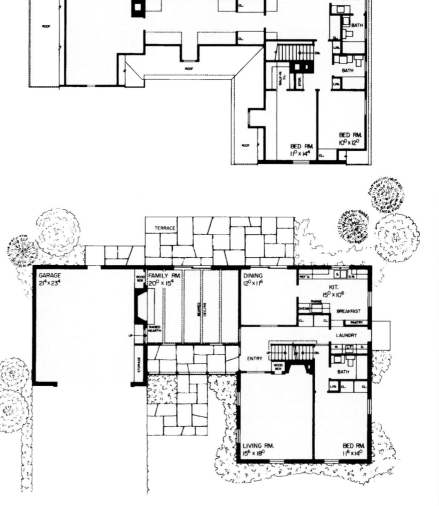

PLAN HPT790021

First Floor: 1,506 square feet
Second Floor: 1,156 square feet
Total: 2,662 square feet
Width: 72'-10"
Depth: 40'-10"

L D

This home, as shown in the photograph, may differ from the actual blueprints.
For more detailed information, please check the floor plans carefully.

Photo by Bob Greenspan

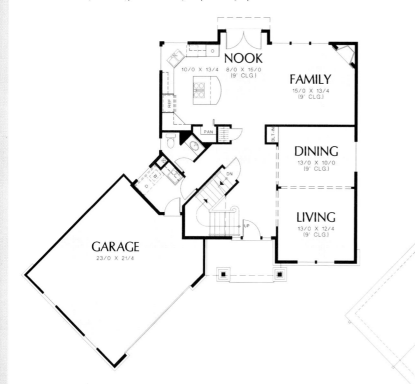

NOOK
10/0 X 13/4   8/0 X 15/0
(9' CLG.)

FAMILY
15/0 X 13/4
(9' CLG.)

REF.

PAN

DN

UP

BLT-IN

DINING
13/0 X 10/0
(9' CLG.)

LIVING
13/0 X 12/4
(9' CLG.)

GARAGE
23/0 X 21/4

SPA TUB

VAULTED
MASTER
12/6 X 16/0

LINEN

BR. 2
10/0 X 12/0

SHLVS

DN

LINEN

BR. 3
13/0 X 11/0

PLANT SHELF

BR. 4
10/8 X 10/0 +

Modern Country

With Craftsman details and modern amenities, this design offers an attractive layout. The long foyer opens to the dining and living rooms, which enjoy a flowing space. To the rear, a family room features a corner fireplace and access to the rear grounds. The breakfast nook sports French doors, which liven up the nearby island kitchen with natural light. Upstairs, the master bedroom is luxurious with a spa tub, dual vanities, a compartmented toilet, shower and a walk-in closet. Three family bedrooms share a full hall bath.

PLAN HPT790022

First Floor: 1,205 square feet
Second Floor: 1,123 square feet
Total: 2,328 square feet
Width: 57'-2"
Depth: 58'-7"

Country Comfort

Inviting porches are just the beginning of this lovely country home. To the left of the foyer, a columned entry supplies a classic touch to the spacious great room, which features a cathedral ceiling, built-in bookshelves and a fireplace that invites you to share its warmth. An octagonal dining room with a tray ceiling provides a perfect setting for formal occasions. The adjacent kitchen is designed to easily serve both formal and informal areas. The master suite, secluded from two family bedrooms, offers privacy and comfort.

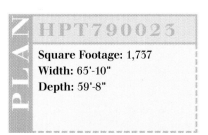

PLAN HPT790023

Square Footage: 1,737
Width: 65'-10"
Depth: 59'-8"

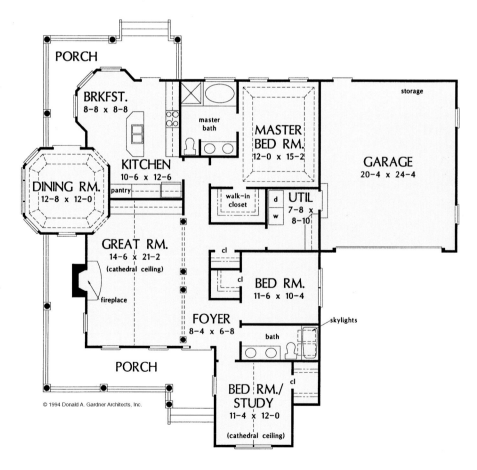

PORCH

BRKFST.
8-8 x 8-8

master
bath

MASTER
BED RM.
12-0 x 15-2

storage

KITCHEN
10-6 x 12-6

DINING RM.
12-8 x 12-0

pantry

walk-in
closet

UTIL
7-8 x
8-10

GARAGE
20-4 x 24-4

d

w

GREAT RM.
14-6 x 21-2
(cathedral ceiling)

cl

cl

cl

BED RM.
11-6 x 10-4

fireplace

FOYER
8-4 x 6-8

skylights

bath

PORCH

© 1994 Donald A. Gardner Architects, Inc.

BED RM./
STUDY
11-4 x 12-0

(cathedral ceiling)

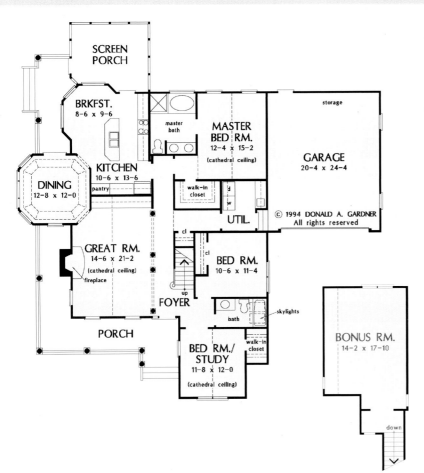

Welcome Retreat

A neighborly porch as friendly as a hand-shake wraps around this charming country home. Inside, cathedral ceilings promote a feeling of spaciousness. The great room is enhanced with a fireplace and built-in bookshelves. A uniquely shaped formal dining room separates the kitchen and breakfast area. Outdoor pursuits—rain or shine—will be enjoyed from the screened porch. The master suite is located at the rear of the plan for privacy and features a walk-in closet and a luxurious bath. Two additional bedrooms—one with a walk-in closet—share a skylit bath.

PLAN

HPT790027

Square Footage: 1,787
Bonus Room: 326 square feet
Width: 66'-2"
Depth: 66'-8"

This home, as shown in the photograph, may differ from the actual blueprints. For more detailed information, please check the floor plans carefully.

Photo by ©1994 Donald A. Gardner Architects, Inc., Photo by Riley & Riley Photography, Inc.

27

This home, as shown in the photograph, may differ from the actual blueprints. For more detailed information, please check the floor plans carefully.

Spacious Flex Room

This gabled and dormered country home with an L-shaped wrapping porch fits unexpected luxury into this compact plan. A balcony adds drama to the vaulted great room, which offers a warming fireplace. The island kitchen includes a bayed breakfast area that opens to the rear porch. The deck holds a spa area for great entertaining. A second bedroom on this floor can be easily converted to an office or study. Upstairs, the master bedroom features a bath with a double-sink vanity, compartmented toilet, walk-in closet, separate shower and skylit tub.

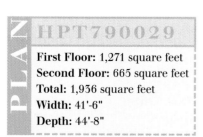

PLAN HPT790029

First Floor: 1,271 square feet
Second Floor: 665 square feet
Total: 1,936 square feet
Width: 41'-6"
Depth: 44'-8"

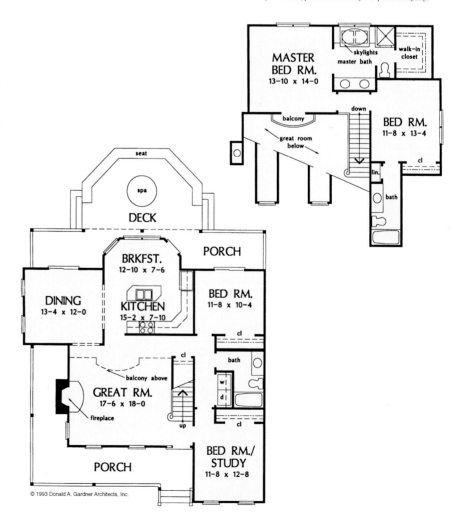

MASTER BED RM. 13-10 x 14-0
skylights
master bath
walk-in closet
balcony
down
great room below
BED RM. 11-8 x 13-4
cl
lin.
bath

seat
spa
DECK
PORCH
BRKFST. 12-10 x 7-6
KITCHEN 15-2 x 7-10
DINING 13-4 x 12-0
BED RM. 11-8 x 10-4
cl
balcony above
cl
bath
w d
GREAT RM. 17-6 x 18-0
fireplace
up
cl
PORCH
BED RM./ STUDY 11-8 x 12-8

© 1993 Donald A. Gardner Architects, Inc.

This home, as shown in the photograph, may differ from the actual blueprints. For more detailed information, please check the floor plans carefully.

Photo by ©1996 Donald A. Gardner Architects, Inc., Photo by Riley & Riley Photography, Inc.

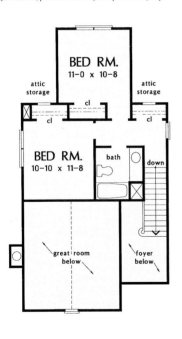

© 1996 Donald A. Gardner Architects, Inc.

A Perfect Place

This home is a great starter for a young family with plans to grow or for empty-nesters with a need for guest rooms. The two secondary bedrooms and shared bath on the second floor could also be used as office space. Additional attic storage is available as family needs expand. On the first floor, the front porch is perfect for relaxing. Inside, the foyer opens through a columned entrance to the large great room with its cathedral ceiling and fireplace. The master bedroom features a walk-in closet and a corner whirlpool tub.

PLAN HPT790028

First Floor: 1,116 square feet
Second Floor: 442 square feet
Total: 1,558 square feet
Width: 49'-0"
Depth: 52'-0"

Beachy Keen

Run up a flight of stairs to an attractive seaside home! With a traditional flavor, this fine pier design is sure to please. The living room features a fireplace and easy access to the L-shaped kitchen. Here, a work island makes meal preparation a breeze. Two family bedrooms share a full bath and access to the laundry facilities. Upstairs, a third bedroom offers a private bath and two walk-in closets. The master suite is complete with a pampering bath, two walk-in closets and a large private balcony. Please specify crawlspace or pier foundation when ordering.

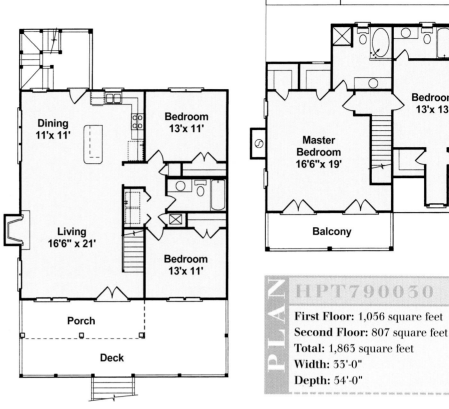

Dining 11'x 11'

Bedroom 13'x 11'

Living 16'6" x 21'

Bedroom 13'x 11'

Porch

Deck

Master Bedroom 16'6"x 19'

Bedroom 13'x 13'

Balcony

PLAN HPT790030

First Floor: 1,056 square feet
Second Floor: 807 square feet
Total: 1,863 square feet
Width: 33'-0"
Depth: 54'-0"

Photo courtesy of Chatham Home Planning

This home, as shown in the photograph, may differ from the actual blueprints. For more detailed information, please check the floor plans carefully.

This home, as shown in the photograph, may differ from the actual blueprints.
For more detailed information, please check the floor plans carefully.

Photo by Andrew Lautman, Lautman Photography

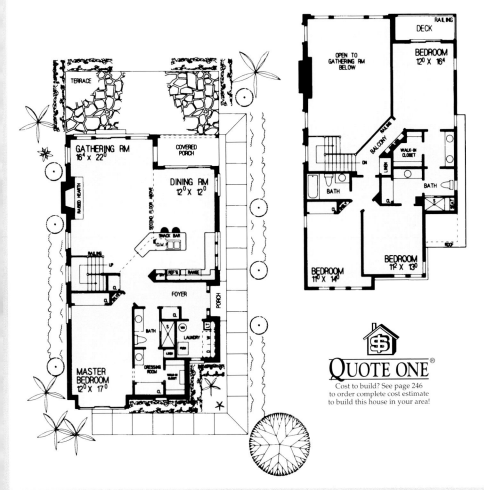

Casual Living

Perfect for a narrow lot, this shingle-and-stone Nantucket Cape home caters to the casual lifestyle. The side entrance gives direct access to the open living areas: the gathering room with its fireplace and abundance of windows; the island kitchen with an angled, pass-through snack bar; and the dining area with sliding glass doors to a covered eating area. Note how the deck further extends the living potential. The master suite boasts a compartmented bath, private dressing room and walk-in closet. Upstairs you'll find three family bedrooms.

PLAN HPT790026

First Floor: 1,387 square feet
Second Floor: 929 square feet
Total: 2,316 square feet
Width: 30'-0"
Depth: 51'-8"

Photo by ©1995 Donald A. Gardner Architects, Inc., Photo by Riley & Riley Photography, Inc.

This home, as shown in the photograph, may differ from the actual blueprints. For more detailed information, please check the floor plans carefully.

Dream Dream

Dormers cast light and interest into the foyer for a grand first impression that sets the tone in a home full of today's amenities. The great room, articulated by columns, features a cathedral ceiling and is conveniently located adjacent to the breakfast room and kitchen. Tray ceilings and picture windows with circle-tops accent the front bedroom and dining room. A secluded master suite, highlighted by a tray ceiling in the bedroom, includes a bath with a skylight, a garden tub, a separate shower, a double-bowl vanity and a spacious walk-in closet.

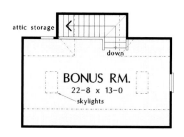

PLAN

HPT790031

Square Footage: 1,879
Bonus Room: 360 square feet
Width: 66'-4"
Depth: 55'-2"

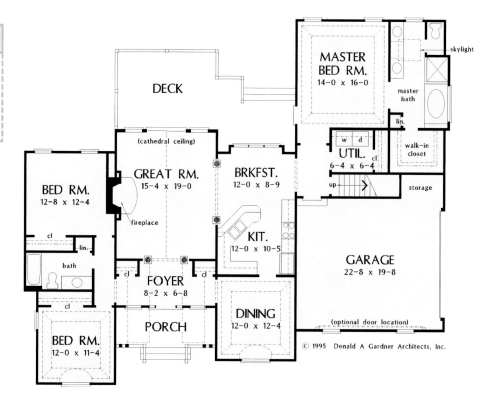

Modern Rustic

Residing peacefully in a serene mountain setting, this small family home brings quaint style to an efficient floor plan. The covered porch leads inside to formal vistas from the dining and great rooms. Warmed by a cozy fireplace, the vaulted great room connects to the kitchen/breakfast area, opening onto a rear patio. The master bedroom is vaulted and includes a walk-in closet and private bath. Three additional family bedrooms share a full hall bath. A two-car garage completes this charming plan.

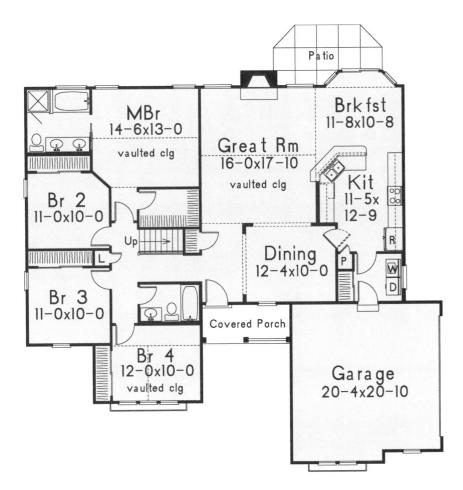

Patio

MBr
14-6x13-0
vaulted clg

Br 2
11-0x10-0

Br 3
11-0x10-0

Up
L

Br 4
12-0x10-0
vaulted clg

Great Rm
16-0x17-10
vaulted clg

Brk fst
11-8x10-8

Kit
11-5x
12-9

Dining
12-4x10-0

Covered Porch

R
P
W
D

Garage
20-4x20-10

PLAN

HPT790032

Square Footage: 1,761
Width: 57'-0"
Depth: 52'-2"

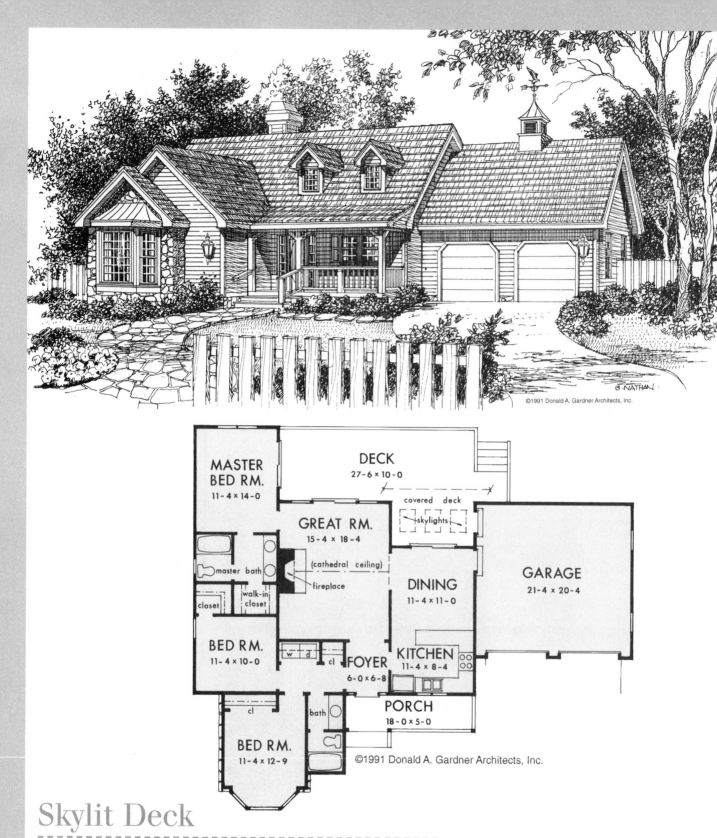

MASTER BED RM.
11-4 × 14-0

DECK
27-6 × 10-0

covered deck
skylights

GREAT RM.
15-4 × 18-4

(cathedral ceiling)
fireplace

master bath

walk-in closet

closet

BED RM.
11-4 × 10-0

w d cl

FOYER
6-0 × 6-8

GARAGE
21-4 × 20-4

DINING
11-4 × 11-0

KITCHEN
11-4 × 8-4

cl

bath

BED RM.
11-4 × 12-9

PORCH
18-0 × 5-0

©1991 Donald A. Gardner Architects, Inc.

©1991 Donald A. Gardner Architects, Inc.

Skylit Deck

A multi-paned bay window, decorative dormers and a covered porch dress up this quaint cottage. The foyer leads to an impressive great room with a cathedral ceiling and fireplace. The U-shaped kitchen, adjacent to the dining room, provides an ideal layout for food preparation. A rear covered deck offers shelter, while admitting cheery sunlight through skylights. The luxurious master bedroom takes advantage of the deck area and is assured privacy from the two other bedrooms at the front of the house. These family bedrooms share a full bath.

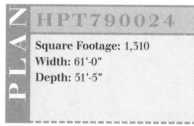

PLAN

HPT790024

Square Footage: 1,310
Width: 61'-0"
Depth: 51'-5"

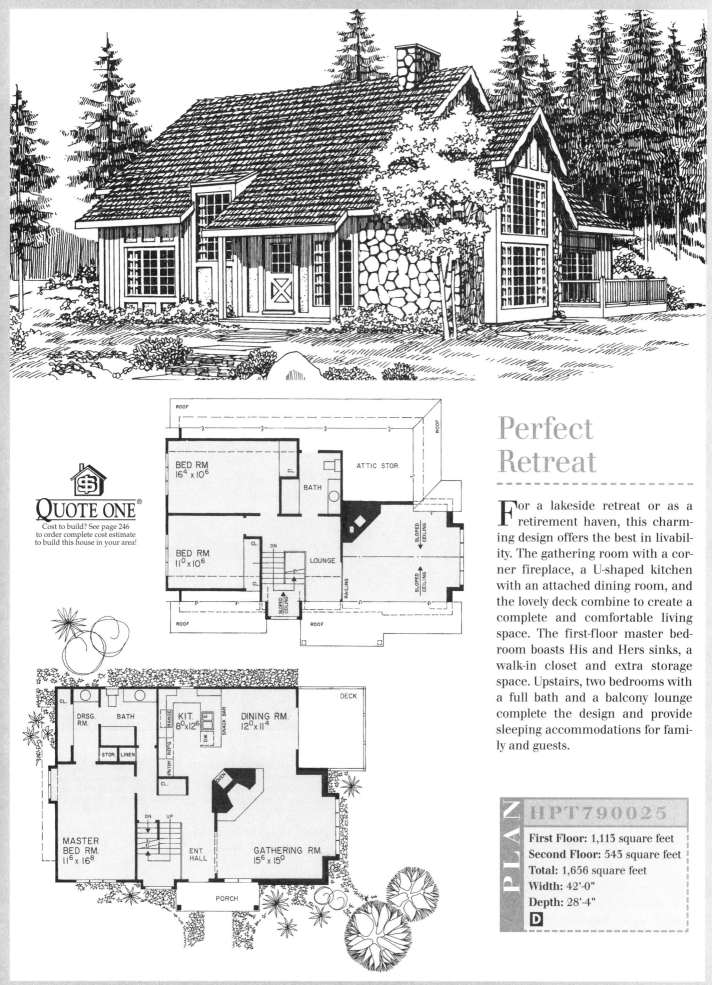

ROOF
ROOF

BED RM
16⁴ x 10⁶

CL.

BATH

ATTIC STOR.

BED RM.
11⁰ x 10⁶

CL.

DN

LOUNGE

SLOPED CEILING

RAILING

SLOPED CEILING

SLOPED CEILING

ROOF
ROOF

CL.

DRSG. RM.

BATH

KIT.
8⁰ x 12⁶

RANGE

SNACK BAR

DINING RM.
12⁰ x 11⁴

DECK

STOR.

LINEN

PANTRY

REFG

DW

S

CL.

OVEN

MASTER
BED RM.
11⁶ x 16⁸

DN UP

ENT.
HALL

GATHERING RM.
15⁶ x 15⁰

PORCH

Perfect Retreat

For a lakeside retreat or as a retirement haven, this charming design offers the best in livability. The gathering room with a corner fireplace, a U-shaped kitchen with an attached dining room, and the lovely deck combine to create a complete and comfortable living space. The first-floor master bedroom boasts His and Hers sinks, a walk-in closet and extra storage space. Upstairs, two bedrooms with a full bath and a balcony lounge complete the design and provide sleeping accommodations for family and guests.

PLAN HPT790025

First Floor: 1,113 square feet
Second Floor: 543 square feet
Total: 1,656 square feet
Width: 42'-0"
Depth: 28'-4"

D

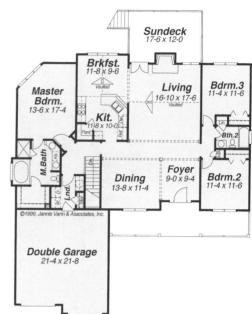

Back at the Ranch

Three dormers and a warming covered front porch would make anyone feel welcome in this country/ranch home. The vaulted ceiling in the living room definitely gives you a feeling of spaciousness along with the cozy fireplace. The elaborate kitchen features lots of counter space, a pantry and a breakfast area. On the far left side of the home, the master bedroom enjoys privacy. The home is completed with a double garage.

PLAN HPT790033

Square Footage: 1,865
Width: 56'-0"
Depth: 58'-0"

PLAN HPT790034

Square Footage: 2,188
Width: 74'-0"
Depth: 49'-4"

Great Retreat

Rustic materials and a ranch-style facade lend this home an easy spirit. Inside, the entry leads to a great room warmed by a corner fireplace. The island kitchen with a snack bar is placed between the dining and breakfast rooms. The three-car garage is located near the laundry room. With a sitting area, two walk-in closets and a private bath, the master suite excels in luxurious style. Please specify crawlspace, slab or basement foundation when ordering.

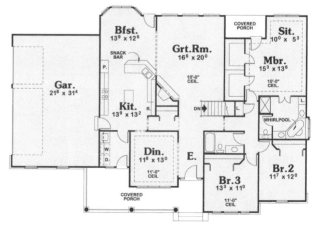

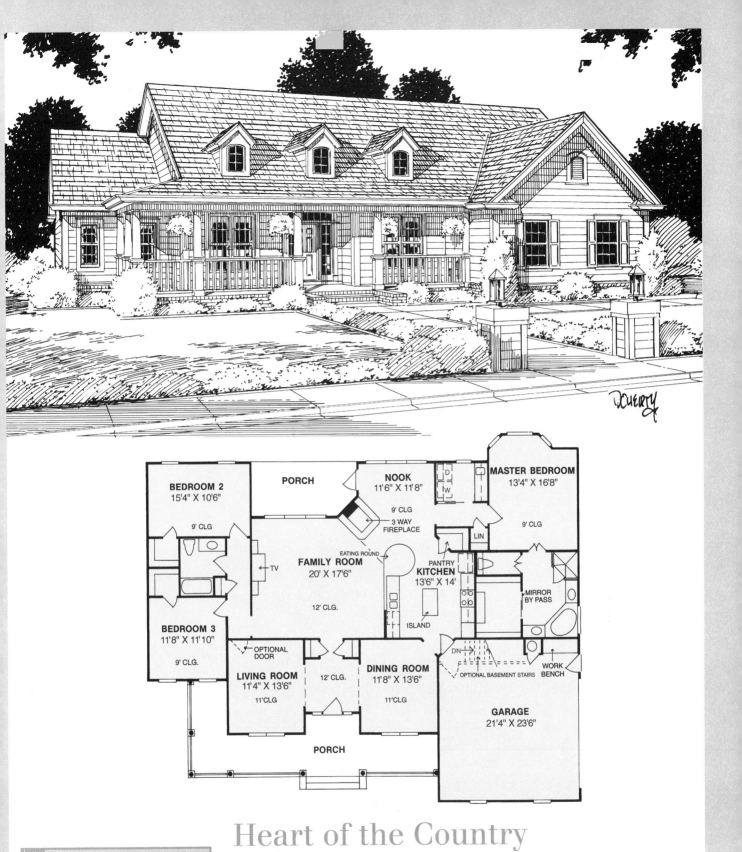

BEDROOM 2
15'4" X 10'6"
9' CLG

PORCH

NOOK
11'6" X 11'8"
9' CLG

MASTER BEDROOM
13'4" X 16'8"
9' CLG

3 WAY FIREPLACE

EATING ROUND

FAMILY ROOM
20' X 17'6"
12' CLG.

LIN

PANTRY

KITCHEN
13'6" X 14'

ISLAND

MIRROR BY PASS

TV

BEDROOM 3
11'8" X 11'10"
9' CLG.

OPTIONAL DOOR

LIVING ROOM
11'4" X 13'6"
11'CLG

12' CLG.

DINING ROOM
11'8" X 13'6"
11'CLG

DN

OPTIONAL BASEMENT STAIRS

WORK BENCH

GARAGE
21'4" X 23'6"

PORCH

Heart of the Country

PLAN

HPT790035

Square Footage: 2,126
Width: 66'-0"
Depth: 54'-0"

This country dream home excels in charm and efficiency. A traditional country porch entices you inside to the formal living and dining rooms flanking the foyer. A three-way fireplace warms the family room, island kitchen and breakfast nook. The secluded master bedroom offers its own bath with a corner soaking tub, two vanities, a separate shower, a compartmented toilet and a walk-in closet. Two additional bedrooms on the other side of the home share a hall bath. Please specify basement, slab or crawlspace foundation when ordering.

Great Views

Two dormers balanced with a double gable and arch-topped windows impart poise and charm upon this efficient home. A cathedral ceiling and windows on two walls lend a bright and fresh feel to the great room. At the rear of the plan, two secondary bedrooms share a full bath. Protected from street noise by the garage, the master suite enjoys a view of the backyard, a private bath and a walk-in closet.

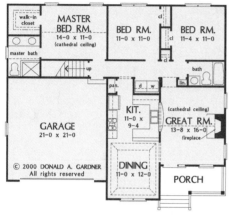

PLAN HPT790037

Square Footage: 1,264
Bonus Room: 397 square feet
Width: 47'-0"
Depth: 40'-4"

PLAN HPT790036

Square Footage: 2,586
Width: 72'-8"
Depth: 64'-8"

Simply Perfect

This splendid ranch home offers an efficient interior with plenty of livability. A front covered porch provides a warm welcome to the entry and the formal living spaces. The island kitchen, breakfast nook and family room with a fireplace create a spacious casual area for family activities. The master suite is brightened by a sitting bay. Bedrooms 2 and 3 have walk-in closets and share a full hall bath.

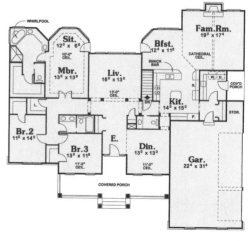

Bedroom 1
11'-10" x 11'-4"
9'-0" Flat Clg.

Bath 2

Porch
39'-6" x 10'-0"
9'-0" Flat Clg.

Nook
9'-4" x 9'-4"
9'-0" Flat Clg.

built-ins

fireplace

Kit.
9'-4" x
8'-6"
9' Clg.

Master Suite
13'-2" x 15'-2"
Tray Clg.

Bedroom 2
11'-10" x 10'-8"
9'-0" Flat Clg.

Living Room
16'-0" x 14'-8"
Vaulted Clg.

WIC

Dining
11'-8" x 10'-4"
Vaulted Clg.

Foyer

Utility
6'-10" x
10'-10'

WIC

M. Bath

Study/Office
12'-6" x 11'-0"
Tray Ceiling

WIC

WIC

Porch
31'-8" x 7'-0"

bench
Dn.

2 Car Garage
20'-4' x 23'-10"

Great Amenities

A quaint mix of materials and an enticing floor plan lend this home modern interest with traditional perks. Inside, the foyer is flanked by a dining room and an optional study/office. The vaulted living room is warmed by a fireplace and connects to the kitchen/nook area. The master suite is secluded and includes a private bath and walk-in closet. Family bedrooms located on the opposite side of the home share a hall bath that accesses the rear porch. Grilling and seasonal activities will be enjoyed on the porch.

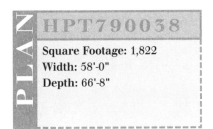

PLAN HPT790038

Square Footage: 1,822
Width: 58'-0"
Depth: 66'-8"

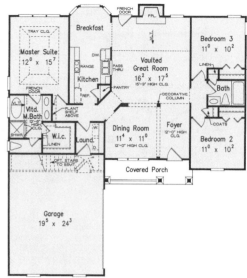

Breakfast by the Bay

Reminiscent of Cape Cod styling, this cozy home boasts a siding-and-brick exterior and two front-facing dormers. The foyer opens to the dining room, complete with decorative entrance columns. The vaulted great room enjoys a fireplace and French doors to the rear property. The bayed breakfast room flows into the kitchen—pantry included. The master suite is secluded for maximum privacy. Please specify crawlspace or basement foundation when ordering.

PLAN

HPT790040

Square Footage: 1,439
Width: 49'-0"
Depth: 54'-10"

PLAN

HPT790039

Square Footage: 1,692
Bonus Room: 358 square feet
Width: 54'-0"
Depth: 56'-6"

Volume Ceilings

This cozy country cottage is enhanced with a front-facing planter box above the garage and a charming covered porch. The foyer leads to a vaulted great room, complete with a fireplace and radius windows. Decorative columns complement the entrance to the dining room, as does a decorative arch. The master suite includes a vaulted sitting room with a radius window. Please specify basement or crawlspace foundation when ordering.

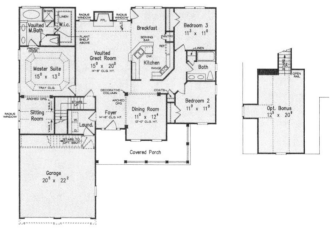

Outdoor Spaces

Cottage accents dazzle the country exterior of this small ranch home, which features rustic dormers. A front covered porch welcomes you inside to a formal living room. Straight ahead, the casual kitchen area with a pantry accesses a rear patio—perfect for outdoor grilling. A laundry room accesses a single-car garage. The master bedroom provides a walk-in closet and shares a full hall bath with two family bedrooms. A linen closet is placed outside the hall bath nearby. Bedroom 3 features a vaulted area that overlooks the front yard.

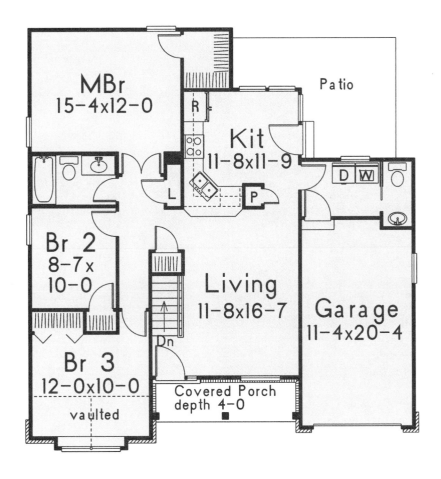

MBr
15-4x12-0

Kit
11-8x11-9

Patio

Br 2
8-7x
10-0

Living
11-8x16-7

Garage
11-4x20-4

Br 3
12-0x10-0

vaulted

Dn

Covered Porch
depth 4-0

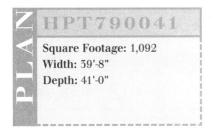

PLAN HPT790041

Square Footage: 1,092
Width: 39'-8"
Depth: 41'-0"

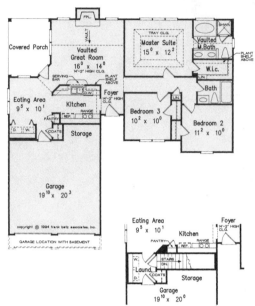

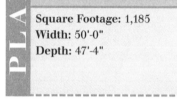

Sweet Retreat

Stone accents, gables and abundant windows make this traditional/ country classic home very charming. The elaborate kitchen features a serving bar, pantry, eating area and access to the washer and dryer. The great room boasts a vaulted ceiling, warm fireplace, built-in plant shelves and access to the covered side porch. The master suite enjoys a tray ceiling, a walk-in closet and a complete master bath with a vaulted ceiling and an oval garden tub.

PLAN

HPT790042

Square Footage: 1,185
Width: 50'-0"
Depth: 47'-4"

PLAN

HPT790043

Square Footage: 1,571
Bonus Room: 334 square feet
Width: 53'-6"
Depth: 55'-10"

Private Suite

Stone trim enhances the siding exterior of this three-bedroom country home. Entertaining will be easy from the centrally located kitchen with its serving bar, pantry and efficient use of space. The nearby breakfast nook enjoys French-door access to the backyard. A warming fireplace adorns the vaulted great room. Privately located off the great room, the master suite features high quality amenities, including a tray ceiling, vaulted bathroom, plant shelf and radius window.

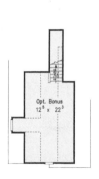

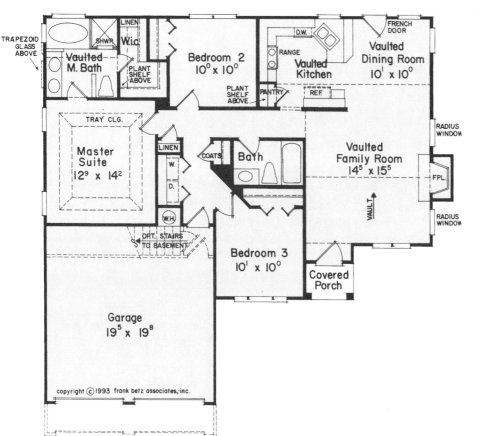

TRAPEZOID GLASS ABOVE

Vaulted M. Bath

LINEN
SHWR W.i.c.

PLANT SHELF ABOVE

Bedroom 2
10⁰ x 10⁰

D.W.

RANGE

Vaulted Kitchen

FRENCH DOOR

Vaulted Dining Room
10¹ x 10⁰

TRAY CLG.

Master Suite
12⁹ x 14²

LINEN
W.
D.

W.H.

COATS

Bath

PLANT SHELF ABOVE

PANTRY

REF.

RADIUS WINDOW

Vaulted Family Room
14⁵ x 15⁵

FPL.

VAULT

RADIUS WINDOW

OPT. STAIRS TO BASEMENT

Bedroom 3
10¹ x 10⁰

Covered Porch

Garage
19⁵ x 19⁸

copyright © 1993 frank betz associates, inc.

Vaulted Ceilings

Numerous extras spice up this elegant traditional home. A covered entry leads into a spacious vaulted family room, enhanced with radius windows and a fireplace. Directly beyond is a vaulted dining room with French doors leading to the rear property. The master suite is greatly enhanced with a tray ceiling, vaulted bath, linen closet and plant shelf above the walk-in closet. Bedrooms 2 and 3 share a full bath and easily access the washer-and-dryer area and the hall coat closet.

PLAN HPT790044

Square Footage: 1,198
Width: 48'-0"
Depth: 44'-0"

Comfort Zones

The country cottage is sure to please with its many amenities! Included in the long list: a fireplace in the family room, a work island in the U-shaped kitchen and a convenient, yet hidden laundry room. Two family bedrooms share a full bath, while the master suite offers a private bath and a large walk-in closet. The large covered front porch adds a country touch to this rustic design.

PLAN **HPT790045**

Square Footage: 1,333
Width: 55'-6"
Depth: 64'-3"

PLAN **HPT790046**

Square Footage: 1,925
Width: 78'-0"
Depth: 52'-0"

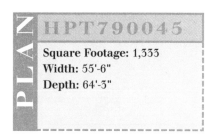

Fine Lines

This three-bedroom traditional beauty offers all the features of a modern home, but with the quaint look of a more established design. The living room features a fireplace, a sloped ceiling and a large rear porch accessible via French doors. The kitchen boasts an ample pantry and easily serves a casual eating area as well as the formal dining room. Please specify crawlspace or slab foundation when ordering.

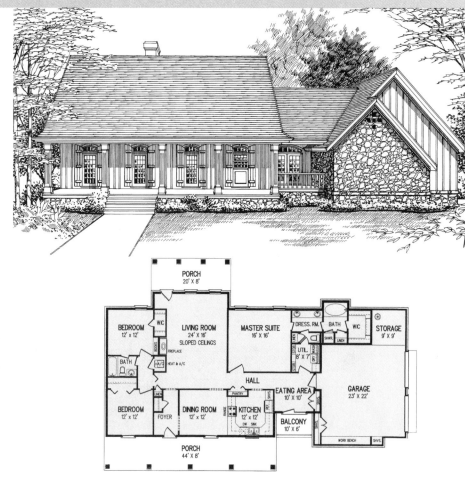

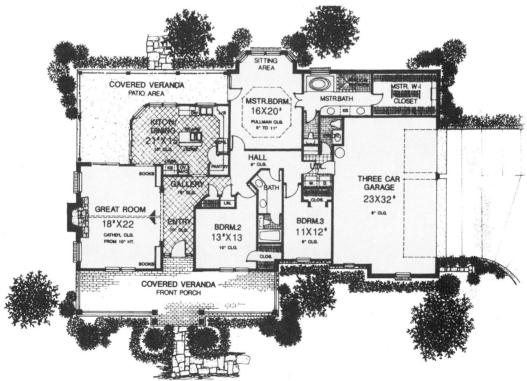

Great Veranda

PLAN

HPT790047

Square Footage: 2,172
Width: 79'-0"
Depth: 47'-0"

The simplicity of the ranch lifestyle is indicated in every detail of this charming country design. Front and rear verandas along with earthy materials combine to give the exterior of this home a true land-lover's look. A central fireplace warms the cathedral-enhanced space of the formal great room. The casual kitchen area features an island workstation overlooking the rear veranda. The master suite is a sumptuous retreat with a sitting area, private bath and walk-in closet. Two additional bedrooms share a full hall bath.

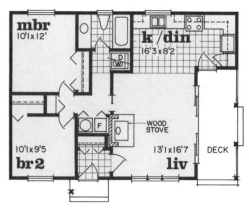

Perfect Getaway

The exterior of this affordable leisure home is enhanced with sliding glass doors under a covered porch and a charming flower box beneath the living-room window. Inside, the living room consists of a warming woodstove and the country kitchen provides ample space for a breakfast table. A linen closet is positioned between the two bedrooms; just around the corner is a full hall bath, plus space for a washer and dryer.

PLAN **HPT790049**

Square Footage: 839
Width: 36'-6"
Depth: 26'-0"

PLAN **HPT790048**

Square Footage: 1,404
Bonus Room: 256 square feet
Width: 54'-7"
Depth: 46'-6"

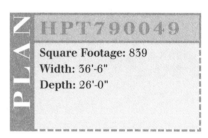

Craftsman Charm

This rustic Craftsman-style cottage provides an open interior with good outdoor flow. The front covered porch invites casual gatherings, while inside, the dining area is set for both everyday and planned occasions. A centered fireplace in the great room shares its warmth with the dining room. A rear hall leads to the master suite with a private bath and a secondary bedroom, while upstairs, a loft provides a space for the family computer.

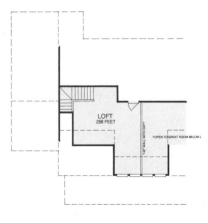

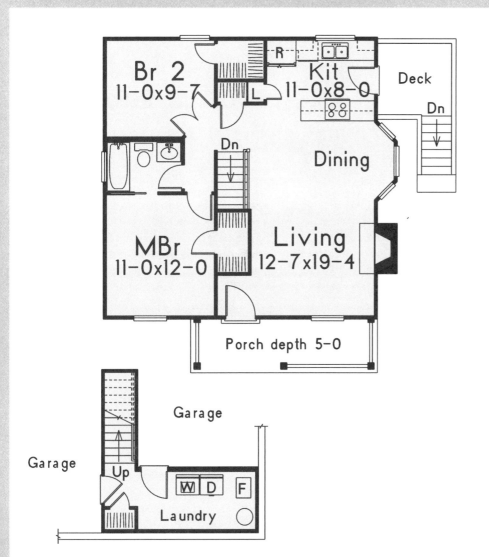

Br 2
11-0x9-7

Kit
11-0x8-0

Deck

Dn

Dn

Dining

MBr
11-0x12-0

Living
12-7x19-4

Porch depth 5-0

Garage

Garage

Up

W D F

Laundry

Real World

Rustic charm and an affordable siding exterior enclose a plan that's perfect for a small or vacationing family. The petite covered front porch opens inside to a formal living room with a country fireplace. The kitchen, offering spacious mountain views, easily serves the bayed dining area for casual or formal occasions. The kitchen also accesses a side deck that leads to the outdoor property. The master bedroom with a walk-in closet privately accesses the hall bath. Double doors open to Bedroom 2, which features its own walk-in closet.

PLAN HPT790050

Square Footage: 796
Basement: 118 square feet
Width: 28'-0"
Depth: 28'-0"

Vaulted Dining Room

This economical, compact home is the ultimate in efficient use of space. The central living room features a cozy fireplace and outdoor access to the front porch. Sliding glass doors lead from the kitchen/dining area to the rear property. The front entry is sheltered by a casual country porch. The master suite offers a walk-in closet and shares a full bath with the secondary bedrooms.

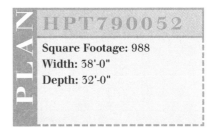

QUOTE ONE®
Cost to build? See page 246
to order complete cost estimate
to build this house in your area!

PLAN HPT790052

Square Footage: 988
Width: 38'-0"
Depth: 32'-0"

PLAN HPT790051

Square Footage: 1,375
Width: 61'-0"
Depth: 35'-0"

Cool Patio

A welcoming front porch opens into the vaulted living room with its warming fireplace. To the left of the living room is the sleeping zone. Two family bedrooms share a full bath. The master suite, shielded from any street noise by the secondary bedrooms, features a roomy walk-in closet and full bath. The U-shaped kitchen opens directly to the dining room and its patio access. Please specify crawlspace or slab foundation when ordering.

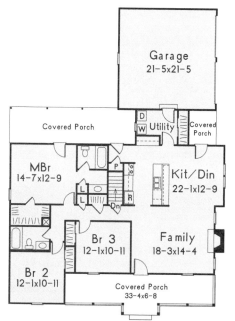

Smart Space

This ranch-style home provides an inviting front covered porch with rustic accents. Inside, the family room provides a lovely fireplace and is open to a kitchen/dining area that accesses a rear covered porch. Nearby, a utility room leads into the two-car garage. The master bedroom provides spacious views of the rear property and privately accesses the rear covered porch. This bedroom also features a walk-in closet and a full bath with linen storage. Bedrooms 2 and 3 share a full hall bath.

PLAN HPT790053

Square Footage: 1,501
Width: 48'-0"
Depth: 57'-4"

PLAN HPT790301

Square Footage: 1,830
Width: 75'-0"
Depth: 43'-5"

L D

Five-Star Ranch

This charming one-story traditional home greets visitors with a front covered porch. A galley-style kitchen shares a snack bar with the spacious gathering room, where a fireplace is the focal point. A spacious master suite includes a luxury bath with a whirlpool tub and a separate dressing room. Two additional bedrooms—one that could double as a study—are located at the front of the home.

QUOTE ONE®
Cost to build? See page 246
to order complete cost estimate
to build this house in your area!

49

High Volume

This long, low ranch home provides outdoor living on two porches—one to the front and one to the rear. Vaulted ceilings in the great room, kitchen and master bedroom add a dimension of extra space. The great room is warmed by a fireplace and is open to the country kitchen with rear-porch access. The master suite is graced by a walk-in closet and a full bath with a garden tub and dual vanities.

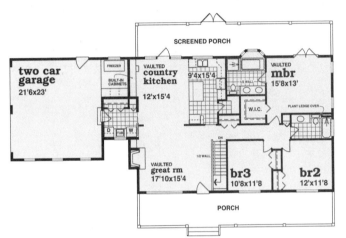

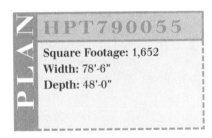

PLAN HPT790055

Square Footage: 1,652
Width: 78'-6"
Depth: 48'-0"

PLAN HPT790054

Square Footage: 2,549
Width: 88'-8"
Depth: 53'-6"

Wide Views

Covered porches to the front and rear will be the envy of the neighborhood when this house is built. The interior plan meets family needs perfectly in well-zoned areas: a sleeping wing with four bedrooms and two baths, a living zone with formal and informal gathering space, and a work zone with a U-shaped kitchen and laundry with a powder room. The two-car garage features a huge storage area.

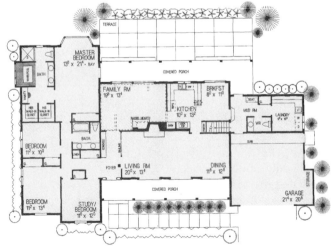

Outdoor Living

Small but inviting, this ranch-style farmhouse is the perfect choice for a small family or empty-nesters. It's loaded with amenities even the most particular homeowner will appreciate. For example, the living room and dining room both have plant shelves, sloped ceilings and built-in cabinetry to enhance livability. The living room also sports a warming fireplace. The master bedroom contains a well-appointed bath with dual vanities and a walk-in closet. The kitchen is separated from the breakfast nook by a bar area.

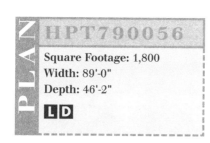

PLAN HPT790056

Square Footage: 1,800
Width: 89'-0"
Depth: 46'-2"

L D

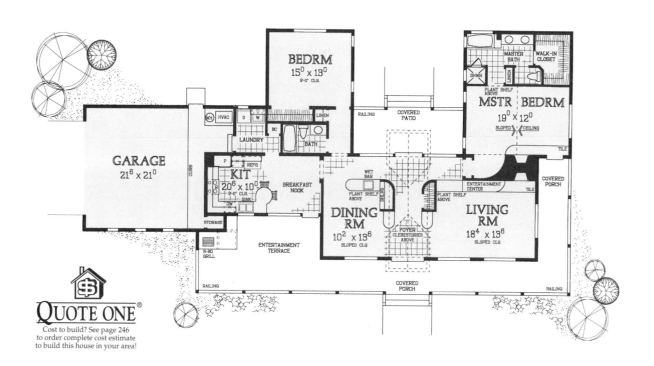

GARAGE 21⁶ x 21⁰

BEDRM 15⁰ x 13⁰ 9'-0" CLG.

KIT 20⁶ x 10⁰ 9'-0" CLG.

LAUNDRY

BATH

LINEN

HVAC

BREAKFAST NOOK

STORAGE

ENTERTAINMENT TERRACE

B-B-Q GRILL

DINING RM 10² x 13⁶ SLOPED CLG.

WET BAR

PLANT SHELF ABOVE

FOYER CLERESTORIES ABOVE

PLANT SHELF ABOVE

LIVING RM 18⁴ x 13⁶ SLOPED CLG.

ENTERTAINMENT CENTER

COVERED PORCH

COVERED PATIO

RAILING

MASTER BATH

WALK-IN CLOSET

PLANT SHELF ABOVE

MSTR BEDRM 19⁰ x 12⁰ SLOPED CEILING

COVERED PORCH

RAILING

QUOTE ONE®
Cost to build? See page 246
to order complete cost estimate
to build this house in your area!

51

PLAN

HPT790058

Square Footage: 2,046
Width: 94'-8"
Depth: 64'-4"

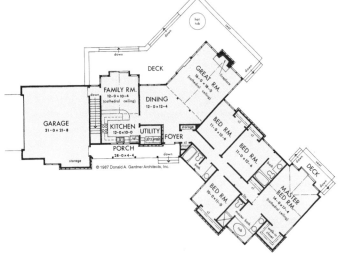

A Full Deck

This country-style ranch is the essence of excitement with its combination of exterior building materials and interesting shapes. Because it is angled, it allows for flexibility in design—the great room and/or the family room can be extended to meet family space requirements. The master bedroom offers a cathedral ceiling, a walk-in closet, a private deck and a spacious master bath with a whirlpool tub. There are three family bedrooms, two of which share a full bath.

PLAN

HPT790057

Square Footage: 2,076
Width: 64'-8"
Depth: 54'-7"

LD

Open Interior

Simple to build, yet loaded with livability, this one-story plan features farmhouse details on the outside and a solid floor plan on the inside. The living areas are the central focus with the kitchen at the hub and the living room/dining room combination to the rear. The master bedroom contains a walk-in closet. The family bedrooms share a full bath that includes dual vanities. This ranch house is eye-catching in any location.

Traditional Charm

Though modest in size, this fetching home offers a great deal of livability with three bedrooms (or two bedrooms and a study) and a spacious gathering room with a fireplace and a sloped ceiling. The galley kitchen, designed to save steps, provides a pass-through snack bar and an attached breakfast room. The private master bath features a large dressing area, a corner vanity and a raised whirlpool tub. Indoor/outdoor living relationships are strengthened by easy access from the dining room, study/bedroom and master suite to the rear terrace.

QUOTE ONE®

Cost to build? See page 246 to order complete cost estimate to build this house in your area!

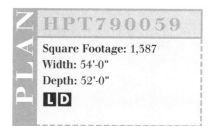

PLAN

HPT790059

Square Footage: 1,387
Width: 54'-0"
Depth: 52'-0"

LD

Formal and Friendly

This ranch-style home is a delight for the small American family. Inside, the open living room extends to a dining room and nearby kitchen area. To the right of the plan, a single carport offers an efficient storage room. The left side of the plan hosts the family bedrooms. The master suite features a walk-in closet and private access to the full bath. Please specify crawlspace or slab foundation when ordering.

PLAN HPT790060

Square Footage: 998
Width: 48'-0"
Depth: 29'-0"

PLAN HPT790061

Square Footage: 2,077
Width: 70'-8"
Depth: 69'-0"

Cool Digs

This country charmer is big on space. Upon entering this beautiful home, notice the family room and dining area separated by an open soffit above. The kitchen and nook area open to the family room, adding to the sense of space. The master suite provides all the elegance of a custom home with its tray ceiling and opulent bath area. The secondary bedrooms share a bath as well as a unique study area.

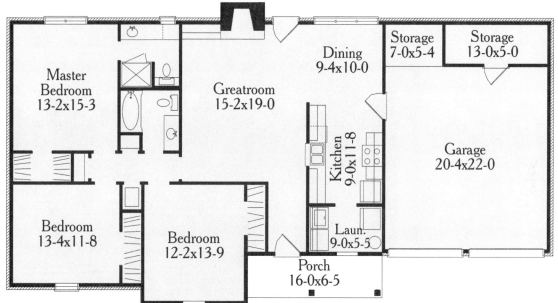

Master Bedroom
13-2x15-3

Greatroom
15-2x19-0

Dining
9-4x10-0

Storage
7-0x5-4

Storage
13-0x5-0

Kitchen
9-0x11-8

Garage
20-4x22-0

Bedroom
13-4x11-8

Bedroom
12-2x13-9

Laun.
9-0x5-5

Porch
16-0x6-5

Great Living Spaces

Ranch-style homes continue to be a popular choice all over the continent because of their casual, rustic appeal. This one is a classic, with a large great room with fireplace, a dining area and a galley-style kitchen. The two-car garage connects to the main home at an entry near the kitchen. This home features two storage areas in the two-car garage. The master bedroom features a private bath and walk-in closet. Please specify basement, crawlspace or slab foundation when ordering.

PLAN HPT790062

Square Footage: 1,441
Width: 67'-0"
Depth: 34'-0"

Skylit Covered Patio

You may decide to build this design simply because of its delightful covered rear patio, as it certainly will provide its share of enjoyment by taking casual living outdoors. The living room/dining area is highlighted by a fireplace, sliding glass doors to the patio and an open staircase with a built-in planter. Notice also how effectively the family bedrooms are arranged away from the main traffic flow of the house.

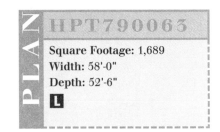

QUOTE ONE®

Cost to build? See page 246 to order complete cost estimate to build this house in your area!

Entertainment Terrace

Country living is the focus of this charming design. From the breakfast room, enter the kitchen with its snack bar pass-through to the gathering room and the entry to the dining area. The master suite features a private bath and access to the rear terrace. Two additional bedrooms share a full bath, and one could be used as a study. The large rear terrace expands the living area to the outdoors.

QUOTE ONE®

Cost to build? See page 246 to order complete cost estimate to build this house in your area!

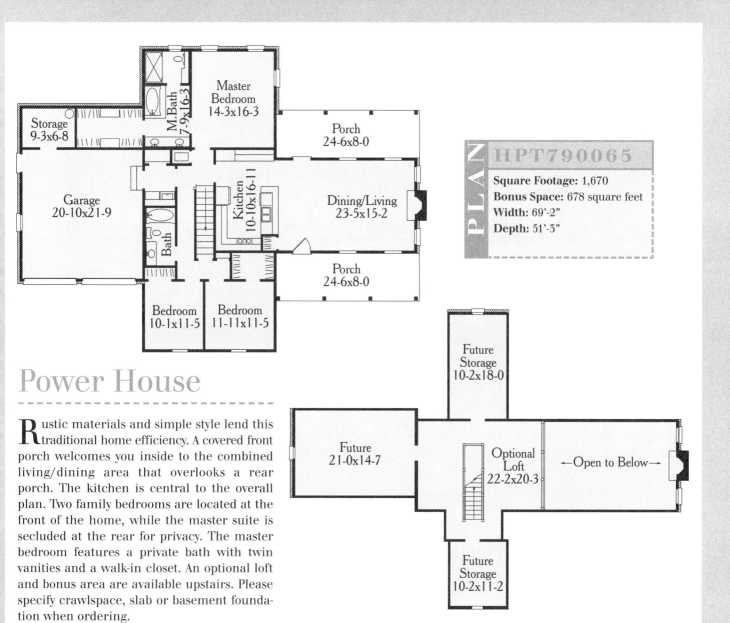

Storage
9-3x6-8

Master
Bedroom
14-3x16-3

M.Bath
7-9x16-3

Porch
24-6x8-0

Garage
20-10x21-9

Kitchen
10-10x16-11

Dining/Living
23-5x15-2

Bath

Porch
24-6x8-0

Bedroom
10-1x11-5

Bedroom
11-11x11-5

PLAN

HPT790065

Square Footage: 1,670
Bonus Space: 678 square feet
Width: 69'-2"
Depth: 51'-3"

Power House

Rustic materials and simple style lend this traditional home efficiency. A covered front porch welcomes you inside to the combined living/dining area that overlooks a rear porch. The kitchen is central to the overall plan. Two family bedrooms are located at the front of the home, while the master suite is secluded at the rear for privacy. The master bedroom features a private bath with twin vanities and a walk-in closet. An optional loft and bonus area are available upstairs. Please specify crawlspace, slab or basement foundation when ordering.

Future
Storage
10-2x18-0

Future
21-0x14-7

Optional
Loft
22-2x20-3

←Open to Below→

Future
Storage
10-2x11-2

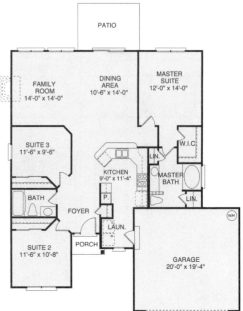

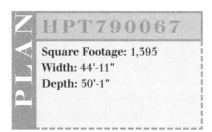

Country Colonial

Quaint cottage style graces the exterior of this lovely home. The bedrooms are made up of two family suites that share a hall bath, and a master bedroom on the opposite side of the home. The master bath includes two linen closets and a garden tub, with a walk-in closet nearby. A family room with a fireplace is open to the dining area, which overlooks the rear patio deck.

PLAN HPT790067

Square Footage: 1,395
Width: 44'-11"
Depth: 50'-1"

PLAN HPT790066

Square Footage: 1,151
Width: 39'-2"
Depth: 42'-0"

Family First

Traditional styling enhances the exterior, while essential family rooms create a beautiful interior. The foyer is flanked on either side by two family bedrooms sharing a full hall bath. The master suite features a private bath with an oval soaking tub and a large walk-in closet. The family room is open to the dining area for easy flow of traffic. The kitchen features a laundry closet and access to the single-car garage.

PATIO

FAMILY ROOM
14'-0" x 14'-0"

DINING AREA
10'-6" x 14'-0"

MASTER SUITE
12'-0" x 14'-0"

SUITE 3
11'-6" x 9'-6"

W.I.C

LIN.

KITCHEN
9'-0" x 11'-4"

MASTER BATH

LIN.

BATH

P.

FOYER

LAUN.

PORCH

SUITE 2
11'-6" x 10'-8"

GARAGE
20'-0" x 19'-4"

W/H

What You Need

A welcoming porch leads to an entry that features a sidelight and transom. Inside, the foyer leads past a utility closet and niche to the island kitchen with a snack bar. The family room with an optional fireplace accesses the rear patio. The secluded master suite provides privacy and features a master bath and walk-in closet. Suites 2 and 3 are separated from the living area and share a full hall bath. The well-placed garage entrance opens to the laundry and kitchen.

PLAN

HPT790068

Square Footage: 1,204
Width: 43'-1"
Depth: 47'-1"

Corner Fireplace

This one-story traditional home caters to family living. The efficient, U-shaped kitchen opens to an adjacent bayed breakfast area. The family room features a corner fireplace and access to the rear yard. Two family bedrooms share a full bath, while the master bedroom offers a private bath with a walk-in closet. A two-car garage with storage completes the plan. Please specify slab or crawlspace foundation when ordering.

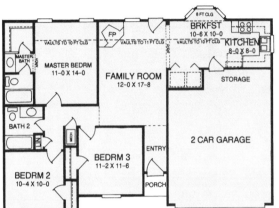

PLAN

HPT790070

Square Footage: 1,142
Width: 48'-10"
Depth: 35'-8"

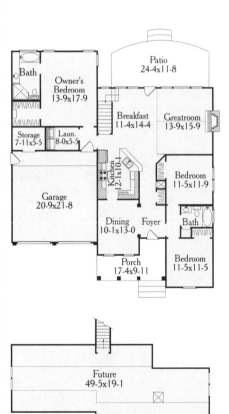

PLAN

HPT790069

Square Footage: 1,689
Bonus Space: 830 square feet
Width: 50'-0"
Depth: 56'-9"

Genuine Retreat

Traditional accents and natural materials create an inviting home perfect for the countryside. A petite covered front porch leads to a foyer flanked by two family bedrooms and a dining room. The great room with a fireplace is open to the breakfast room, with the kitchen just a few steps away. Please specify basement, crawlspace or slab foundation when ordering.

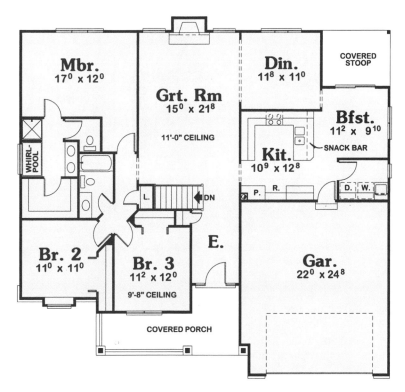

Mbr.
17⁰ x 12⁰

Grt. Rm
15⁰ x 21⁸

11'-0" CEILING

Din.
11⁸ x 11⁰

COVERED STOOP

Bfst.
11² x 9¹⁰

Kit.
10⁹ x 12⁸

SNACK BAR

L.

DN

E.

P. R.

D. W.

Br. 2
11⁰ x 11⁰

Br. 3
11² x 12⁰

9'-8" CEILING

Gar.
22⁰ x 24⁸

COVERED PORCH

WHIRL-POOL

New Tradition

Transom lights and a columned front porch give country charm to this home. The entry leads to a comforting fireplace and a vaulted ceiling in the great room. The master suite is complete with a walk-in closet and private bath including a whirlpool tub and a separate shower. Two family bedrooms share a full bath nearby. An efficient U-shaped kitchen adjoins a breakfast nook. A ribbon of windows lights the dining room naturally and allows a great view of the backyard. Please specify basement or crawlspace foundation when ordering.

PLAN

HPT790071

Square Footage: 1,758
Width: 55'-4"
Depth: 49'-8"

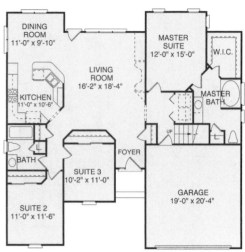

Classic Style

This efficient design looks good anywhere—in an established neighborhood or a new lot. The foyer opens directly onto a sunlit living room with an optional fireplace. The kitchen features a serving bar to both the dining and living rooms. Two family bedrooms share a bath. To the right of the living room sits a luxurious master suite. A set of stairs between the master suite and garage leads to an optional bonus room.

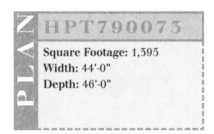

PLAN

HPT790072

Square Footage: 1,458
Bonus Room: 256 square feet
Width: 47'-7"
Depth: 46'-5"

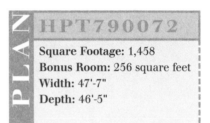

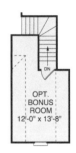

PLAN

HPT790073

Square Footage: 1,395
Width: 44'-0"
Depth: 46'-0"

Second Glance

Traditional peaks and a beautiful brick facade grace the exterior of this lovely home. Inside, the foyer is flanked by a two-car garage and two family bedrooms sharing a hall bath. Straight ahead, the living room with a fireplace is open to the dining area and kitchen. The master bedroom features a walk-in closet. Please specify crawlspace, slab or basement foundation when ordering.

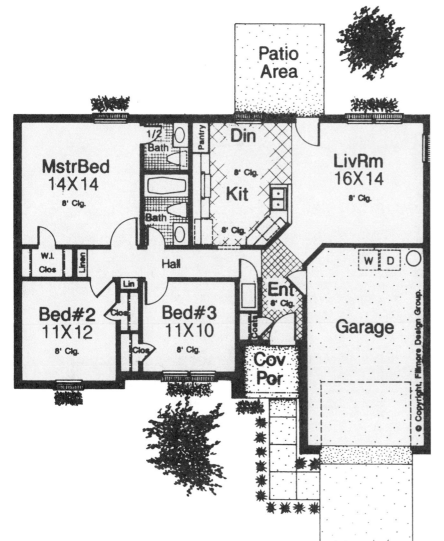

Easy Living

This petite ranch home will charm the landscape of any neighborhood setting. A small covered front porch welcomes you into the entryway. The formal living room connects to the kitchen/dinette space and offers access to the rear patio area—a perfect spot to relax and enjoy outdoor grilling. Down the hall, the master bedroom features a private half bath and a walk-in closet. Bedrooms 2 and 3 face the front of the property and share a full hall bath with the master bedroom.

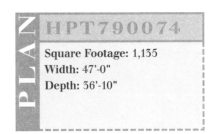

PLAN HPT790074

Square Footage: 1,135
Width: 47'-0"
Depth: 36'-10"

Country Home

This small family home offers many traditional features and efficient amenities within. A petite porch enters into a spacious living room area with a fireplace. An open dining room for formal or casual occasions connects to the U-shaped kitchen and overlooks the rear deck. The master bedroom with a walk-in closet privately accesses the full hall bath. Two additional family bedrooms located nearby overlook the front of the property.

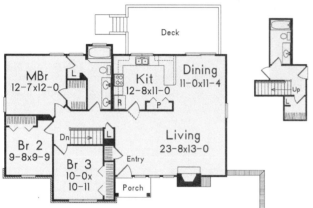

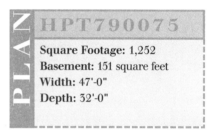

PLAN HPT790075

Square Footage: 1,252
Basement: 151 square feet
Width: 47'-0"
Depth: 32'-0"

Step Inside

A stone-and-siding exterior easily combines with the front covered porch on this three-bedroom ranch home. Inside, columns define the great room, which holds a warming fireplace framed by windows. The master bedroom enjoys a walk-in closet and a luxurious bath including a separate shower and a whirlpool tub. Two family bedrooms share a full bath and views of the front yard. Note the two-car side-access garage—perfect for a corner lot.

PLAN HPT790076

Square Footage: 1,611
Width: 66'-4"
Depth: 43'-10"

Home Suite Home

MBR.
16'4" X 13'0"

DIN.
12'0" X 11'8"

COV. PORCH
9'8" X 12'0"

GRT. RM.
VAULTED CEILING
16'0" X 21'6"

KIT.
10'4" X 13'4"

NK.
11'0" X 9'6"

STORAGE

BR. #3
13'0" X 11'0"

BR. #2
11'-1 1/8" CEILING HGT.
11'0" X 11'8"

F.
VAULTED

3 CAR GARAGE
21'8" X 31'4"

T his traditional home exhibits a Western-ranch style. Brick and traditional siding grace the exterior. Inside, a vaulted and tiled foyer welcomes you into the home. Straight ahead, the great room is warmed by a fireplace. The island kitchen serves the nook and the dining room with ease. The rear covered porch is perfect for outdoor grilling. Family bedrooms include a master suite with a private bath and two additional bedrooms that share a hall bath. A three-car garage with storage, a laundry room and powder room complete the floor plan.

PLAN HPT790077

Square Footage: 1,907
Width: 66'-4"
Depth: 56'-0"

Interior Vistas

This traditional home offers all the amenities of a larger plan in a compact layout. Ten-foot ceilings give this home an expansive feel. An angled eating bar separates the kitchen and the great room, while leaving these areas open for family gatherings and entertaining. The master bedroom includes a huge walk-in closet and a superior master bath with a whirlpool and a separate shower. Please specify crawlspace or slab foundation when ordering.

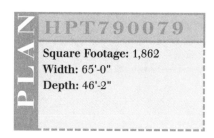

PLAN HPT790079

Square Footage: 1,862
Width: 65'-0"
Depth: 46'-2"

PLAN HPT790078

Square Footage: 1,557
Width: 53'-0"
Depth: 49'-0"

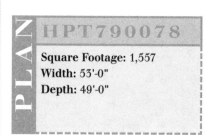

Spacious Suite

Traditional wood siding and compact designing enclose a plan perfect for a young family. This floor plan offers a great room enhanced by a cathedral ceiling with a fireplace and a kitchen open to the spacious dining room. The master bedroom features a tray ceiling, walk-in closet and a private bath. Two bedrooms reside just across the hall. A laundry room and two-car garage complete this plan.

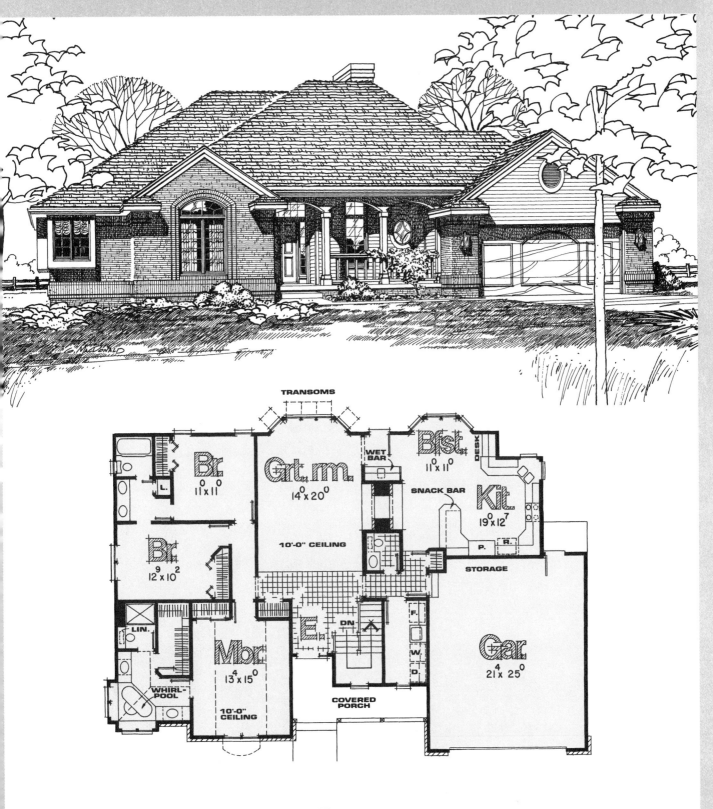

Smart Rooms

PLAN

HPT790080

Square Footage: 1,808
Width: 64'-0"
Depth: 44'-0"

Discriminating buyers will love the refined yet inviting look of this three-bedroom home plan. A tiled entry with a ten-foot ceiling leads into the spacious great room with a large bay window. An open-hearth fireplace warms both the great room and the kitchen. The sleeping area features a spacious master suite with a dramatic arched window and a bath with a whirlpool tub, twin vanities and a walk-in closet. Two secondary bedrooms each have private access to the shared bath. Don't miss the storage space in the oversized garage.

New South

Two arched dormers and a wide open porch welcome guests into this charming home. The entry opens to a skylit and hearth-warmed living room with two French doors opening to the rear porch. Two family bedrooms reside to the right, sharing a full hall bath. The dining room views the front porch. Nearby, the kitchen features a built-in desk and snack bar angled to complement the adjoining bayed breakfast nook. Secluded to the rear of the plan, the comforting master suite provides a luxurious bath. Please specify crawlspace or slab foundation when ordering.

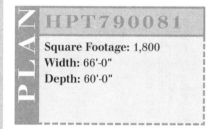

PLAN

HPT790081

Square Footage: 1,800
Width: 66'-0"
Depth: 60'-0"

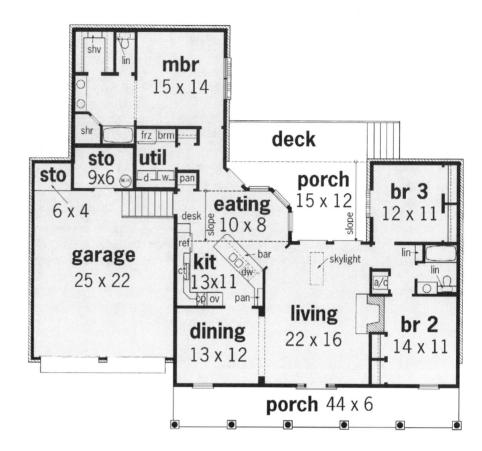

mbr 15 x 14

shv
lin
shr
sto 9x6
sto 6 x 4
util
d w pan
W.H.
frz brm

garage 25 x 22

deck

porch 15 x 12
slope
slope
skylight

br 3 12 x 11
lin
lin

desk
eating 10 x 8
ref
ct
kit 13x11
bar
dw
cp ov
pan

a/c

living 22 x 16

br 2 14 x 11

dining 13 x 12

porch 44 x 6

Hip Chateau

PLAN

HPT790082

Square Footage: 1,770
Width: 64'-0"
Depth: 48'-0"

Keystones and segmental arches draw attention to the beautifully covered porch on this French-style home. Quoins accent the stucco, along with shutters that outline the windows to make a versatile facade. A conveniently placed kitchen and breakfast nook greet the homeowner or guest upon entry—no more carrying groceries through the house! The living room and dining room are open to each other. A fireplace and entertainment center are built-in, creating a focal point. The well-lit master suite includes dual vanities and a spacious walk-in closet. Please specify crawlspace or slab foundation when ordering.

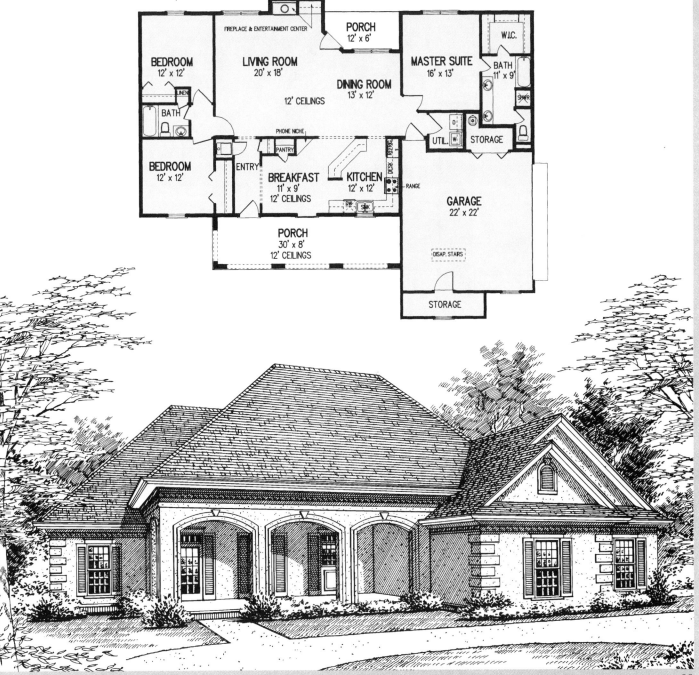

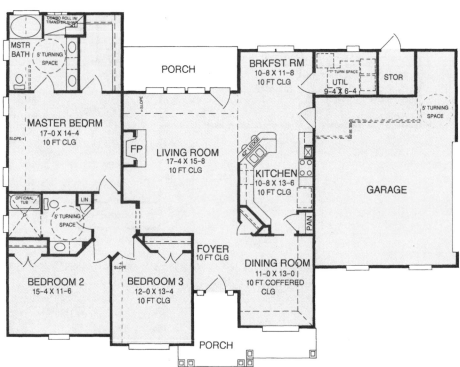

Heart of Luxury

PLAN

HPT790083

Square Footage: 2,000
Width: 65'-10"
Depth: 51'-11"

An arched entrance, a sunburst and sidelights around the four-panel door provide a touch of class to this European-style home. An angled bar opens the kitchen and breakfast room to the living room with bookcases and a fireplace. The master suite boasts a sloped ceiling and private bath with a five-foot turning radius, dual vanity, and a separate tub and shower. Two family bedrooms provide ample closet space and share a full hall bath and linen closet. Don't miss the two-car garage located to the far right of the plan.

Lavish Amenities

Enter this beautiful home through graceful archways and columns. The foyer, dining room and living room are one open space, defined by a creative room arrangement. The living room opens to the breakfast room and porch. The bedrooms are off a small hall reached through an archway. Two family bedrooms share a bath, while the master bedroom enjoys a private bath with a double-bowl vanity. A garage with storage and a utility room complete the floor plan. Please specify slab or crawlspace foundation when ordering.

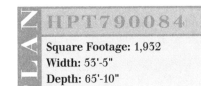

PLAN

HPT790084

Square Footage: 1,932
Width: 53'-5"
Depth: 65'-10"

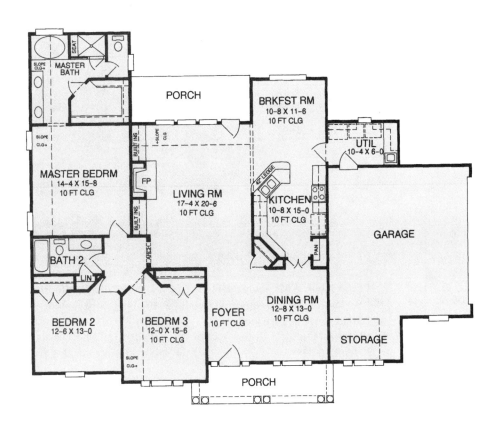

All the Angles

Palladian windows, underscored by a soaring covered portico, unite the foyer, living and dining rooms in splendid, sunlit radiance. A corner fireplace enhances the family room. The kitchen serves the dining room through a pocket door and opens to the breakfast area with a garden window and patio access. The master bedroom offers a sliding door to the patio and a pocket door to a full bath with a walk-in closet and spa tub.

PLAN HPT790085

Square Footage: 2,041
Width: 60'-0"
Depth: 56'-0"

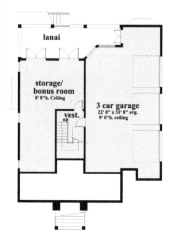

PLAN HPT790086

First Floor: 1,671 square feet
Second Floor: 846 square feet
Total: 2,517 square feet
Width: 44'-0"
Depth: 55'-0"

Wide Veranda

This magnificent villa boasts a beautiful stucco exterior, Spanish-tiled roof and Old World details such as arches and accent columns framing the spectacular entry. The striking interior revisits the past in glorious style and sets a new standard for comfort and luxury. Open rooms, French doors and vaulted ceilings add an air of spaciousness throughout the home. To the right of the foyer, an open formal dining room provides dazzling views.

Haute House

Bedroom 2
volume ceiling
11⁰ • 10⁰

Covered Patio

opt.
summer
kitchen

Master
Bedroom
volume ceiling
15⁰ • 12⁰

Bath

m   opt. media center
or fireplace

sh

Family Room
volume ceiling
16⁸ • 14⁴

lin

sh   w.i.c.

Bath

pan

Bedroom 3
volume ceiling
11⁰ • 10⁰

ref

dw

Kitchen
volume ceiling

w

d

ac

Living Room
13⁶ • 11⁰
volume ceiling

ac

wh

Dining
11⁴ • 11⁰

Double Garage

© 91 HOME DESIGN SERVICES, INC.

Foyer

Entry

Enjoy resort-style living in this striking sun-country home. Guests will always feel welcome when entertained in the formal living and dining areas, but the eat-in country kitchen overlooking the family room will be the center of attention. Casual living will be enjoyed in the large family room and out on the patio with the help of an optional summer kitchen and view of the fairway. Built-in shelves and an optional media center provide decorating options. The master suite features a volume ceiling and a spacious master bath.

PLAN

HPT790087

Square Footage: 1,550
Width: 43'-0"
Depth: 59'-0"

SEN PTL.

PLAN HPT790089

Square Footage: 1,118
Width: 30'-0"
Depth: 60'-0"

Great Outdoors

Decorative stucco touches, an impressive entry and muntin windows grace the exterior of this home. The living room flows easily into the dining room—both boast volume ceilings. The galley kitchen looks over to the dining room. A patio or optional screened porch is accessed from the dining area. The master bath is located to the rear of the plan, away from street traffic, and sports a full bath.

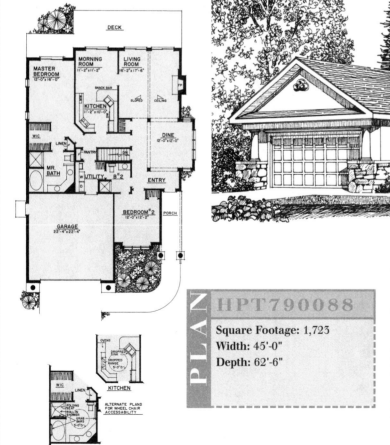

PLAN HPT790088

Square Footage: 1,723
Width: 45'-0"
Depth: 62'-6"

Entertainment Deck

A new-age contemporary touch graces the exterior of this impressive yet affordable home. The entry leads to the formal areas in the open dining room and vaulted living room. The kitchen overlooks a quaint morning room. The rear deck will host a variety of outdoor activities. With a walk-in closet and private bath, homeowners will be pampered in the master suite. The second bedroom, two-car garage and utility room complete the plan.

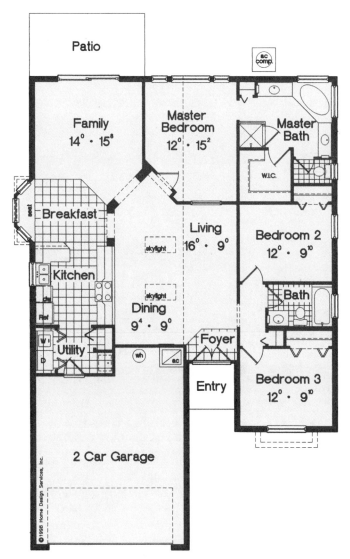

Tomorrow House

A simple yet detailed design, the exterior of this home boasts keystone lintels, muntin windows, French-style shutters and a stucco facade. Volume ceilings in all rooms, arches, plant shelves and look-over walls make this home feel much larger. A large transom above the front double doors floods the foyer with natural light. Sleeping quarters take up residence on the right side of the plan, including a large master bedroom with a full bath. The spacious dining/living room is complemented with skylights.

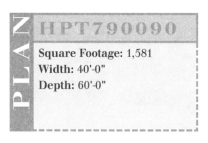

PLAN HPT790090

Square Footage: 1,581
Width: 40'-0"
Depth: 60'-0"

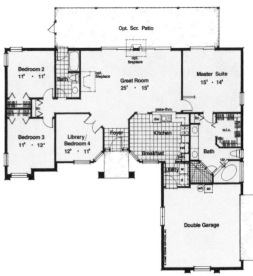

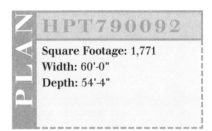

Grand Spaces

A home reminiscent of Mediterranean influences, this plan displays stucco, a high entry and an abundance of windows. The expansive great room is truly the *piece de resistance* in this home—it boasts space for two optional fireplaces and looks to the rear patio through lovely muntin windows. The master suite is secluded for increased privacy and boasts sliding glass doors to the patio, a garden tub, separate shower and a spacious walk-in closet.

PLAN HPT790092

Square Footage: 1,771
Width: 60'-0"
Depth: 54'-4"

PLAN HPT790091

Square Footage: 1,702
Width: 55'-0"
Depth: 76'-4"

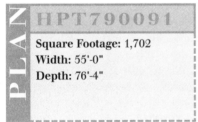

Euro-American Charm

Arched lintels, shutters and a welcoming covered entryway lend this home country charm. Inside, the foyer leads directly to the great room with a fireplace and built-ins along two walls. The sleeping quarters all reside on the left of this design. The master suite includes a lavish bath with a garden tub, separate shower, dual vanity sinks and a compartmented toilet. Two secondary bedrooms share a bath. Please specify basement, crawlspace or slab foundation when ordering.

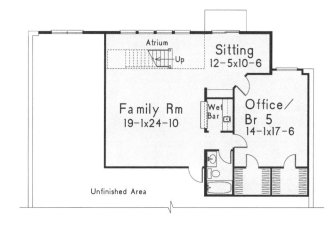

Atrium

Sitting
12-5x10-6

Up

Family Rm
19-1x24-10

Wet
Bar

Office/
Br 5
14-1x17-6

Unfinished Area

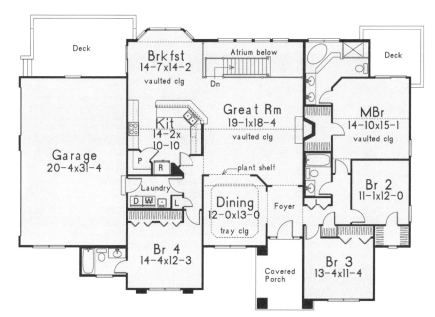

Deck

Brkfst
14-7x14-2
vaulted clg

Atrium below

Dn

Deck

Kit
14-2x
10-10

Great Rm
19-1x18-4
vaulted clg

MBr
14-10x15-1
vaulted clg

Garage
20-4x31-4

P

R

plant shelf

Laundry

D W L

Dining
12-0x13-0

tray clg

Foyer

Br 2
11-1x12-0

Br 4
14-4x12-3

Covered
Porch

Br 3
13-4x11-4

Sunset House

Contemporary and Mediter-ranean influences shape the spirit and inner spaces of this new-age home. An arched entrance and front covered porch welcome you inside to the formal dining room and great room. The relaxing kitchen/breakfast area is reserved for more intimate and casual occasions. The master suite provides a walk-in closet and private bath. Bedrooms 2 and 3 share a hall bath. Bedroom 4 makes the perfect guest suite. A family room, sitting area, wet bar, office and additional bath reside upstairs.

PLAN HPT790093

Square Footage: 2,408
Width: 75'-8"
Depth: 52'-6"

Fabulous Retreat

Quoins, keystone lintels and two picture windows adorn the stucco exterior of this charming four-bedroom home. Inside, the foyer introduces a dining room adorned with graceful columns. The nearby kitchen features a sunny breakfast nook, walk-in pantry and an angled serving bar to the living room. A hearth with built-in shelves enhances the living room, which also includes rear porch access. A tray ceiling accents the master suite, which also enjoys a luxurious bath.

PLAN

HPT790095

Square Footage: 2,391
Width: 61'-10"
Depth: 64'-11"

Juliet's Balcony

This wonderful transitional plan combines the best of contemporary and traditional styling. Its stucco exterior is enhanced by arched windows and a recessed arched entry plus a lovely balcony off the second floor master bedroom. The family room is set off behind the garage and features a sloped ceiling and fireplace. Sleeping quarters consist of two secondary bedrooms with a shared bath and a generous master suite with a well-appointed bath.

PLAN

HPT790094

First Floor: 1,023 square feet
Second Floor: 866 square feet
Total: 1,889 square feet
Width: 52'-4"
Depth: 34'-8"

L D

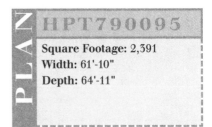

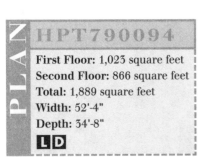

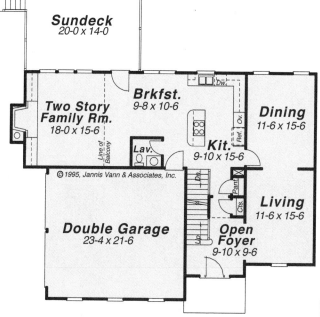

Sundeck
20-0 x 14-0

Two Story Family Rm.
18-0 x 15-6

Brkfst.
9-8 x 10-6

Dw.

Dining
11-6 x 15-6

Ref. | Ov.

Kit.
9-10 x 15-6

Line of Balcony

Lav.

© 1995, Jannis Vann & Associates, Inc.

Dn.

Pant.

Clts.

Living
11-6 x 15-6

Double Garage
23-4 x 21-6

Up

Open Foyer
9-10 x 9-6

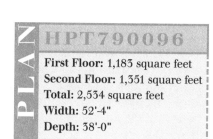

PLAN

HPT790096

First Floor: 1,183 square feet
Second Floor: 1,351 square feet
Total: 2,534 square feet
Width: 52'-4"
Depth: 38'-0"

Sun Deck

Stucco and corner quoins adorn this wonderful home, which features a two-story family room, a spacious island kitchen with a breakfast area, and formal dining and living rooms. The rear sun deck will be enjoyed throughout seasonal summer barbecues. A two-car garage completes the first floor. All four family bedrooms are upstairs, including the master bedroom with its tray ceiling, private bath and impressive walk-in closet. Bedroom 4 also features its own private bath. Please specify basement, crawlspace or slab foundation when ordering.

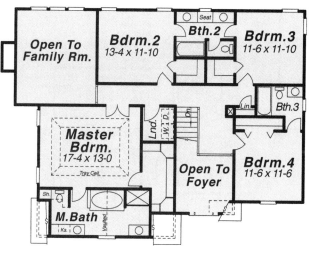

Open To Family Rm.

Seat

Bdrm.2
13-4 x 11-10

Bth.2

Bdrm.3
11-6 x 11-10

Lin.

Bth.3

Master Bdrm.
17-4 x 13-0

Lnd.

W.D.

Dn.

Up

Tray Ceil.

Open To Foyer

Bdrm.4
11-6 x 11-6

Sh.

M.Bath

Lks.

Vaulted

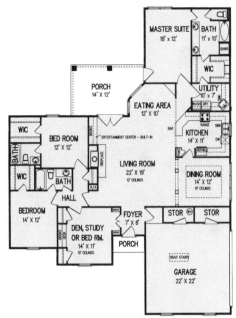

Provençal Cool

A versatile swing room highlights this charming French-style home. At the center of the plan is a spacious living room with a fireplace and a built-in entertainment center. Enjoy entertaining in the dining room, complete with columns and arches at the entry and a ribbon of windows to let in sunlight or moonbeams. The king-sized master suite is isolated for privacy and furnishes a spacious bath and walk-in closet. Please specify crawlspace or slab foundation when ordering.

PLAN HPT790098

Square Footage: 2,200
Width: 56'-0"
Depth: 74'-0"

PLAN HPT790097

Square Footage: 1,828
Width: 64'-0"
Depth: 62'-0"

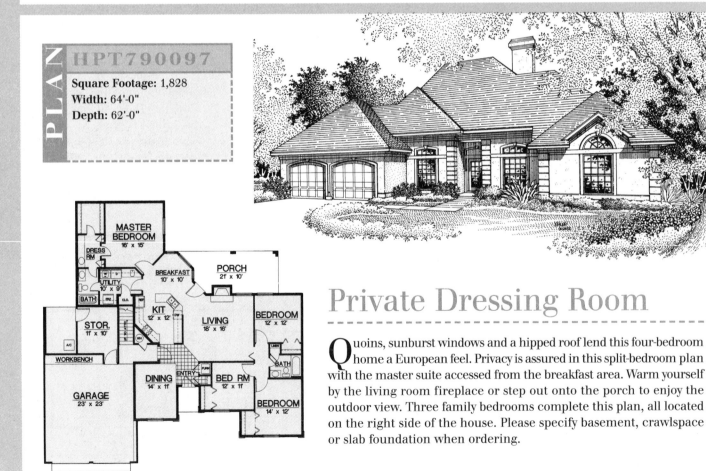

Private Dressing Room

Quoins, sunburst windows and a hipped roof lend this four-bedroom home a European feel. Privacy is assured in this split-bedroom plan with the master suite accessed from the breakfast area. Warm yourself by the living room fireplace or step out onto the porch to enjoy the outdoor view. Three family bedrooms complete this plan, all located on the right side of the house. Please specify basement, crawlspace or slab foundation when ordering.

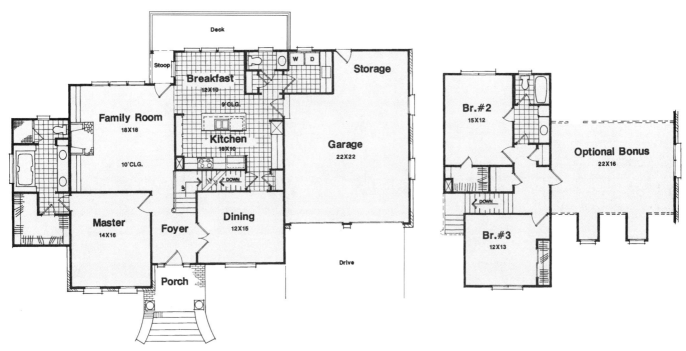

Curb Appeal

PLAN

HPT790099

First Floor: 1,633 square feet
Second Floor: 624 square feet
Total: 2,257 square feet
Width: 70'-0"
Depth: 47'-0"

Unique rooflines, strong graceful pillars and a covered front porch all combine to give this home plenty of curb appeal. With a first-floor master suite, this home is great for a growing family or for empty-nesters. The master bath includes a spacious walk-in closet. The family room features a fireplace, while the kitchen is placed conveniently between the dining and breakfast rooms. An optional bonus room on the second floor could provide plenty of expansion space if needed. Note the handy storage in the two-car garage.

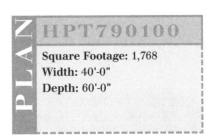

Old World Charm

All of the negatives of a narrow plan have been overcome in this ingenious design. All entrances to major spaces of this home are at an angle to give a feeling of spaciousness. The living/dining room is entered through a distinct foyer, complete with decorative niche and low walls which define the space. An angled archway next to another niche brings you into the family center. The master suite, with panoramic views, boasts a generous bath.

PLAN HPT790100

Square Footage: 1,768
Width: 40'-0"
Depth: 60'-0"

PLAN HPT790101

Square Footage: 1,890
Width: 65'-10"
Depth: 53'-5"

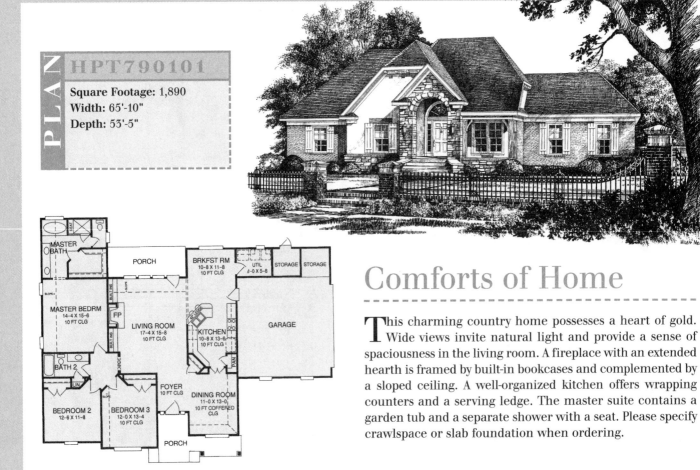

Comforts of Home

This charming country home possesses a heart of gold. Wide views invite natural light and provide a sense of spaciousness in the living room. A fireplace with an extended hearth is framed by built-in bookcases and complemented by a sloped ceiling. A well-organized kitchen offers wrapping counters and a serving ledge. The master suite contains a garden tub and a separate shower with a seat. Please specify crawlspace or slab foundation when ordering.

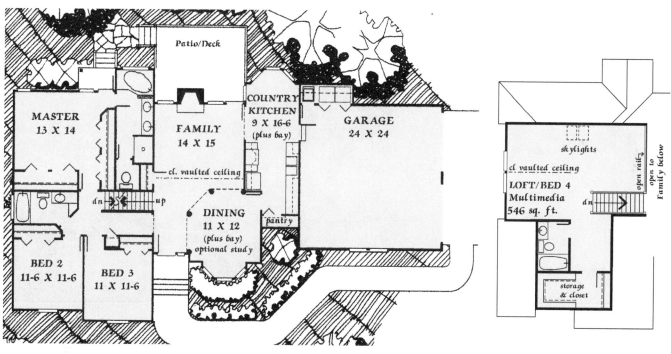

Patio/Deck

MASTER
13 X 14

FAMILY
14 X 15

COUNTRY
KITCHEN
9 X 16-6
(plus bay)

GARAGE
24 X 24

cl. vaulted ceiling

dn   up

DINING
11 X 12
(plus bay)
optional study

pantry

BED 2
11-6 X 11-6

BED 3
11 X 11-6

skylights

cl vaulted ceiling

LOFT/BED 4
Multimedia
546 sq. ft.

open rail

open to
Family below

dn

storage
& closet

Country Kitchen

The short-hipped gabled roof, the attention to detail around the vents, vertical corner stone, period shutters and stone treatment above and below the windows identify this as a refined stucco-and-stone home in traditional European Country style. The dramatic open entry—illuminated by an arched window—gives first hints to a well-planned ranch home. Three amply sized bedrooms are secluded to one side of the house for privacy. The country kitchen serves the dining room, which is open to the family room with fireplace. A vaulted ceiling enhances a loft upstairs.

PLAN **HPT790102**

First Floor: 1,490 square feet
Second Floor: 549 square feet
Total: 2,039 square feet
Width: 72'-0"
Depth: 42'-0"

Great Classic

This elaborate exterior expresses a transitional-style home. The brick-and-stone facade with rich, strong accents gives a solid look to the overall plan. The large foyer introduces an elegantly turned staircase and a spacious great room. The large kitchen with an angled island serves the formal and informal dining areas with equal ease. A loft overlooks the two-story great room and provides room for a library or computer space.

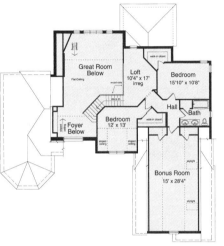

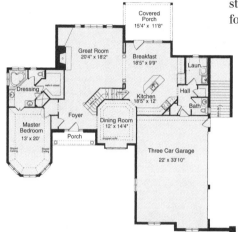

PLAN HPT790103

First Floor: 1,823 square feet
Second Floor: 761 square feet
Total: 2,584 square feet
Bonus Room: 492 square feet
Width: 63'-6"
Depth: 62'-1"

PLAN HPT790104

Square Footage: 1,175
Width: 44'-0"
Depth: 46'-0"

Dinner by the Bay

Contemporary style and European influences shape this brick exterior. The entry opens to a living room area warmed by a fireplace. The island snack-bar kitchen combines with a circular bayed breakfast room for casual family meals. The two family bedrooms share a hall bath with a corner tub, separate shower and a double-bowl vanity. This home is designed with a basement foundation.

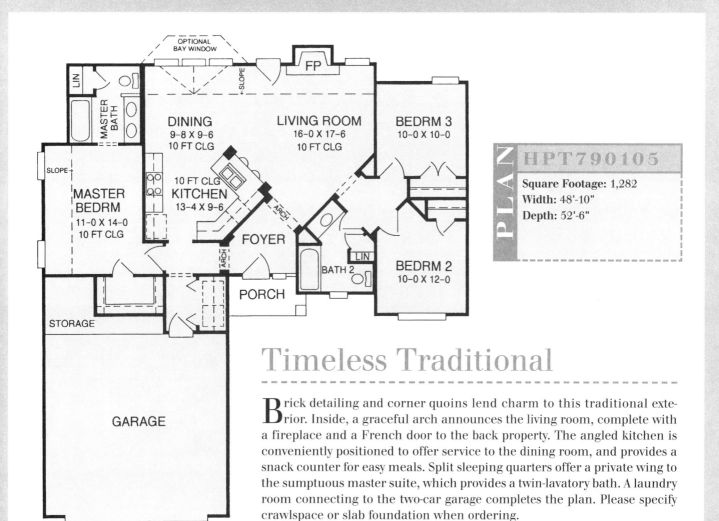

DINING
9–8 X 9–6
10 FT CLG

LIVING ROOM
16–0 X 17–6
10 FT CLG

BEDRM 3
10–0 X 10–0

OPTIONAL BAY WINDOW

SLOPE

FP

LIN

MASTER BATH

SLOPE

MASTER BEDRM
11–0 X 14–0
10 FT CLG

10 FT CLG
KITCHEN
13–4 X 9–6

ARCH

ARCH

FOYER

ARCH

BATH 2

LIN

BEDRM 2
10–0 X 12–0

PORCH

STORAGE

GARAGE

PLAN

HPT790105

Square Footage: 1,282
Width: 48'-10"
Depth: 52'-6"

Timeless Traditional

Brick detailing and corner quoins lend charm to this traditional exterior. Inside, a graceful arch announces the living room, complete with a fireplace and a French door to the back property. The angled kitchen is conveniently positioned to offer service to the dining room, and provides a snack counter for easy meals. Split sleeping quarters offer a private wing to the sumptuous master suite, which provides a twin-lavatory bath. A laundry room connecting to the two-car garage completes the plan. Please specify crawlspace or slab foundation when ordering.

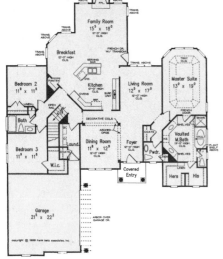

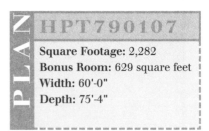

Optional Basement
Stair Location

Feng Shui

Columns and keystone lintels lend a European aura to this stone-and-siding home. Arched openings and decorative columns define the formal dining room to the left of the foyer. A ribbon of windows with transoms above draws sunshine into the living room. The master suite enjoys a tray ceiling and a vaulted bathroom. Transoms abound in the open informal living areas. Please specify basement or crawlspace foundation when ordering.

PLAN HPT790107

Square Footage: 2,282
Bonus Room: 629 square feet
Width: 60'-0"
Depth: 75'-4"

Living In Style

An appealing blend of stone, siding and stucco announces a 21st-Century floor plan. A formal dining area defined by decorative columns opens to a grand great room with a centered hearth. The gourmet kitchen overlooks the great room and enjoys natural light brought in by the bayed breakfast nook. The sleeping wing, to the right of the plan, includes a sumptuous master suite with a tray ceiling and a skylit bath with twin vanities. The secluded study and a family bedroom share a bath.

PLAN HPT790106

Square Footage: 1,912
Bonus Room: 398 square feet
Width: 67'-7"
Depth: 56'-7"

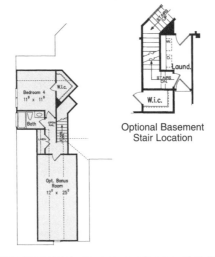

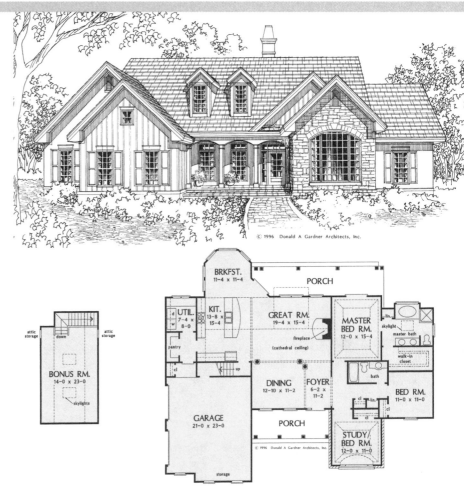

© 1996 Donald A Gardner Architects, Inc.

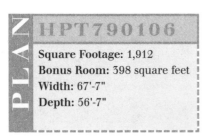

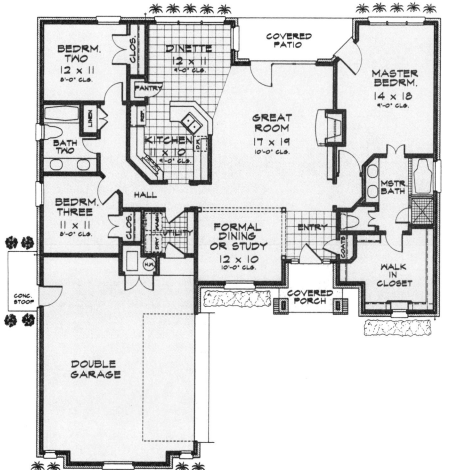

Flex Space

Corner quoins, French shutters and rounded windows provide an Old World feel to this modern cottage design. A stunning brick facade hints at the exquisite beauty of the interior spaces. The great room is warmed by a fireplace and accesses the rear patio. The casual kitchen/dinette area provides pantry space. The master suite offers a private bath and a walk-in closet. Two family bedrooms on the opposite side of the home share a full hall bath and linen storage. A double garage and laundry room are located nearby.

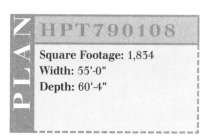

PLAN HPT790108

Square Footage: 1,834
Width: 55'-0"
Depth: 60'-4"

Ceramic Tile Floors

European influences subtly enhance the appearance of this modern-day cottage. Brick and stone and a brilliant bay window add alluring textures to the exterior. Inside, the foyer is flanked by formal living and dining rooms. The family room features a fireplace, while the kitchen/breakfast area is nearby for convenience. The master suite and breakfast room access the rear covered patio. Three additional family bedrooms share a hall bath, located behind the three-car garage.

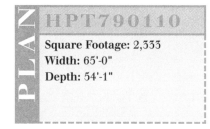

PLAN
HPT790110

Square Footage: 2,333
Width: 65'-0"
Depth: 54'-1"

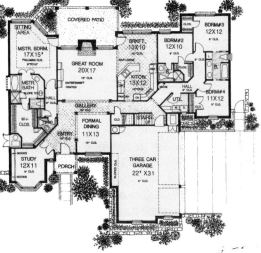

PLAN
HPT790109

Square Footage: 2,630
Bonus Room: 627 square feet
Width: 73'-6"
Depth: 67'-7"

Head Space

Straight out of a fairy tale, this charming European cottage will catch of the eye of neighborhood onlookers. Inside, a study with space for computers and books opens from the foyer. The master suite features a private bath, walk-in closet and access to the rear patio. Two family bedrooms share a Jack-and-Jill bath, while another bedroom offers its own bath. Upstairs, a recreation room illuminated by skylights provides plenty of room for the whole family.

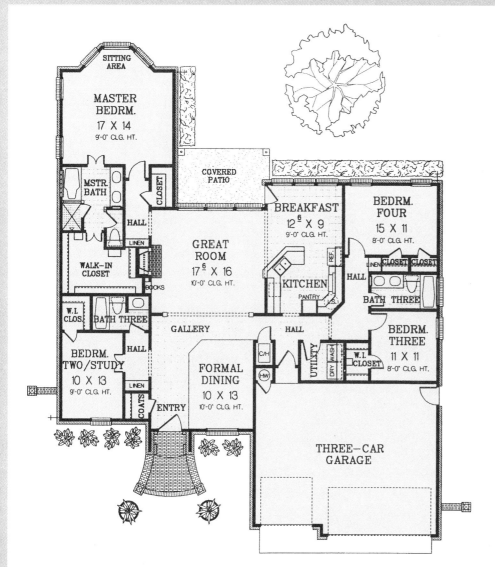

Floor plan labels:

SITTING AREA

MASTER BEDRM.
17 X 14
9'-0" CLG. HT.

MSTR. BATH

HALL

CLOSET

COVERED PATIO

BREAKFAST
12⁶ X 9
9'-0" CLG. HT.

BEDRM. FOUR
15 X 11
8'-0" CLG. HT.

GREAT ROOM
17⁶ X 16
10'-0" CLG. HT.

KITCHEN

PANTRY

REF.

LINEN

CLOSET CLOSET

HALL

BATH THREE

LINEN

BOOKS

WALK-IN CLOSET

W.I. CLOS.

BATH THREE

GALLERY

HALL

C/H

UTILITY

DRY WASH

W.I. CLOSET

BEDRM. THREE
11 X 11
8'-0" CLG. HT.

BEDRM. TWO/STUDY
10 X 13
9'-0" CLG. HT.

HALL

LINEN

COATS

ENTRY

FORMAL DINING
10 X 13
10'-0" CLG. HT.

HW

THREE-CAR GARAGE

Euro Hip

Intermingled European influences dazzle the exterior of this quaint cottage design. Inside, a gallery separates the great room, which boasts a fireplace, from the formal dining room. Bedroom 2 with a walk-in closet is flexible as a quiet study. The kitchen is open to the casual breakfast area, accessing the rear covered patio. The master bedroom offers a private bath and huge walk-in closet. Two additional family bedrooms on the opposite side of the home share a full hall bath. A spacious three-car garage completes the floor plan.

PLAN

HPT790111

Square Footage: 2,324
Width: 60'-0"
Depth: 74'-1"

Outer Space

Exquisite French style overwhelms the exterior of this modern European cottage. A porch leads to an entry introducing a study and an open great room. The kitchen is open to a dinette area that accesses the rear porch. The master suite features a private bath and walk-in closet. Bedrooms 2 and 3 share a full hall bath. Down the hall, a utility room connects to the two-car garage.

PLAN HPT790113

Square Footage: 1,736
Width: 50'-0"
Depth: 62'-10"

Five-Star Screen Porch

This Western ranch features the most traditional and modern amenities for family comfort. The two-car garage opens into the tiled entry. The dining room opens to the great room with a fireplace and built-ins. Double doors open to a screened porch. The first-floor master suite offers a private bath and walk-in closet. On the lower level, an optional third bedroom is placed next to a full bath. An optional recreation room is provided.

PLAN HPT790112

Square Footage: 1,675
Basement: 729 square feet
Width: 68'-4"
Depth: 45'-0"

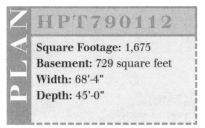

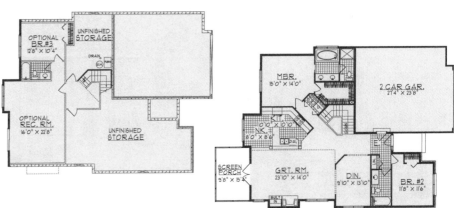

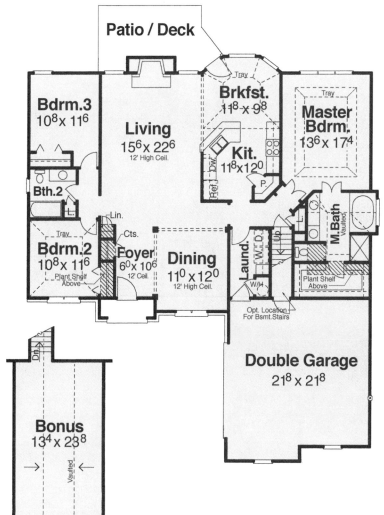

Patio / Deck

Bdrm.3
10^8 x 11^6

Living
15^6 x 22^6
12' High Ceil.

Brkfst.
11^8 x 9^8

Tray

Master Bdrm.
13^6 x 17^4

Tray

Kit.
11^8 x 12^0

Ref.
D.w.

P.

Bth.2

Lin.
Cts.
Tray

Bdrm.2
10^8 x 11^6
Plant Shelf Above

Foyer
6^0 x 10^6
12' Ceil.

Dining
11^0 x 12^0
12' High Ceil.

Laund.
W./D.

Up.

M.Bath
Vaulted

Plant Shelf Above

Opt. Location
For Bsmt.Stairs

W/H

Double Garage
21^8 x 21^8

Dn.

Bonus
13^4 x 23^8
Vaulted

Fun Sun Deck

A rustic exterior of shingles, siding and stone provides a sweet country look. Inside, the foyer is flanked by the dining room and family bedrooms. Bedrooms 2 and 3 share a full hall bath. The master suite is located on the opposite side of the home and features a private bath and walk-in closet. The kitchen opens to a breakfast room that accesses the rear sun deck. The spacious living room is warmed by a central fireplace. The laundry room and double-car garage complete this plan. Please specify crawl-space, slab or basement foundation when ordering.

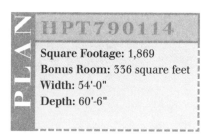

PLAN
HPT790114
Square Footage: 1,869
Bonus Room: 336 square feet
Width: 54'-0"
Depth: 60'-6"

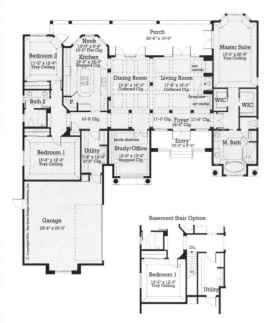

Arts and Crafts

The modern rustic look of this cottage lends a unique charm to the overall plan. Inside, the foyer faces a formal area made up of the combined living and dining rooms. The island kitchen expands into a bayed nook. The study/office is placed just off the entry. Two family bedrooms share a hall bath. Double doors open into the master suite, which offers two walk-in closets and a private bath. Please specify slab or basement foundation when ordering.

Great Digs

Contemporary European accents define the exterior, while modern amenities are plentiful within. The formal dining room and study flank the foyer. The master suite offers its own bath and walk-in closet. The enormous great room boasts a fireplace and accesses the rear porch. Two family bedrooms are placed on the other side of the kitchen and breakfast room. The three-car garage offers a space for every family member.

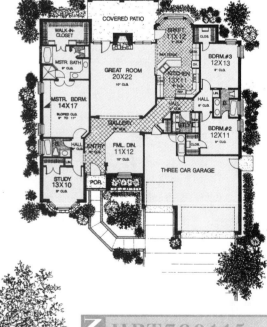

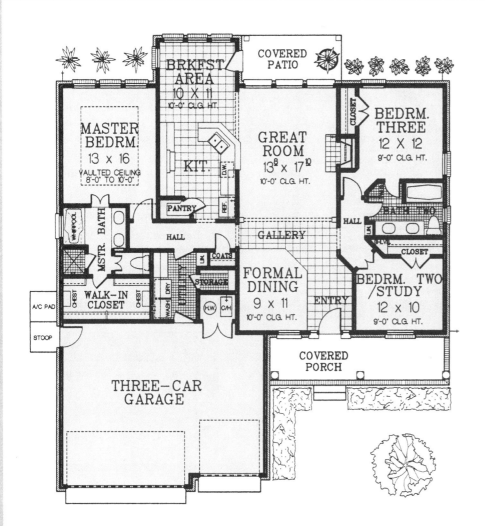

MASTER
BEDRM.
13 x 16
VAULTED CEILING
8'-0" TO 10'-0"

BRKFST
AREA
10 X 11
10'-0" CLG. HT.

COVERED
PATIO

GREAT
ROOM
13⁸ x 17¹⁰
10'-0" CLG. HT.

BEDRM.
THREE
12 X 12
9'-0" CLG. HT.

KIT.

CLOSET

PANTRY

REF.

D.W.

MSTR. BATH

W-POOL

GALLERY

HALL

BATH TWO

CLOSET

HALL

COATS

FORMAL
DINING
9 x 11
10'-0" CLG. HT.

ENTRY

BEDRM. TWO
/STUDY
12 x 10
9'-0" CLG. HT.

WALK-IN
CLOSET

CHEST

CHEST

A/C PAD

STOOP

STORAGE

UTILITY

WASH

DRY

H-W

C/H

THREE-CAR
GARAGE

COVERED
PORCH

From the Heart

The popular appeal of this pampering classic home is all about the amenities found within. A covered front porch welcomes you inside to a foyer flanked on either side by a study and formal dining room. Across the gallery, the great room features a fireplace. The kitchen with pantry opens to the breakfast room accessing the rear porch. The master suite boasts a private bath with a walk-in closet. The study converts to a second family bedroom and shares a hall bath with Bedroom 3. A laundry and three-car garage complete this efficient family plan.

PLAN HPT790117

Square Footage: 1,797
Width: 53'-0"
Depth: 60'-1"

Easy Breezy

This trendy cabin is the ideal vacation home for a mountain retreat. The stone-and-siding exterior blends well into any country scene. Inside, the study is enhanced by a vaulted ceiling and double doors, which open onto the front balcony. This room is a perfect home office for quiet escapes. Vaulted ceilings create a spacious feel throughout the home, especially in the central great room, which overlooks the rear deck—perfect for summertime entertainment.

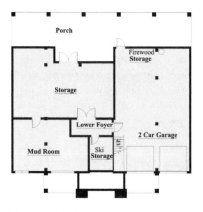

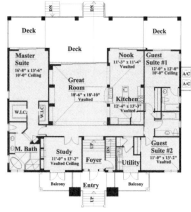

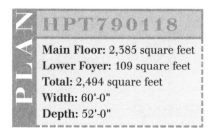

PLAN HPT790118

Main Floor: 2,385 square feet
Lower Foyer: 109 square feet
Total: 2,494 square feet
Width: 60'-0"
Depth: 52'-0"

Grand Manor

With a rugged blend of stone and siding, an inviting mix of details creates the kind of comfortable beauty that every homeowner craves. Craftsman elements easily take on the most modish of neighborhoods but speak of personal taste too. Massive stone columns support a striking pediment entry, which leads up to the dazzling main-level landing and great room. A spacious formal dining room complements a gourmet kitchen designed to serve any occasion.

PLAN HPT790119

Square Footage: 2,430
Width: 70'-2"
Depth: 53'-0"

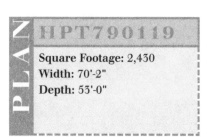

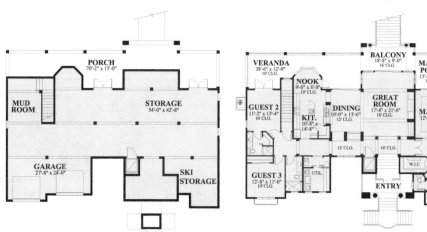

History Lesson

The horizontal lines and straightforward details of this rustic plan borrow freely from the Arts and Crafts style, remembered with a dash of traditional warmth. Gallery porches open the indoors to nature, and classy windows add plenty of wide views. An intelligent arrangement of rooms provides both formal and casual living space to the left of the plan. The master retreat is all decked out with a wall of glass, two walk-in closets and generous dressing space.

firewood storage

covered porch
9' 4"h. ceiling

Mud Area
9' 0"h. ceiling

up foyer

storage/
bonus room
9' 0"h. ceiling

2 car garage
9' 0"h. ceiling

ski storage

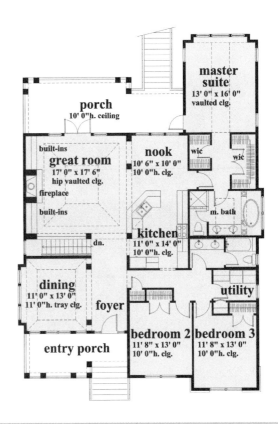

porch
10' 0"h. ceiling

master suite
13' 0" x 16' 0"
vaulted clg.

built-ins

great room
17' 0" x 17' 6"
hip vaulted clg.

nook
10' 6" x 10' 0"
10' 0"h. clg.

wic

wic

fireplace

built-ins

m. bath

dn.

kitchen
11' 0" x 14' 0"
10' 0"h. clg.

dining
11' 0" x 13' 0"
11' 0"h. tray clg.

foyer

utility

bedroom 2
11' 8" x 13' 0"
10' 0"h. clg.

bedroom 3
11' 8" x 13' 0"
10' 0"h. clg.

entry porch

P L A N
HPT790120

Square Footage: 2,137
Width: 44'-0"
Depth: 63'-0"

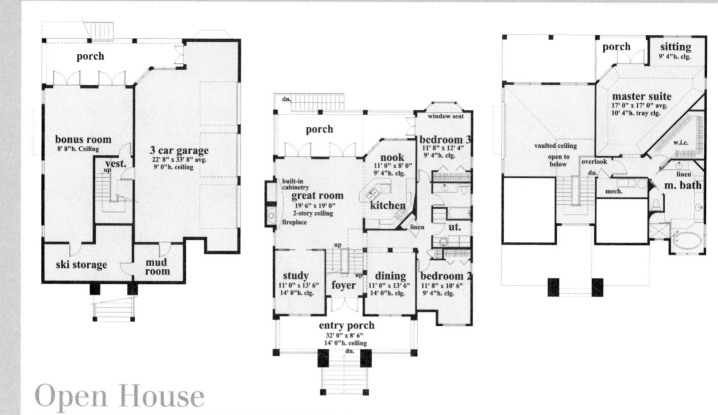

porch

bonus room
8' 8"h. Ceiling

3 car garage
22' 8" x 33' 8" avg.
9' 0"h. ceiling

vest.
up

ski storage

mud room

---

dn.

porch

built-in cabinetry

great room
19' 6" x 19' 0"
2-story ceiling
fireplace

nook
11' 0" x 8' 0"
9' 4"h. clg.

kitchen

window seat

bedroom 3
11' 8" x 12' 4"
9' 4"h. clg.

linen

ut.

up

study
11' 0" x 13' 6"
14' 0"h. clg.

up

foyer

dining
11' 0" x 13' 6"
14' 0"h. clg.

bedroom 2
11' 8" x 10' 6"
9' 4"h. clg.

entry porch
32' 0" x 8' 6"
14' 0"h. ceiling
dn.

---

porch

sitting
9' 4"h. clg.

master suite
17' 0" x 17' 0" avg.
10' 4"h. tray clg.

vaulted ceiling
open to below

overlook

dn.

w.i.c.

linen

mech.

m. bath

Open House

P L A N

HPT790121

First Floor: 1,671 square feet
Second Floor: 846 square feet
Vestibule: 140 square feet
Total: 2,657 square feet
Width: 44'-0"
Depth: 55'-0"

An array of elegant details creates a welcoming entry to this new-century home, with massive stone pillars, a matchstick pediment and a stunning turret. The mid-level foyer leads up to the spacious living area and down to the lower-level bonus room, which boasts a covered porch, ski storage, a mud room and a three-car garage. A vaulted ceiling highlights the great room, and a fireplace warms the open interior. French doors bring in a feeling of nature. Upstairs, a rambling master suite enjoys a luxury bath and a walk-in closet with a dressing area.

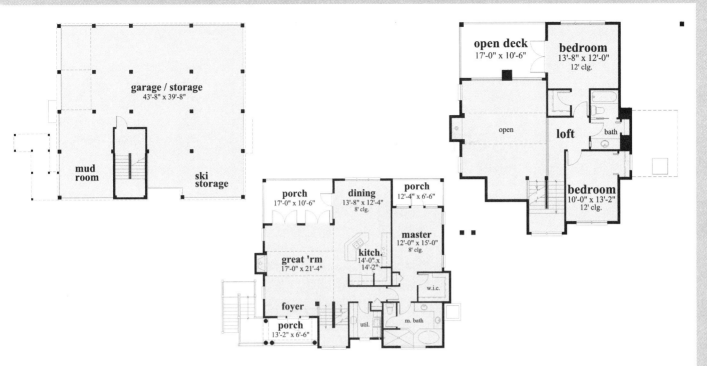

garage / storage
43'-8" x 39'-8"

mud room

ski storage

open deck
17'-0" x 10'-6"

bedroom
13'-8" x 12'-0"
12' clg.

open

loft

bath

bedroom
10'-0" x 13'-2"
12' clg.

porch
17'-0" x 10'-6"

dining
13'-8" x 12'-4"
8' clg.

porch
12'-4" x 6'-6"

great 'rm
17'-0" x 21'-4"

kitch.
14'-0" x 14'-2"

master
12'-0" x 15'-0"
8' clg.

w.i.c.

foyer

util.

m. bath

porch
13'-2" x 6'-6"

Porches, Porches, Porches

Matchstick details and a careful blend of stone and siding lend a special style and spirit to this stately retreat. Multi-pane windows take in the scenery and deck out the refined exterior of this cabin-style home designed for a life of luxury. An open foyer shares its natural light with the great room—a bright reprieve filled with its own outdoor light. Dinner guests may wander from the coziness of the hearth space into the crisp night air through lovely French doors. The master retreat is an entire wing of the main level.

PLAN

HPT790122

First Floor: 1,342 square feet
Second Floor: 511 square feet
Total: 1,853 square feet
Width: 44'-0"
Depth: 40'-0"

PLAN HPT790124

First Floor: 993 square feet
Second Floor: 642 square feet
Total: 1,635 square feet
Width: 28'-0"
Depth: 44'-0"

Open Shutters

This modern three-level home is just right for a young family. The main level features a study, kitchen, dining room, laundry and two-story living room with a corner fireplace. A rear patio makes summertime grilling fun. The master bedroom is vaulted and features a double-bowl vanity bath and walk-in closet. Bedroom 2 offers its own full bath as well. The basement level boasts a spacious garage and storage area.

Pure and Simple

A mixture of materials and modern styling offers a lovely home plan for the small family. The main level provides formal living and dining rooms as well as a kitchen area. The quiet study may be converted to an additional bedroom as space is needed. A laundry and powder room are located nearby. The vaulted master bedroom boasts a private bath with a double-bowl vanity and a walk-in closet. Bedroom 2 provides its own bath.

PLAN HPT790123

First Floor: 1,005 square feet
Second Floor: 620 square feet
Total: 1,625 square feet
Width: 30'-0"
Depth: 44'-6"

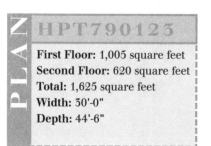

On Another Level

The contemporary look of this modern country design is both impressive and unique. Enormous windows brighten and enliven every interior space. The vaulted family room features a fireplace, while a two-sided fireplace warms the formal living and dining rooms. The gourmet island kitchen opens to a nook. Double doors open into a den that accesses the front deck. Upstairs, the master bedroom features a private bath with linen storage, along with a walk-in closet. Two family bedrooms share a Jack-and-Jill bath. The two-car garage features a storage area on the lower level.

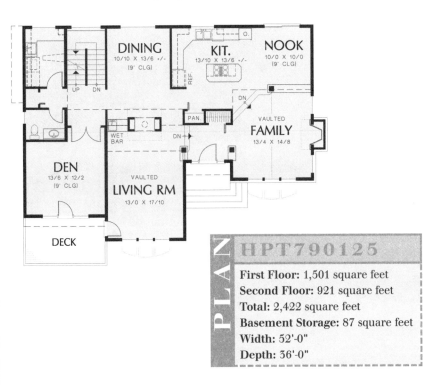

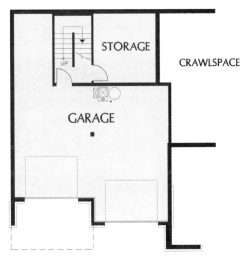

PLAN
HPT790125

First Floor: 1,501 square feet
Second Floor: 921 square feet
Total: 2,422 square feet
Basement Storage: 87 square feet
Width: 52'-0"
Depth: 36'-0"

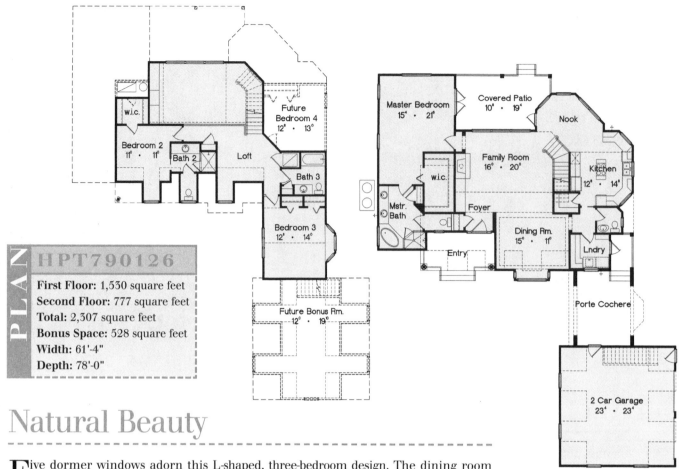

HPT790126

First Floor: 1,530 square feet
Second Floor: 777 square feet
Total: 2,307 square feet
Bonus Space: 528 square feet
Width: 61'-4"
Depth: 78'-0"

Natural Beauty

Five dormer windows adorn this L-shaped, three-bedroom design. The dining room sits to the right of the foyer and showcases a beautiful box-bay window. Nearby, the family room features a warming fireplace. The master suite enjoys French-door access to the rear patio, an oval tub and a separate shower. Conveniently near the garage, the kitchen provides a walk-in pantry, cooktop island, bayed nook and powder room. The second floor includes two family bedrooms, two baths and the possibility for a future bonus room and future bedroom when space is needed.

VAULTED
DINING
11/0 X 14/0

DW

PAN.

DN.

SHLVS

SHLVS

LINEN

VAULTED
PORCH
11/0 X 10/6

VAULTED
LIVING
17/8 X 15/10

VAULTED
MASTER
13/0 X 14/8 + BAY

Pleasure Principle

This design looks cozy yet the interior provides all the amenities an owner could want. A covered porch leads to the vaulted dining area, directly next to the island kitchen, complete with plenty of counter space and a pantry. The vaulted living room is graced with a fireplace, perfect for chilly evenings. The second-floor, vaulted master suite enjoys a linen closet, a large walk-in closet, and separate tub and shower. Two additional bedrooms sharing a hall bath reside downstairs. Bedroom 2 boasts a desk/seat area, perfect for studying.

PLAN

HPT790127

First Floor: 630 square feet
Second Floor: 1,039 square feet
Total: 1,669 square feet
Width: 44'-6"
Depth: 32'-0"

BR. 2
10/0 X 11/0
(9' CLG.)

LINEN

W.   D.

UP

BR. 3
10/6 X 11/4
(9' CLG.)

DESK OR
SEAT

GARAGE
12/10 X 28/10

Perfect Neighbor

Though this home gives an impression of the Northwest, it will be a winner in any neighborhood. Craftsman style is evident both on the outside and the inside of this three-bedroom home. A few steps up from the foyer, the two-story living room features a through-fireplace. A spacious family room—enhanced by built-ins—shares the fireplace with the living room and offers a quiet deck for stargazing. Please specify basement or slab foundation when ordering.

GARAGE
28/2 X 29/10

BR. 3
11/0 X 10/8

BR. 2
11/0 X 10/0

LOFT

FOYER
BELOW

LIVING
BELOW

VAULTED
MASTER
15/2 X 12/0

OPT. FR.
DRS.

DINING
10/6 X 12/0

15/0 X 9/0

NOOK
13/10 X 8/4

2 STORY
LIVING
13/0 X 14/0

FAMILY
13/10 X 20/8

DECK

PLAN HPT790129

Main Level: 1,106 square feet
Upper Level: 872 square feet
Total: 1,978 square feet
Width: 38'-0"
Depth: 35'-0"

Optional Bonus
24/7 x 11/4

Kid's Living
10/8 x 11/3
8' Clg.

Attic Storage

Bedroom #3
13/4 x 11
8' Clg.
Sloped Clg.

Bedroom #2
14/4 x 15/7
8' Clg.

Garage
22 x 24/7

Dining
13 x 11
9' Clg.

Utility

Kitchen
Bar
12/11 x 11/9

Stoop

Master
13/4 x 18
9' Clg.

Family Room
14/3 x 18
9' Clg.

Foyer

Porch
21 x 8

American Cool

Here's a highly livable plan with a new look that's right for any region. An open arrangement of the interior boasts good flow from the public realm to the private. A side entry and staircase lead up to the secondary bedrooms and a kid's living space. The master suite features two walk-in closets and a privacy door. A food preparation island in the kitchen provides a snack bar for on-the-go meals and spontaneous family gatherings.

PLAN HPT790128

First Floor: 1,269 square feet
Second Floor: 741 square feet
Total: 2,010 square feet
Bonus Room: 313 square feet
Width: 43'-0"
Depth: 69'-4"

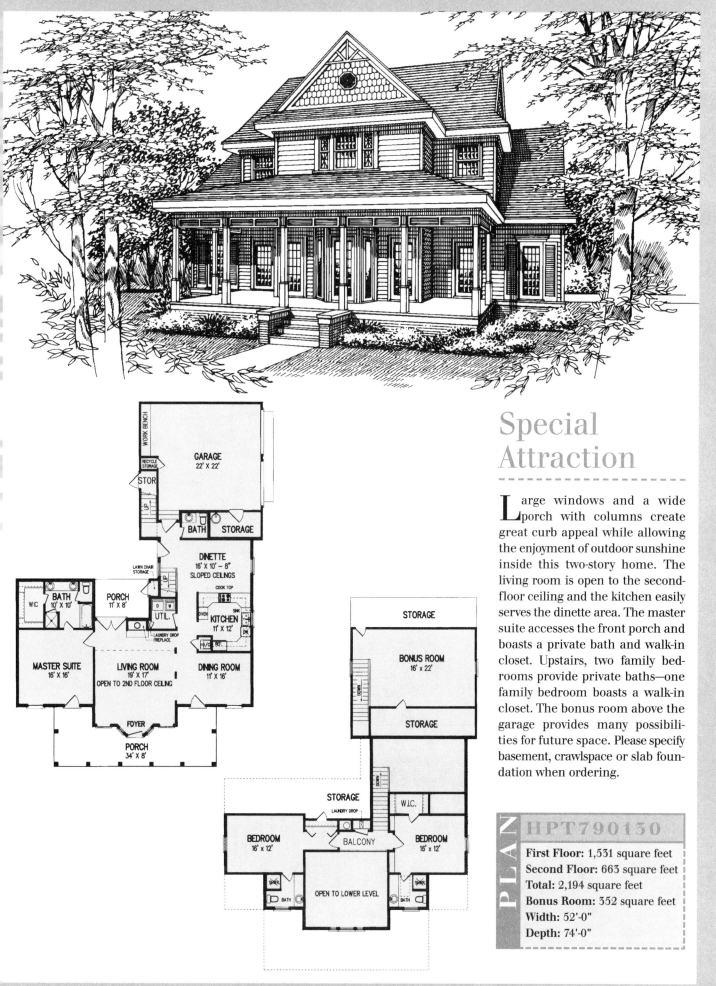

Special Attraction

Large windows and a wide porch with columns create great curb appeal while allowing the enjoyment of outdoor sunshine inside this two-story home. The living room is open to the second-floor ceiling and the kitchen easily serves the dinette area. The master suite accesses the front porch and boasts a private bath and walk-in closet. Upstairs, two family bedrooms provide private baths—one family bedroom boasts a walk-in closet. The bonus room above the garage provides many possibilities for future space. Please specify basement, crawlspace or slab foundation when ordering.

PLAN HPT790130

First Floor: 1,531 square feet
Second Floor: 663 square feet
Total: 2,194 square feet
Bonus Room: 352 square feet
Width: 52'-0"
Depth: 74'-0"

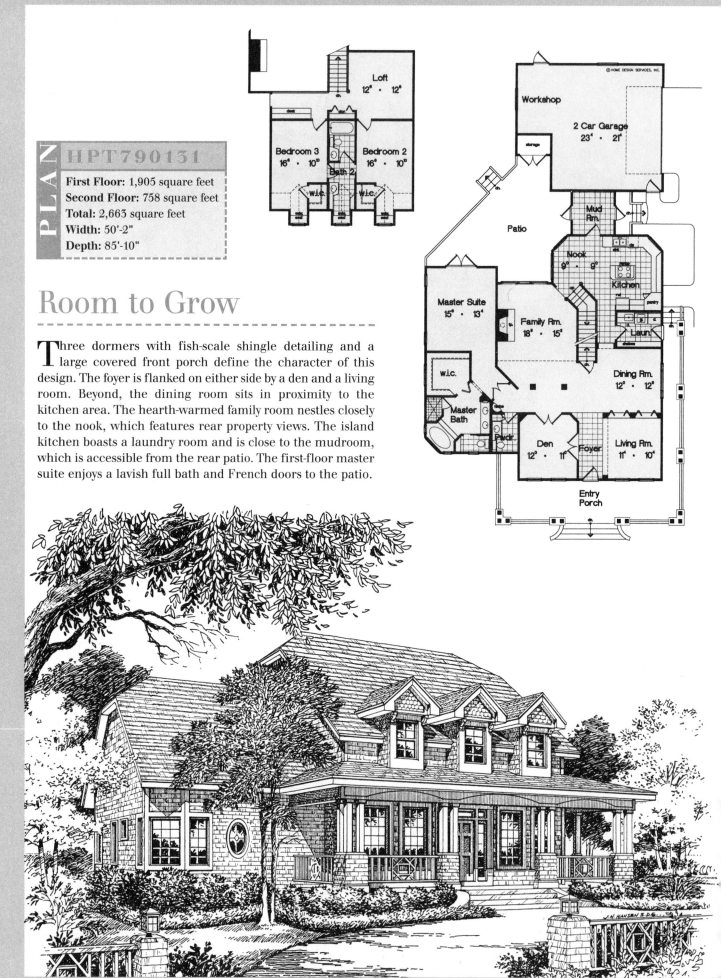

HPT790131

First Floor: 1,905 square feet
Second Floor: 758 square feet
Total: 2,663 square feet
Width: 50'-2"
Depth: 85'-10"

Room to Grow

Three dormers with fish-scale shingle detailing and a large covered front porch define the character of this design. The foyer is flanked on either side by a den and a living room. Beyond, the dining room sits in proximity to the kitchen area. The hearth-warmed family room nestles closely to the nook, which features rear property views. The island kitchen boasts a laundry room and is close to the mudroom, which is accessible from the rear patio. The first-floor master suite enjoys a lavish full bath and French doors to the patio.

PLAN

HPT790132

Square Footage: 2,595
Bonus Space: 1,480 square feet
Width: 78'-8"
Depth: 67'-0"

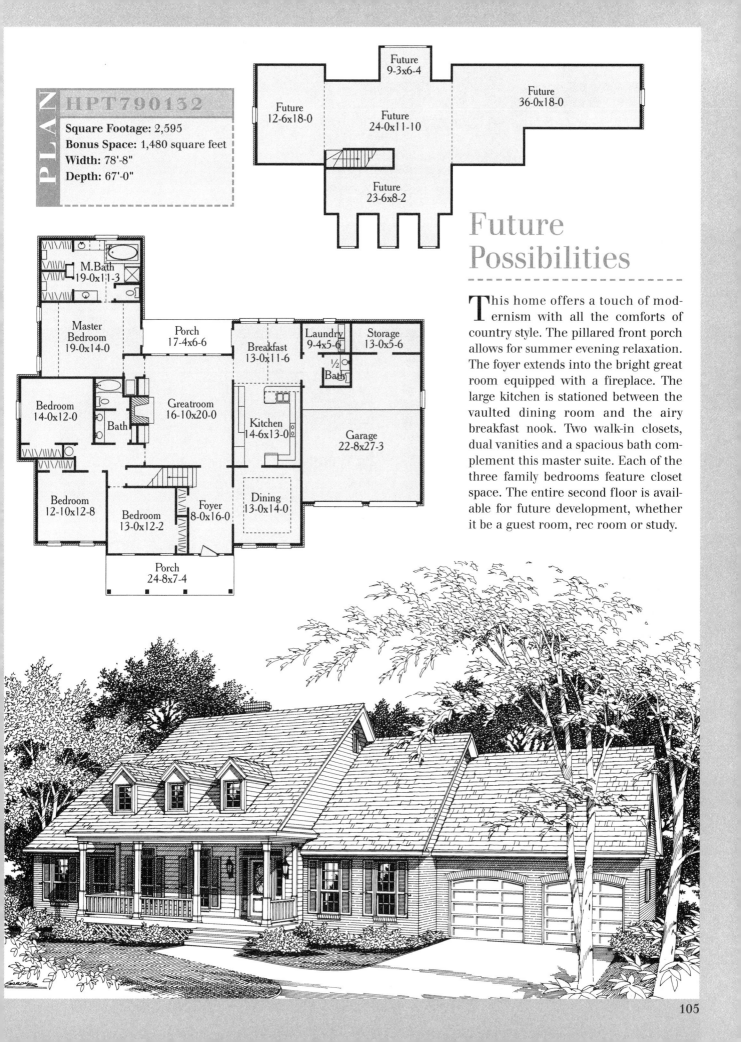

Future
9-3x6-4

Future
12-6x18-0

Future
24-0x11-10

Future
36-0x18-0

Future
23-6x8-2

M.Bath
19-0x11-3

Master
Bedroom
19-0x14-0

Porch
17-4x6-6

Breakfast
13-0x11-6

Laundry
9-4x5-6

Storage
13-0x5-6

½
Bath

Bedroom
14-0x12-0

Bath

Greatroom
16-10x20-0

Kitchen
14-6x13-0

Garage
22-8x27-3

Bedroom
12-10x12-8

Bedroom
13-0x12-2

Foyer
8-0x16-0

Dining
13-0x14-0

Porch
24-8x7-4

Future Possibilities

This home offers a touch of modernism with all the comforts of country style. The pillared front porch allows for summer evening relaxation. The foyer extends into the bright great room equipped with a fireplace. The large kitchen is stationed between the vaulted dining room and the airy breakfast nook. Two walk-in closets, dual vanities and a spacious bath complement this master suite. Each of the three family bedrooms feature closet space. The entire second floor is available for future development, whether it be a guest room, rec room or study.

Superb Starter

This is a superb home-building candidate for those with a narrow, relatively inexpensive building site. Inside, the rounded corners of the foyer add appeal and foster a feeling of spaciousness. Separate formal and informal dining areas are achieved through the incorporation of a breakfast bar. The kitchen will be a joy in which to work. The spacious living room features a sloped ceiling, a central fireplace and cheerful windows.

PLAN

HPT790134

Square Footage: 1,273
Width: 40'-8"
Depth: 59'-0"

L D

QUOTE ONE®
Cost to build? See page 246
to order complete cost estimate
to build this house in your area!

Country Chic

Gables, dormers and an old-fashioned covered porch create a winsome, country look for this transitional exterior. Inside, an upscale, educated floor plan starts with the great room, which offers a sloped ceiling, a fireplace with an extended hearth, and built-in shelves for an entertainment center. Gourmet features in the kitchen include a cooktop island counter, easy-care ceramic tile flooring and a divided sink. A split bedroom plan allows a separate wing for the master suite.

QUOTE ONE®
Cost to build? See page 246
to order complete cost estimate
to build this house in your area!

PLAN

HPT790133

Square Footage: 1,937
Bonus Room: 414 square feet
Width: 76'-4"
Depth: 73'-4"

L

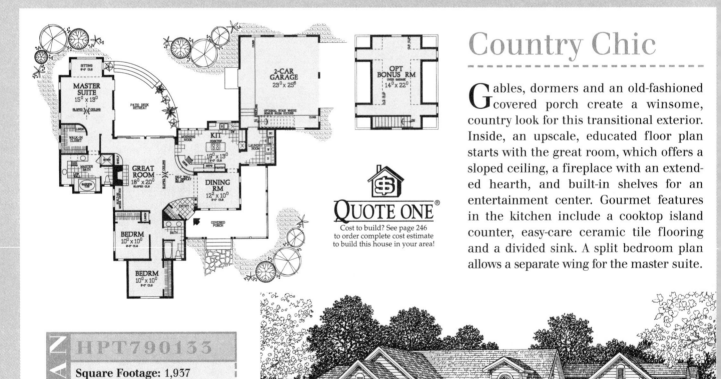

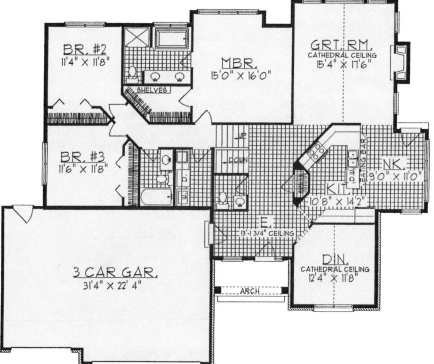

Unique Ranch

This unique ranch offers all the modern amenities you're searching for in a new home. The open great room provides a cozy fireplace. Designed with a busy family in mind, the kitchen offers ample counter space, an eating bar, and a generous nook for family dining. The cathedral ceiling in the formal dining room provides an elegant atmosphere for entertaining. With built-in shelves in the walk-in closet, and a dual vanity and spa tub in the bath, the master suite allows an area of solitude. Two additional bedrooms share a full bath.

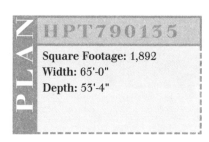

PLAN HPT790135

Square Footage: 1,892
Width: 65'-0"
Depth: 53'-4"

Wraparound Views

Ideal as a starter or as an empty-nester home, this efficient floor plan features many amenities found in larger homes. A wraparound porch sets the scene for relaxing and a lovely place for outdoor dining. A fireplace gives a stunning focal point to the great room that is heightened with a sloped ceiling. The master suite is full of luxurious touches such as a walk-in closet and a lush private bath.

QUOTE ONE®

Cost to build? See page 246
to order complete cost estimate
to build this house in your area!

PLAN HPT790136

Square Footage: 1,295
Width: 48'-0"
Depth: 59'-0"

L D

Hillside Home

The entry of this transitional home, which is designed for a hillside lot, takes you downstairs to a two-story living room. The dining room/kitchen combination shares a three-way gas fireplace with the living room. The master bedroom on this floor includes a private bath, a walk-in closet and a nearby laundry room. Two bedrooms on the upper level share a full bath.

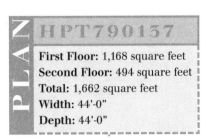

PLAN HPT790137

First Floor: 1,168 square feet
Second Floor: 494 square feet
Total: 1,662 square feet
Width: 44'-0"
Depth: 44'-0"

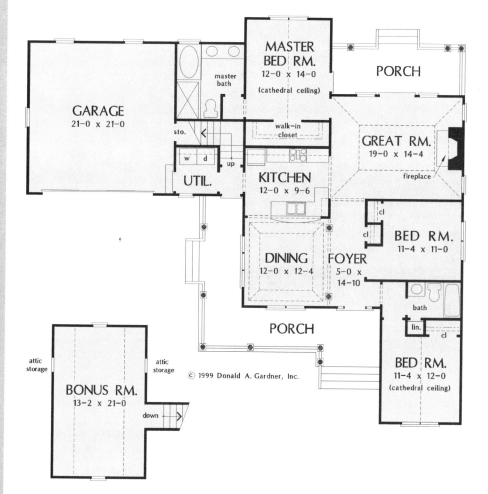

MASTER BED RM.
12-0 x 14-0
(cathedral ceiling)

master bath

GARAGE
21-0 x 21-0

PORCH

sto.

walk-in closet

GREAT RM.
19-0 x 14-4

fireplace

w   d   up

UTIL.

KITCHEN
12-0 x 9-6

BED RM.
11-4 x 11-0

cl

cl

DINING
12-0 x 12-4

FOYER
5-0 x
14-10

bath

lin.

cl

attic storage

attic storage

BONUS RM.
13-2 x 21-0

down

PORCH

© 1999 Donald A. Gardner, Inc.

BED RM.
11-4 x 12-0
(cathedral ceiling)

Cool Country

Striking gables, arched windows and a wrapping front porch grace the facade of this modest three-bedroom home. The dining room, kitchen and great room separate the master suite from the two family bedrooms. An efficient kitchen is placed to serve both the dining room and great room with ease. Tray ceilings in the dining room and great room add volume and interest, while the master bedroom and front family room are expanded by cathedral ceilings. The master suite features back-porch access, a walk-in closet and private bath.

PLAN

HPT790138

Square Footage: 1,469
Bonus Room: 383 square feet
Width: 63'-4"
Depth: 57'-0"

© 1999 Donald A. Gardner, Inc.

New Classic

European charm cleverly frames this home with keystone lintels, columns on the porch, and a sunburst transom over the door. The columned foyer radiates to the living, dining and great rooms. A fireplace with built-ins sets off the great room. Ribbon windows in the great room, breakfast area and study take full advantage of a backyard view. The master suite includes a lavish bath, walk-in closets and a private study. The kitchen is full of helpful amenities, such as a built-in desk, large pantry and snack bar. Please specify basement, crawlspace or slab foundation when ordering.

PLAN | **HPT790139**

Square Footage: 2,570
Width: 73'-0"
Depth: 71'-0"

Master Bedroom

Laundry
12-0x6-6

Basement Stair Location

Study
8-10x9-4

M. Bath
8-4x23-5

Master Bedroom
15-3x12-9

Porch
17-0x10-6

Breakfast
12-8x10-8

Laundry
12-0x10-0

Bedroom
11-6x13-0

Greatroom
14-9x19-4

Kitchen
12-8x14-2

1/2 Bath

Garage
23-10x23-6

Pantry

Desk

Bedroom
11-6x11-4

Living
11-6x11-6

Foyer

Dining
11-6x11-6

Storage
15-6x5-8

Porch
33-0x9-8

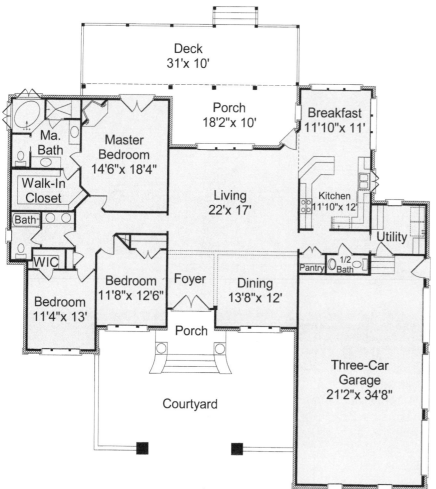

Deck
31'x 10'

Porch
18'2"x 10'

Breakfast
11'10"x 11'

Ma.
Bath

Master
Bedroom
14'6"x 18'4"

Living
22'x 17'

Kitchen
11'10"x 12'

Walk-In
Closet

Utility

Bath

WIC

Bedroom
11'8"x 12'6"

Foyer

Dining
13'8"x 12'

Pantry

1/2
Bath

Bedroom
11'4"x 13'

Porch

Courtyard

Three-Car
Garage
21'2"x 34'8"

Colonial Spirit

A luscious courtyard introduces you into the presence of this petite formal home. Interesting rooflines, keystone arches atop fanlight windows and a dramatic covered entry precede the masterful plan within. The foyer opens to the dining room on the right and to the living room, which boasts a wonderful view to the rear porch and deck. A sunny breakfast nook adjoins the angled kitchen on the right. The master suite on the left delights with a cozy corner fireplace, access to the deck and a lavish bath. Two additional bedrooms share a full bath.

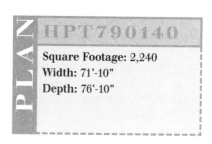

PLAN HPT790140

Square Footage: 2,240
Width: 71'-10"
Depth: 76'-10"

PLAN HPT790142

Square Footage: 2,197
Width: 60'-0"
Depth: 64'-0"

Grand Vistas

Corner quoins, a Palladian window, open gables and a hipped roof embellish this traditional design. The open foyer introduces the dining room on the right accented by columns and a private den on the left. The great room repeats the open style with smooth interaction to the breakfast nook and kitchen. The secluded master suite enjoys its own bath and elegant Palladian window. Two family bedrooms complete the plan.

PLAN HPT790141

Square Footage: 1,500
Width: 59'-10"
Depth: 44'-4"

Classic Bay Window

A spacious interior is implied from the curb with the lofty, hipped rooflines of this economical family home. From the entry, the large living room is fully visible, as is the rear yard, through windows flanking the fireplace. The kitchen is partially open to the living room via a snack bar and offers full access to the breakfast room. A formal dining room just off the kitchen will serve entertaining needs with style. Please specify crawlspace or slab foundation when ordering.

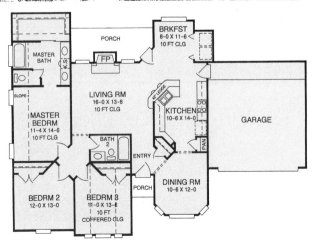

Sunshine and Trees

A striking mix of traditional brick and siding enhances the exterior of this home, enclosing a floor plan of family luxury. A petite porch welcomes you inside to a two-story entry. The U-shaped kitchen with pantry is placed between the breakfast and dining rooms for optimal convenience. The family room with fireplace overlooks the rear patio—a seasonal outdoor necessity. A powder room, laundry and two-car garage complete the first floor. Upstairs, the master bedroom features a private bath and walk-in closet for the homeowners. Three additional family bedrooms share a full hall bath and a linen storage closet.

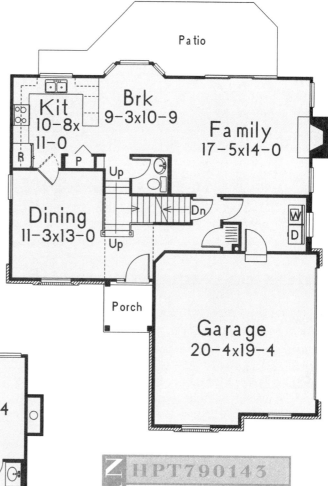

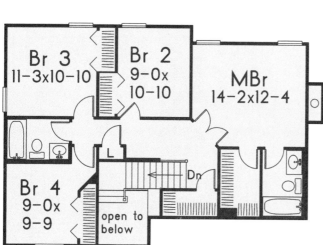

PLAN HPT790143

First Floor: 896 square feet
Second Floor: 804 square feet
Total: 1,700 square feet
Width: 39'-0"
Depth: 42'-8"

PLAN

HPT790144

Square Footage: 2,670
Width: 70'-6"
Depth: 72'-4"

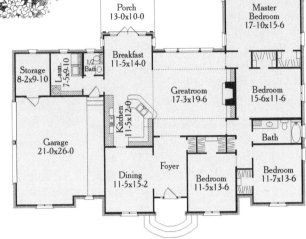

Spacious Sleeping Wing

This comforting cottage's lovely brick facade is decorated with shutters, arched and straight lintels, and a transom with sidelights on the entry. At the center of the house, the great room holds a ribbon of bright windows and a fireplace sided with built-ins. A roomy master suite includes a garden tub and a compartmented shower and toilet. Three secondary bedrooms give this house long-lasting appeal. Please specify crawlspace or slab foundation when ordering.

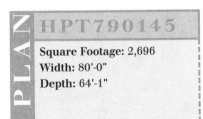

Pretty Facade

A brick archway covers the front porch of this European-style home, creating a grand entrance. Situated beyond the entry, the living room takes center stage with a fireplace flanked by tall windows that overlook the rear yard. To the right is a bayed eating area and an efficient kitchen. Steps away, the formal dining room is perfect for holidays and special occasions. The master suite features a luxurious bath and private patio access.

PLAN

HPT790145

Square Footage: 2,696
Width: 80'-0"
Depth: 64'-1"

Porch
18-10x9-4

Master
Bedroom
15-2x12-0

M.Bath

Greatroom
17-6x14-6

Storage
9-0x6-6

Pantry

Laundry
9-0x7-8

Garage
21-4x23-6

Bedroom
10-0x12-4

Dining
11-7x11-6

Desk

Bedroom
12-4x12-2

Bath

Foyer

Kitchen
12-0x10-0

Storage
5-7x6-6

Laundry
5-7x7-8

Basement Stair
Location

Great Personality

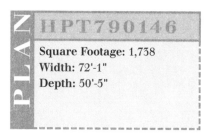

HPT790146

Square Footage: 1,738
Width: 72'-1"
Depth: 50'-5"

The charming brick facade of this home will warm any family's heart. Walk through the grand entry to the great room where a magnificent fireplace awaits. Entertaining is a delight with the kitchen easily accessible from the dining room. A storage room is conveniently located off the garage. Dual sinks are featured in the master bath. Two additional bedrooms located to the left of the plan share a bath. Please specify crawlspace, slab or basement foundation when ordering.

Grand and Cozy

With traditional style and transitional accents, this modern plan is a stunning neighborhood charmer. Inside, the two-story entry is flanked on either side by a den with a cathedral ceiling and a formal dining room. Straight ahead, the living room offers a fireplace flanked by built-in cabinets. The U-shaped island kitchen is open to the breakfast nook. A hallway flanked by a powder room, walk-in closet and a laundry room leads to the two-car garage. Upstairs, the master bedroom offers a private bath with linen storage and a walk-in closet.

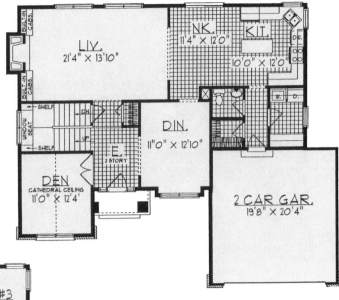

PLAN

HPT790147

First Floor: 1,339 square feet
Second Floor: 1,081 square feet
Total: 2,420 square feet
Width: 52'-8"
Depth: 48'-0"

PLAN

HPT790148

First Floor: 1,554 square feet
Second Floor: 695 square feet
Total: 2,249 square feet
Width: 56'-0"
Depth: 49'-0"

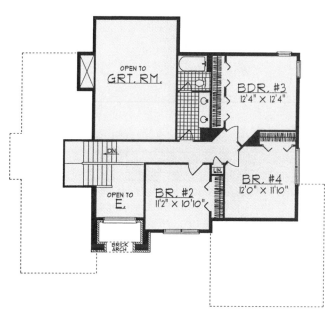

Space for Computers

In the transitional times of the modern era, this lovely traditional home is a truly luxurious retreat. Inside, the two-story entry opens to a dining room on the right. The vaulted great room features a fireplace and built-in cabinets. Through an archway, the island kitchen opens to a nook. A two-car garage, laundry and powder room reside nearby. A secluded master bedroom offers a cathedral ceiling, private bath and walk-in closet. Upstairs, three additional family bedrooms share a full hall bath.

New Country

Enjoy the elegance of the stone-and-stucco exterior on this amenity-filled four-bedroom home. Columns define the dining room to the right of the foyer. The nearby kitchen features a pantry, a serving bar to the great room, and a view of the backyard through the breakfast area. An impressive fireplace features built-ins to each side within the great room. The secondary bedroom on the first floor—or make it a study—provides access to a full bath, while the tray-ceilinged master suite includes a sumptuous bath, two walk-in closets and a bay window.

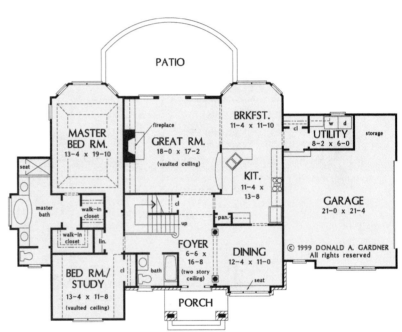

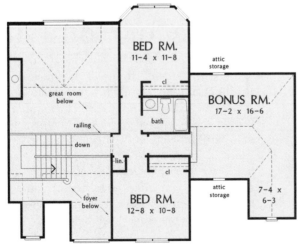

PLAN HPT790149

First Floor: 1,918 square feet
Second Floor: 469 square feet
Total: 2,387 square feet
Bonus Room: 374 square feet
Width: 73'-3"
Depth: 43'-6"

Simply Perfect

The stately and formal exterior of this traditional home leaves a lasting impression. Inside, the foyer is flanked by a home office and dining room. The open great room, featuring a fireplace and built-ins, opens onto the rear patio through double doors. The master suite privately accesses the rear patio as well. The kitchen with a walk-in pantry overlooks a bayed breakfast room. A powder room, laundry and two-car garage complete the first floor. Upstairs, a balcony overlooks the two-story great room. Two family bedrooms share a hall bath.

PLAN HPT790150

First Floor: 1,688 square feet
Second Floor: 986 square feet
Total: 2,674 square feet
Bonus Room: 341 square feet
Width: 63'-11"
Depth: 68'-11"

Stately Disposition

This European charmer is a cottage hideaway not to be forgotten. The dramatic high arched entryway gives an elegant first impression. Enter through the front portico—notice the dining room to the right. The kitchen overlooks a small breakfast room. A rear terrace can be accessed from the family room, or by a private door from the master suite. The master suite is a pampering haven for any homeowner—two walk-in closets sit on either side of the entryway to the master bath. Suite 4 shares a bath with the bonus room.

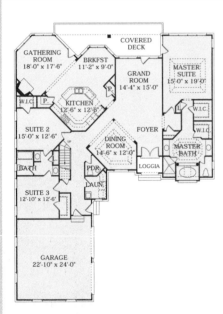

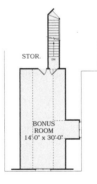

PLAN HPT790152

First Floor: 1,688 square feet
Second Floor: 986 square feet
Total: 2,674 square feet
Bonus Room: 341 square feet
Width: 63'-11"
Depth: 68'-11"

Corner Quoins

The facade of this cozy home displays brick quoins, keystone lintels, hipped rooflines and muntin windows. A grand room accesses the rear covered deck. A snug hearth-warmed gathering room nestles close to the breakfast room and kitchen. Suites 2 and 3 reside on the left side of the design, while the master suite takes up the right side. A bonus room is ideal for an exercise room or extra storage area.

PLAN HPT790151

Square Footage: 2,700
Bonus Room: 477 square feet
Width: 61'-10"
Depth: 80'-10"

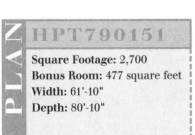

Two-Story Delight

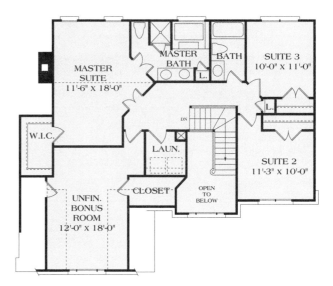

PATIO / DECK

FAMILY ROOM
18'-4" x 13'-6"

BREAKFAST
9'-4" x 12'-0"

KITCHEN
11'-2" x 14'-0"

P.

PDR.

FOYER

GARAGE
20'-0" x 22'-0"

DINING ROOM
11'-3" x 11'-10"

UP

PORCH

MASTER SUITE
11'-6" x 18'-0"

MASTER BATH

BATH

L.

SUITE 3
10'-0" x 11'-0"

W.I.C.

DN

LAUN.

L.

SUITE 2
11'-3" x 10'-0"

UNFIN. BONUS ROOM
12'-0" x 18'-0"

CLOSET

OPEN TO BELOW

Palladian windows and columns at the entry of this spectacular home give it an early Classical feeling. The foyer leads to a powder room to the left and the dining room to the right. The family room includes a cozy fireplace and two large windows to let in natural light. The breakfast area with a sliding door to the rear patio/deck leads to the U-shaped kitchen with lots of space and a walk-in pantry. The second floor includes a laundry room, two family bedrooms and the master suite.

PLAN HPT790153

First Floor: 900 square feet
Second Floor: 921 square feet
Total: 1,821 square feet
Bonus Room: 276 square feet
Width: 45'-10"
Depth: 37'-5"

Rosy Outlook

A classic mixture of brick and siding make this home appealing in any region of the country. Triple-wide windows enhance the facade while illuminating the interior rooms of this two-story plan. The library is tucked in the front of the house and designed for both relaxation and convenience with built-in bookshelves lining two walls. The master suite is secluded on the first floor while three additional bedrooms share a full bath on the second floor.

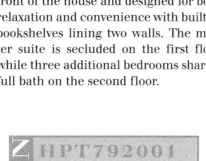

PLAN

HPT792001

First Floor: 1,624 square feet

Second Floor: 566 square feet

Total: 2,190 square feet

Width: 55'-8"

Depth: 52'-0"

Room to Grow

This European design is filled with space for formal and informal occasions. Informal areas include an open kitchen, breakfast room and family room with a fireplace. Formal rooms surround the foyer, with the living room on the left and dining room on the right. The master suite is conveniently placed on the first floor, with a gorgeous private bath and a walk-in closet. This home is designed with a walkout basement foundation.

QUOTE ONE®

Cost to build? See page 246
to order complete cost estimate
to build this house in your area!

PLAN

HPT790154

First Floor: 1,660 square feet

Second Floor: 665 square feet

Total: 2,325 square feet

Bonus Room: 240 square feet

Width: 64'-0"

Depth: 48'-6"

PLAN

HPT790156

First Floor: 1,216 square feet
Second Floor: 1,275 square feet
Total: 2,491 square feet
Bonus Room: 154 square feet
Width: 54'-0"
Depth: 44'-0"

Just Right

Agraceful sloped roof adorns the two-story canted wall that is the focal point of this design. Equally beautiful is the molded arch detailing of its portal. Inside, three fireplaces spread luxurious warmth throughout the home. The island countertop kitchen is open to both the breakfast and keeping rooms. A garage conveniently close to the kitchen completes the first floor. All bedrooms are located upstairs, with the master suite featuring a sloped ceiling and His and Hers walk-in closet space. Sleeping quarters upstairs enjoy a useful second-floor laundry.

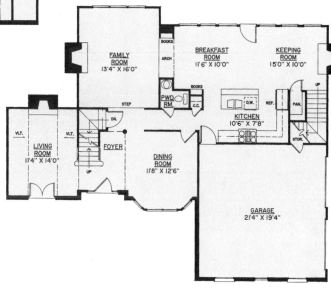

Cozy Cottage

Stately brick and jack-arch detailing create an exterior with an established look, yet the floor plan offers 21st-Century livability. A dramatic two-story entry is framed by formal living and dining areas. The cheery breakfast nook allows rear covered porch access and opens to a kitchen loaded with modern amenities. A coffered ceiling, His and Hers vanities and a walk-in closet highlight the master suite. This home is designed with a walkout basement foundation.

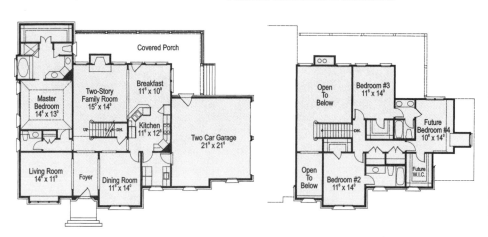

Single-Story Splendor

Delightfully different, this brick one-story home offers everything for the active family. The entry foyer opens to a formal dining room, accented with four columns, and a great room with a fireplace and French doors to the rear deck. The master suite features a tray ceiling, His and Hers walk-in closets, a double vanity and a garden tub. This home is designed with a walkout basement foundation.

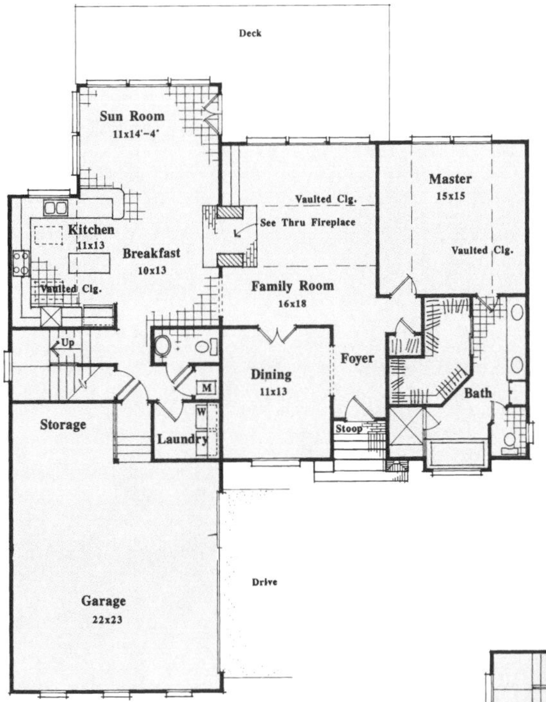
Deck
Sun Room
11x14'-4"
Kitchen
11x13
Breakfast
10x13
Vaulted Clg.
Vaulted Clg.
See Thru Fireplace
Master
15x15
Vaulted Clg.
Family Room
16x18
Up
Dining
11x13
Foyer
M
W
Bath
Storage
Laundry
Stoop
Garage
22x23
Drive

Pretty And Smart

Shutters, multi-pane windows and corner quoins add to this great design, featuring copper bays and interesting rooflines. A separate dining room flows into the vaulted family room with a through-fireplace, which opens into the breakfast area. This large vaulted kitchen/breakfast area with eat-in bar becomes a sun room overlooking a large deck. The vaulted master bedroom features a large angled closet. The convenient stair location allows upstairs traffic to flow to the kitchen area.

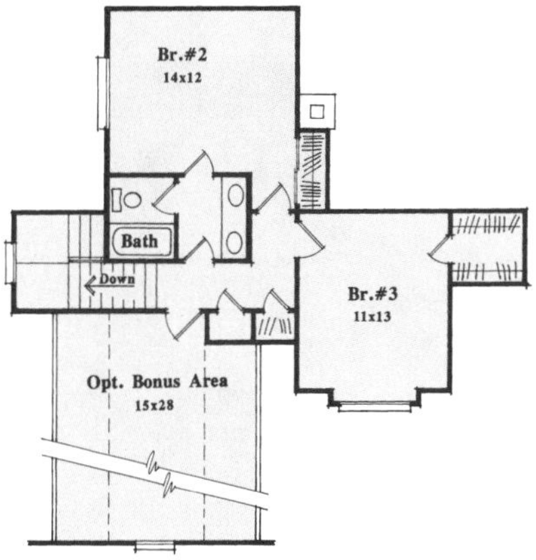
Br.#2
14x12
Bath
Down
Br.#3
11x13
Opt. Bonus Area
15x28

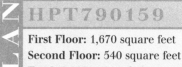

PLAN HPT790159

First Floor: 1,670 square feet
Second Floor: 540 square feet
Total: 2,210 square feet
Bonus Room: 455 square feet
Width: 54'-0"
Depth: 61'-0"

Stately Traditional

The entry of this lovely home opens to the great room, which features a corner fireplace and wide views of the rear property. A snack counter connects the kitchen with a spacious breakfast area/hearth room. Access to the rear covered porch is provided from this casual space and from the master suite. The homeowner's retreat opens through French doors from a private vestibule that provides linen storage. Please specify basement or block foundation when ordering.

PLAN HPT790161

Square Footage: 2,579
Width: 66'-0"
Depth: 68'-0"

PLAN HPT790160

Square Footage: 2,377
Width: 69'-0"
Depth: 49'-6"

QUOTE ONE®
Cost to build? See page 246
to order complete cost estimate
to build this house in your area!

House Blend

One-story living takes a lovely traditional turn in this brick home. The entry foyer opens to the formal dining room and the great room through graceful columned archways. The open gourmet kitchen, bayed breakfast nook and keeping room with a fireplace will be a magnet for family activity. Two family bedrooms and a rambling master suite with a bayed sitting area and sensuous bath are offered. This home is designed with a walkout basement foundation.

Savory Simplicity

PLAN HPT790162

Square Footage: 2,077
Width: 66'-0"
Depth: 54'-0"

This American classic begins with a recessed entry that announces a modern interior designed for entertaining as well as relaxed gatherings. The foyer leads to the living room, which opens through French doors to the back property, and to a banquet-sized dining room through a splendid colonnade. The spacious kitchen offers a work island and a sunlit breakfast area that shares the warmth of a hearth in the great room. French doors open to the master suite, which features a lovely bay window and a lavish bath. This home is designed with a walkout basement foundation.

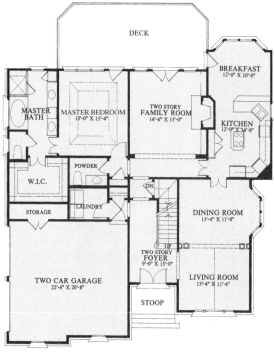

DECK

BREAKFAST
12'-0" X 10'-0"

**MASTER
BATH**

MASTER BEDROOM
13'-0" X 15'-4"

**TWO STORY
FAMILY ROOM**
14'-6" X 15'-0"

KITCHEN
12'-0" X 14'-8"

POWDER

W.I.C.

DINING ROOM
13'-4" X 11'-8"

LAUNDRY

STORAGE

DN

UP

**TWO STORY
FOYER**
9'-0" X 15'-0"

TWO CAR GARAGE
22'-4" X 20'-8"

LIVING ROOM
13'-4" X 11'-4"

STOOP

QUOTE ONE®
Cost to build? See page 246
to order complete cost estimate
to build this house in your area!

BEDROOM NO. 3
11'-10" X 12'-0"

OPEN TO BELOW

BATH

BALCONY

**FUTURE
BEDROOM NO. 4**
13'-6" X 12'-0"

DN.

**FUTURE
BATH**

**BEDROOM
NO. 2**
13'-0" X 12'-0"

**OPEN TO
BELOW**

**FUTURE
STORAGE**

Cozy Elegance

The foyer opens to the living and dining areas, providing a spectacular entrance to this English country cottage. Just beyond the dining room is the gourmet kitchen with a work island and a food bar opening to the breakfast room. Accented by a fireplace, built-in bookcases and a ribbon of windows, the family room is an excellent setting for casual gatherings. Remotely located off the central hallway, the master suite includes rectangular ceiling detail and access to the rear deck. The central staircase leads to the balcony overlook. This home is designed with a walkout basement foundation.

PLAN

HPT790163

First Floor: 1,720 square feet
Second Floor: 545 square feet
Total: 2,265 square feet
Bonus Space: 365 square feet
Width: 50'-0"
Depth: 53'-6"

First Impression

Floor Plan Labels:

- BEDROOM NO. 3 11'-6" X 11'-0"
- BATH
- BEDROOM NO. 2 11'-4" X 11'-0"
- SUN ROOM 12'-0" X 13'-9"
- PORCH
- MASTER BATH
- W.I.C.
- MASTER BEDROOM 13'-4" X 15'-8"
- BREAKFAST 10'-0" X 9'-0"
- FAMILY ROOM 18'-0" X 14'-0"
- LAUNDRY
- KITCHEN 12'-0" X 13'-9"
- BATH
- DN.
- DINING ROOM 10'-6" X 13'-6"
- FOYER
- DEN 11'-4" X 12'-6"
- TWO CAR GARAGE 20'-4" X 20'-8"
- STOOP

Arch-top windows act as grace-ful accents for this wonderful design. Inside, the floor plan is compact but commodious. The family room serves as the center of activity. It provides a fireplace and connects to a lovely sun room with rear-porch access. A private den opens off the foyer with double doors and boasts its own cozy fire-place. The kitchen area opens to the sun room and contains an island work counter. Bedrooms are split, with the master suite to the right side of the design. This home is designed with a walkout base-ment foundation.

PLAN HPT790164

Square Footage: 2,120
Width: 62'-0"
Depth: 62'-6"

Mbr.
15⁰ x 13⁰

Grt. Rm.
18⁰ x 15¹⁰

10'-0" CEILING

Bfst.
12⁴ x 10⁰

SNACK BAR

P.

R.

Kit.
12⁴ x 11⁴

UP

DN

W. D.

E.

Din. Rm.
11⁰ x 14⁴

Study
10⁰ x 10⁰

COVERED PORCH

Gar.
21⁸ x 23⁸

PLAN
HPT 790165

First Floor: 1,569 square feet
Second Floor: 598 square feet
Total: 2,167 square feet
Width: 55'-8"
Depth: 52'-4"

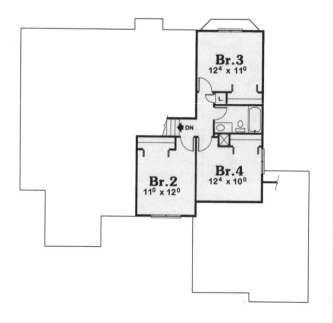

Br.3
12⁴ x 11⁰

L

DN

Br.2
11⁰ x 12⁰

Br.4
12⁴ x 10⁰

Rustic Charm

A mix of gables and hipped roofs and a grand porch present an attractive facade for this traditional home. Inside, the four-bedroom home begins with a study on the left and a spacious dining room to the right. The great room includes a fireplace and accesses the breakfast room and U-shaped kitchen. The master suite resides on the first floor, secluded for privacy. The second floor is perfect for additional family members; it holds three family bedrooms and a full hall bath. The two-car garage provides an entrance to the utility room and kitchen.

Winning Personality

This early American creation features a distinct Cape Cod spirit, perfect for the New England coast. Elegance reigns within, beyond the arched entryway framed by classic columns. The spacious two-story foyer is open to the formal dining hall. Graceful interior columns separate the dining hall from the two-story living room, which offers a massive fireplace, built-ins and double-door access to the rear covered porch. A beautiful arch leads to the casual areas. The island kitchen overlooks the vaulted octagonal breakfast room and the vaulted keeping room. The master suite is an immaculate escape, enhanced by a vaulted ceiling.

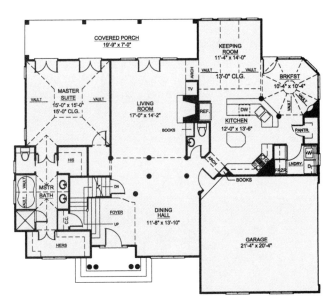

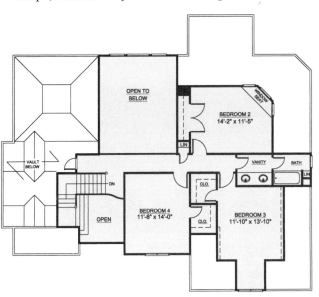

PLAN **HPT790166**

First Floor: 1,704 square feet
Second Floor: 818 square feet
Total: 2,522 square feet
Width: 54'-0"
Depth: 51'-0"

Warmth and Grace

A sophisticated stone-and-siding facade goes well with the windows that align this home. The covered entry opens to the sunny living room which is in turn connected to the dining room. The adjoining island kitchen serves both the dining room and the breakfast nook with ease and efficiency. The family room enjoys a hearth and a beautiful view. Three family bedrooms and a master suite are located upstairs. Please specify basement, crawlspace or slab foundation when ordering.

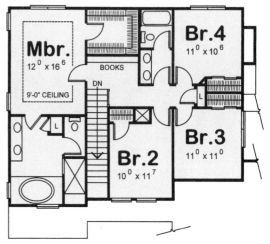

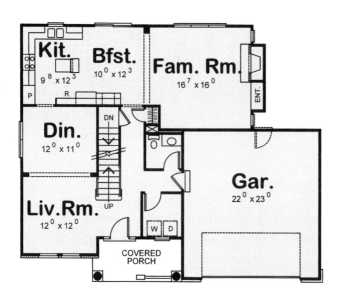

PLAN

HPT792002

First Floor: 1,130 square feet
Second Floor: 1,070 square feet
Total: 2,200 square feet
Width: 49'-0"
Depth: 40'-0"

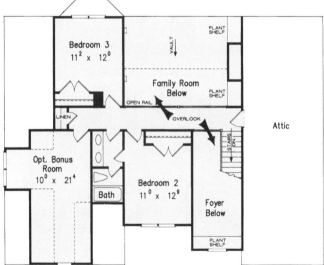

Plain and Fancy

This stately home provides the homeowner with a winning combination of efficiency and luxury. The interior features sets of decorative columns that allow open views from dining room to family room to breakfast nook. In the right wing, the master suite offers a vaulted sitting room and a spacious bath. The great room also enjoys a vaulted ceiling as well as a fireplace and built-in shelves. An upstairs hall connects two secondary bedrooms with an optional bonus room. Please specify basement, crawlspace or slab foundation when ordering.

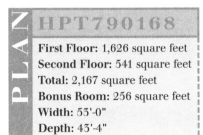

PLAN HPT790168

First Floor: 1,626 square feet
Second Floor: 541 square feet
Total: 2,167 square feet
Bonus Room: 256 square feet
Width: 53'-0"
Depth: 43'-4"

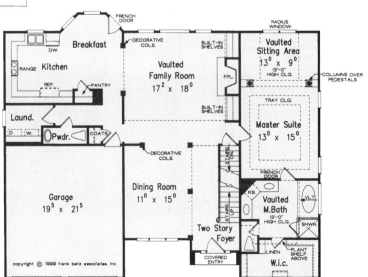

Upscale Traditional

This beautiful home is highlighted by keystones and lintels decorating the windows and garage doors. The pedimented entryway leads to a lavish living room where a large fireplace and a ribbon of windows await. The cozy breakfast room and L-shaped kitchen are quite spacious and include access to the rear deck. The stairs wrap around and lead the family up to the sleeping quarters. The master suite is completed with a walk-in closet and bath.

PLAN HPT790169

First Floor: 869 square feet
Second Floor: 963 square feet
Total: 1,832 square feet
Width: 44'-0"
Depth: 36'-0"

Rear Deck

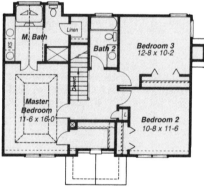

Great for a sloped lot, this three-bedroom home is sure to please. Inside, the foyer opens to the formal dining room to the right and double doors to the kitchen on the left. The large living area features a fireplace and a wall of windows. The U-shaped kitchen easily serves the sunny bayed breakfast nook. Upstairs, two family bedrooms share a full hall bath while the master suite offers a private bath.

PLAN HPT790170

First Floor: 830 square feet
Second Floor: 861 square feet
Total: 1,691 square feet
Width: 34'-0"
Depth: 31'-5"

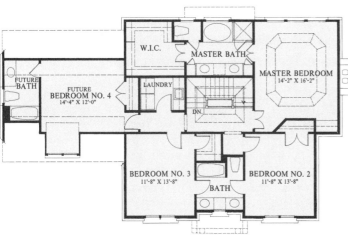

PLAN HPT790171

First Floor: 1,165 square feet
Second Floor: 1,050 square feet
Total: 2,215 square feet
Bonus Space: 265 square feet
Width: 58'-0"
Depth: 36'-0"

QUOTE ONE®
Cost to build? See page 246
to order complete cost estimate
to build this house in your area!

Elegant Attitude

No detail is left to chance in this classically designed two-story home. A formal entry opens to the living and dining rooms through graceful arches. The family room provides ample space for large gatherings and features a fireplace and access to the rear deck through double doors. A triple window bathes the breakfast area in natural light. The L-shaped kitchen handles any occasion with ease. Upstairs, the master suite runs the width of the house and includes a generous walk-in closet and a bath. This home is designed with a walkout basement foundation.

PATIO

GREAT RM.
16-4 x 17-6

PORCH

MASTER BED RM.
14-0 x 15-4

fireplace
(cathedral ceiling)

BRKFST.
10-0 x 11-8

KIT.
9-0 x 15-4

up

storage

walk-in closet · walk-in closet

pd. rm.

FOYER
10-8 x 6-0

DINING
12-0 x 14-0

UTILITY
12-4 x 5-8

w d

master bath

PORCH

GARAGE
20-10 x 21-8

great room below

attic storage

BED RM.
12-4 x 12-8
(vaulted ceiling)

bath

down

BED RM.
12-0 x 11-8
(vaulted ceiling)

attic storage

BONUS RM.
13-8 x 21-8

HPT790172

First Floor: 1,588 square feet
Second Floor: 487 square feet
Total: 2,075 square feet
Bonus Room: 363 square feet
Width: 60'-1"
Depth: 50'-11"

Sweetness and Light

With its hipped roof, gables, covered entry, and brick and siding exterior, this home possesses the enduring style of traditional elegance. The generous great room with a cathedral ceiling and fireplace is centrally located and open to the home's breakfast area and spacious island kitchen. A patio extends living space beyond the great room. The master suite is located on the first floor with a private bath. Two bedrooms and a bonus room share a full bath upstairs.

Individual Character

Multiple gables, columns and a balustrade add stature to the facade of this four-bedroom traditional home. Both the foyer and great room have impressive two-story ceilings and clerestory windows. The great room is highlighted by built-in bookshelves and French doors that lead to the back porch. The breakfast bay features a rear staircase to the upstairs bedrooms and the bonus room. Downstairs, the master suite enjoys an indulgent bath with a walk-in closet.

PORCH

MASTER BED RM.
15-0 x 14-0

fireplace

GREAT RM.
15-4 x 19-7
(two story ceiling)

BRKFST.
13-0 x 11-9

KIT.
13-0 x 12-2

UTILITY
8-0 x 10-0

storage

master bath

walk-in closet

BED RM./ STUDY
12-6 x 11-0

FOYER
8-1 x 10-8
(two story ceiling)

DINING
14-0 x 13-4

GARAGE
22-0 x 23-0

PORCH

storage

great room below

BED RM.
13-0 x 12-0

walk-in closet

bath

lin.

down

down

(optional bedroom)
12-4 x 10-0

foyer below

BED RM.
14-0 x 13-4

walk-in closet

built-in cabinet

BONUS RM.
16-8 x 15-0

attic storage

HPT790173

First Floor: 2,067 square feet
Second Floor: 615 square feet
Total: 2,682 square feet
Bonus Space: 394 square feet
Width: 73'-0"
Depth: 60'-6"

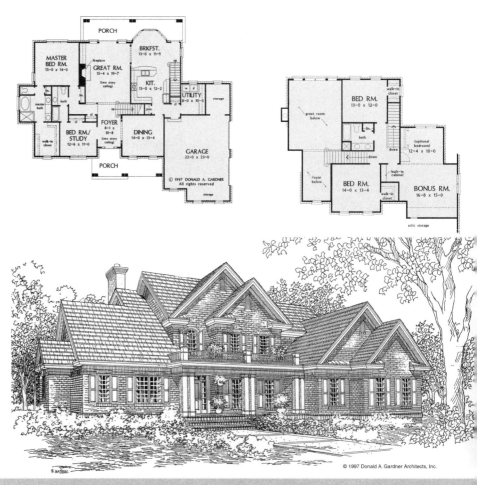

Absolutely Great

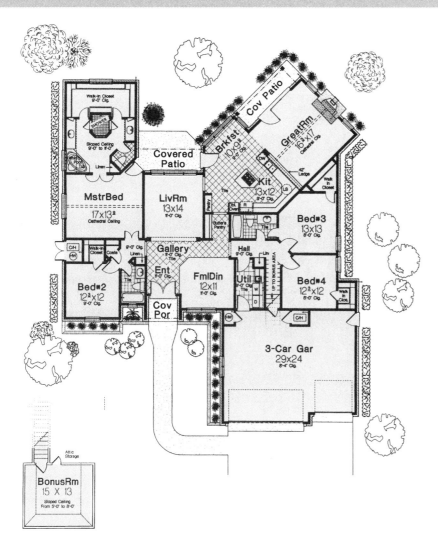

Plan floor layout showing:
- Walk-in Closet 9'-0" Clg
- MstrBed 17x13² Cathedral Ceiling
- Covered Patio
- LivRm 13x14 9'-0" Clg
- Brkfst 10x9 9'-0" Clg
- GreatRm 16³x17 Cathedral Clg
- Cov Patio
- Kit 13x12 9'-0" Clg
- Bed#3 13x13 8'-0" Clg
- Walk in Closet
- Gallery
- Butler's Pantry
- Ent 9'-0" Clg
- FmlDin 12x11 9'-0" Clg
- Hall 9'-0" Clg
- Util
- Bed#4 12³x12 8'-0" Clg
- Bed#2 12³x12 9'-0" Clg
- Cov Por
- 3-Car Gar 29x24 8'-4" Clg
- Attic Storage
- BonusRm 15 X 13 Sloped Ceiling From 9'-0" to 8'-0"

Brick and stone and European accents create a plan filled with family amenities. A petite covered porch welcomes you inside to a gallery leading through the formal areas of the home to the casual areas at the rear of the plan. The master suite features an impressive bath with a walk-in closet. Bedroom 2 easily accesses a full hall bath. The island kitchen is open to the breakfast and great rooms, which offer rear patio access. Bedrooms 3 and 4 share a bath near a utility room that connects to the three-car garage.

PLAN HPT790174

Square Footage: 2,515
Bonus Room: 200 square feet
Width: 63'-10"
Depth: 73'-1"

Octagons and Light

Double columns and an arch-top clerestory window create an inviting entry to this fresh interpretation of traditional style. The two-story foyer features a decorative ledge—perfect for displaying a tapestry. Decorative columns and arches open to the formal dining room and to the octagonal great room, which provides a ten-foot tray ceiling. The kitchen looks over an angled counter to a breakfast bay that brings in the outdoors and shares a through-fireplace with the great room. Please specify basement, crawlspace or slab foundation when ordering.

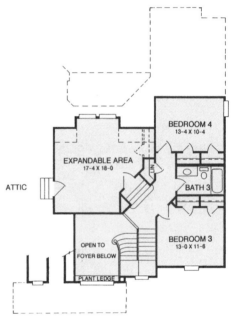

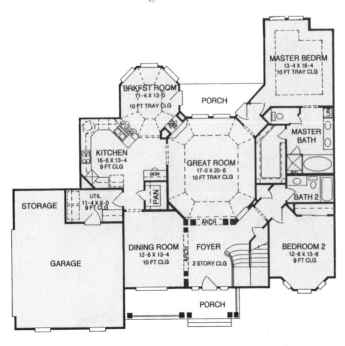

PLAN HPT790175

First Floor: 2,028 square feet
Second Floor: 558 square feet
Total: 2,586 square feet
Bonus Room: 272 square feet
Width: 64'-10"
Depth: 61'-0"

Fine Welcome

This charming exterior conceals a perfect family plan. The formal dining and living rooms reside on either side of the foyer. At the rear of the home is a family room with a fireplace and access to a deck and veranda. The modern kitchen features a sunlit breakfast area. The second floor provides four bedrooms, one of which may be finished at a later date and used as a guest suite. Note the extra storage space in the two-car garage. This home is designed with a walkout basement foundation.

PLAN HPT790176

First Floor: 1,205 square feet
Second Floor: 1,160 square feet
Total: 2,365 square feet
Bonus Space: 350 square feet
Width: 52'-6"
Depth: 43'-6"

Cost to build? See page 246 to order complete cost estimate to build this house in your area!

Bright and Airy

There's nowhere to go but up in this bright and airy three-bedroom home. Nearly every room offers a volume ceiling, including the living and dining rooms, breakfast nook, master suite and T-shaped additional bedroom on the second floor. Natural light fills this extra space via a ribbon of windows in the formal dining room and bay windows in the living room, breakfast and master bedrooms. Fireplaces in the living room and great room will keep these spaces cozy. A master suite featuring a sumptuous bath resides on the first floor. The upstairs loft overlooks the main floor below. This home is designed with a walkout basement foundation.

PLAN HPT790177

First Floor: 1,724 square feet
Second Floor: 700 square feet
Total: 2,424 square feet
Width: 47'-10"
Depth: 63'-6"

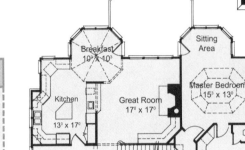

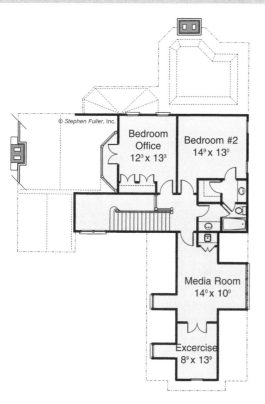

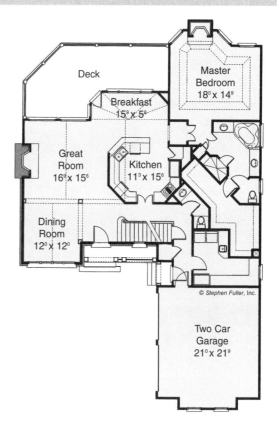

Beautiful Floors

At the heart of this home, a gourmet kitchen provides beautiful hardwood floors, a snack counter and a walk-in pantry. Double doors open to a gallery hall that leads to the formal dining room. A classic great room—perfect for both formal and casual family gatherings—is warmed by a cozy fireplace and brightened by a wall of windows. The master retreat is a luxurious addition to this beautiful plan. The suite is brightened by sweeping views of the backyard and a romantic fireplace just for two. This home is designed with a walkout basement foundation.

PLAN HPT790178

First Floor: 1,746 square feet
Second Floor: 651 square feet
Total: 2,397 square feet
Width: 50'-0"
Depth: 75'-4"

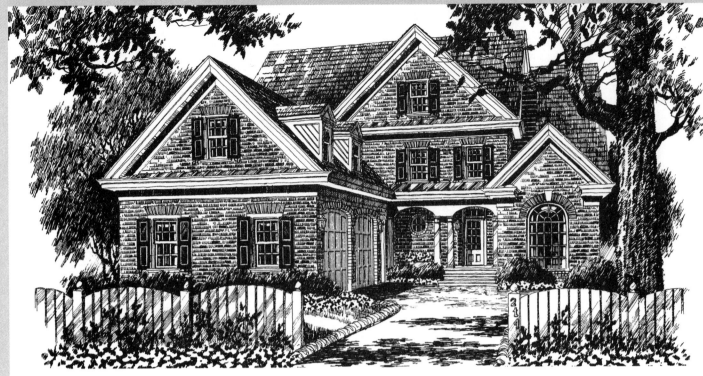

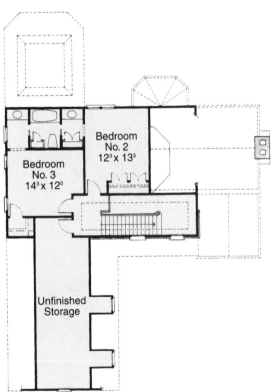

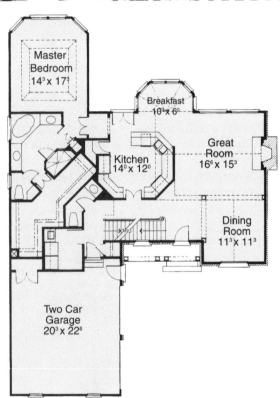

Within the floor plans:

Bedroom No. 3
14³ x 12⁰

Bedroom No. 2
12³ x 13³

Unfinished Storage

Master Bedroom
14³ x 17³

Breakfast
10³ x 6⁰

Kitchen
14⁰ x 12⁰

Great Room
16⁶ x 15³

Dining Room
11³ x 11³

Two Car Garage
20³ x 22⁶

Colonial Style

This plan marries the best of both casual and elegant elements to create a home that breathes with individual style. The formal dining room opens through decorative pillars to the two-story great room, which features a fireplace. French doors lead from the bayed breakfast area to the private master suite, a retreat with a lavish bath with an angled whirlpool tub, glass-enclosed shower, twin vanities and rambling walk-in closet. Two family bedrooms share a bath upstairs. This home is designed with a walkout basement foundation.

PLAN

HPT790179

First Floor: 1,580 square feet
Second Floor: 595 square feet
Total: 2,175 square feet
Width: 48'-0"
Depth: 69'-6"

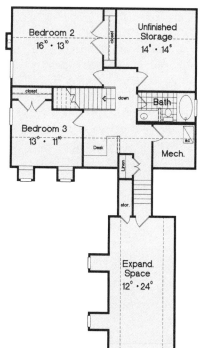

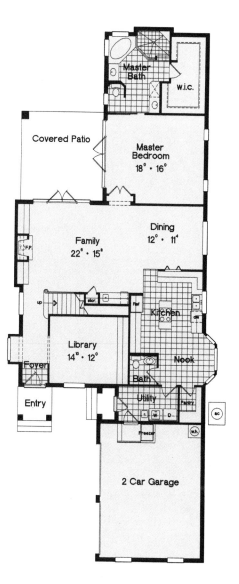

PLAN

HPT790180

First Floor: 1,889 square feet
Second Floor: 798 square feet
Total: 2,687 square feet
Bonus Space: 356 square feet
Width: 38'-8"
Depth: 95'-0"

French-Style Shutters

Interesting rooflines, dormers, French-style shutters and a country cupola complete the exterior of this plan. The foyer leads to a library with built-in bookshelves—perfect for quiet reading. The hearth-warmed family room flows into the dining room, which easily accesses the kitchen and bayed breakfast nook. The island kitchen is graced with plentiful counter space. The master suite is located at the rear of the plan for increased privacy and includes a walk-in closet, access to a covered patio and a full bath. Two family bedrooms reside upstairs. Unfinished storage and expandable space complete this floor.

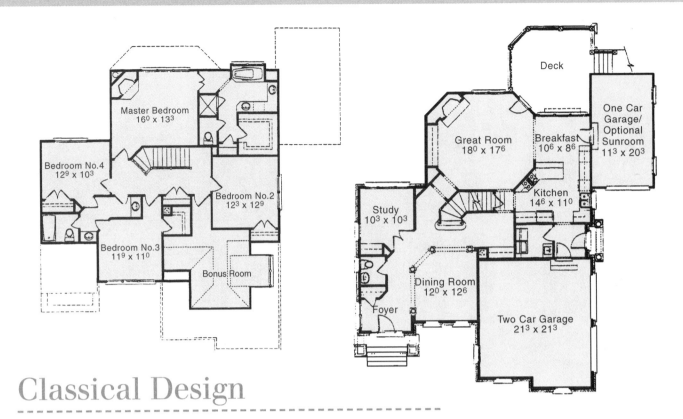

Classical Design

The stately columns and stunning pediment of this classical design will bring a fresh new look to any community. A box-paneled door topped by a transom leads to a spacious foyer that opens to the formal dining room through decorative columns. Double doors in the foyer open to a compact study with built-in bookshelves. An octagonal great room features a fireplace, built-in shelves and access to the rear deck. The well-organized kitchen offers plenty of counter space. Second-floor sleeping quarters include three family bedrooms and the master suite with a corner fireplace. This home is designed with a basement foundation.

PLAN HPT790181

First Floor: 1,330 square feet
Second Floor: 1,244 square feet
Total: 2,574 square feet
Bonus Room: 273 square feet
Width: 56'-0"
Depth: 57'-6"

Master Sitting
11⁶ x 7⁹

Porch

Breakfast
11⁶ x 9⁰

Master
Bedroom
14⁰ x 18⁶

Great Room
16⁰ x 16⁶

Kitchen
11⁶ x 16⁰

Two-Car
Garage
21⁶ x 22⁹

Dining
Room
14⁰ x 14⁰

Stoop

Future
Bedroom
14⁰ x 11⁰

Bedroom
#3
12⁰ x 10⁹

Future Bedroom
19⁰ x 10⁰

Bedroom
#2
21⁶ x 22⁹

Suite Drama

Double doors crowned by a fanlight provide an impressive entry to this stately home. Inside, built-in bookshelves and a fireplace occupy one wall of the great room, where double doors lead to a rear porch. The gourmet kitchen includes a walk-in pantry and built-in cabinets. Family and friends can share meals in a snug, well-lit breakfast room or an elegant, formal dining room. A dramatic master suite features a private sitting area with back-porch access. Two second-floor bedrooms share a full bath, while two spacious future bedroom areas border another full bath. This home is designed with a basement foundation.

PLAN

HPT790182

First Floor: 1,966 square feet
Second Floor: 696 square feet
Total: 2,662 square feet
Bonus Space: 458 square feet
Width: 56'-6"
Depth: 60'-0"

Natural Beauty

Brick jack-arches, flat lintels and flower boxes enhance the facade of this majestic brick home. The pedimented porch and paneled front door of this spacious country home open to a foyer. The octagonal great room provides a fireplace, built-in bookshelves and access to a rear deck. A gourmet kitchen adjoins a breakfast room brightened by an optional box-bay window. A one-car garage supplements the side-loading two-car garage, and may be converted to a stunning sun room. A winding central staircase leads to the second-floor master suite, where a corner fireplace provides warmth. This home is designed with a basement foundation.

PLAN HPT790183

First Floor: 1,327 square feet
Second Floor: 1,222 square feet
Total: 2,549 square feet
Bonus Room: 296 square feet
Width: 55'-9"
Depth: 57'-6"

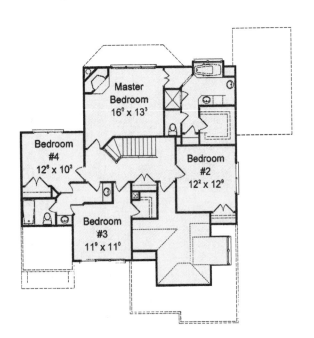

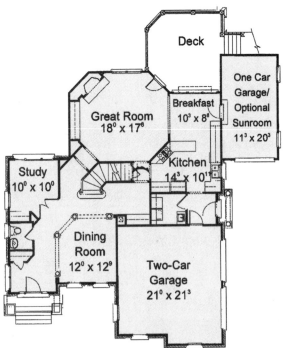

Outside In

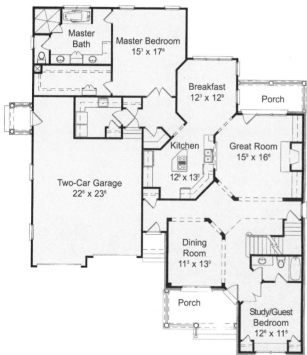

Multiple gables and a myriad of stylish windows make this home a standout. Wood siding and stacked-stone accents provide depth and character for an elevation that will easily be the prettiest in the neighborhood. A study is followed by a formal dining room and a full bath. A fireplace, built-ins and access to a covered back porch create comfort in the great room, while a sunny breakfast room provides a less formal place. The kitchen offers an island cooktop and lots of counter space. This home is designed with a basement foundation.

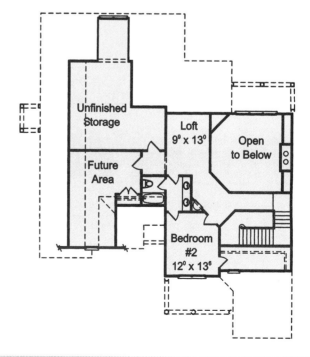

P L A N

HPT790184

First Floor: 1,990 square feet
Second Floor: 615 square feet
Total: 2,605 square feet
Bonus Space: 292 square feet
Width: 56'-0"
Depth: 69'-0"

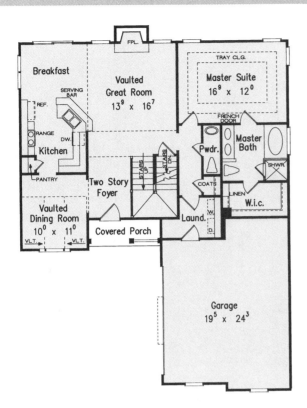

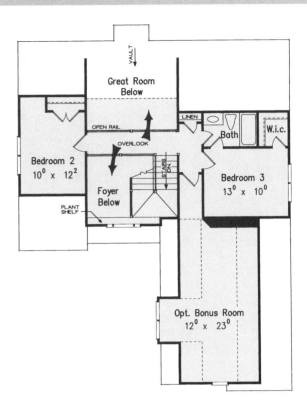

A Wealth of Light

With vaulted ceilings in the dining room and the great room, a tray ceiling in the master suite and a sunlit two-story foyer, this inviting design offers a wealth of light and space. The counter-filled kitchen opens to a large breakfast area with backyard access. The master suite is complete with a walk-in closet and pampering bath. Upstairs, two secondary bedrooms share a hall bath and access to an optional bonus room. Note the storage space in the two-car garage. Please specify basement or crawlspace foundation when ordering.

PLAN HPT790185

First Floor: 1,179 square feet
Second Floor: 460 square feet
Total: 1,639 square feet
Bonus Room: 350 square feet
Width: 41'-6"
Depth: 54'-4"

Deluxe Bath

A careful blend of siding and stone lends eye-catching appeal to this traditional plan. Vaulted ceilings grace the great room, master bath and dining room. The master suite features a tray ceiling and a deluxe private bath. A bedroom/study is located on the first floor. Two second-floor bedrooms easily access a full bath. An optional bonus room offers plenty of room to grow—making it perfect for a guest suite, home office or exercise room. Please specify basement or crawlspace foundation when ordering.

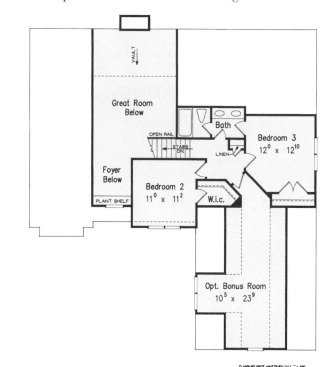

PLAN HPT790186

First Floor: 1,559 square feet
Second Floor: 475 square feet
Total: 2,034 square feet
Bonus Room: 321 square feet
Width: 50'-0"
Depth: 56'-4"

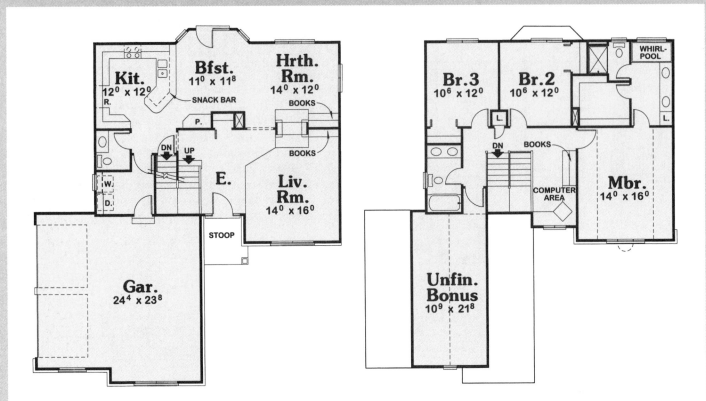

Through-Fireplace

Brick and siding combine over the exterior of this handsome traditional home. A spacious living room and hearth room share a see-through fireplace. Adjoining the kitchen and breakfast room is a convenient snack bar. Just around the corner is a powder room and laundry room. Upstairs, the master suite features a private bath with a whirlpool tub, separate shower and walk-in closet. Two additional family bedrooms share a full hall bath that includes dual vanities. An unfinished bonus room is available above the two-car garage.

PLAN HPT790187

First Floor: 1,002 square feet
Second Floor: 926 square feet
Total: 1,928 square feet
Bonus Room: 262 square feet
Width: 46'-0"
Depth: 51'-0"

Family Plan

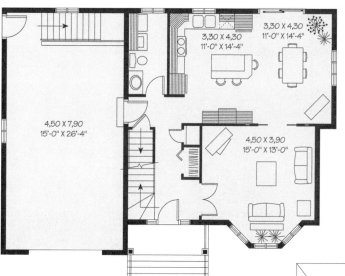

4,50 X 7,90
15'-0" X 26'-4"

3,30 X 4,30
11'-0" X 14'-4"

3,30 X 4,30
11'-0" X 14'-4"

4,50 X 3,90
15'-0" X 13'-0"

The traditional facade of this country-style two-story home is both charming and family-oriented. A porch welcomes you inside, where a living room is found to the right. The kitchen with a snack bar is open to the dining area—perfect for casual or formal occasions. The laundry room is placed right outside the spacious garage. Upstairs, the master suite features a roomy walk-in closet. Two additional family bedrooms share a huge hall bathroom that includes a corner tub and a separate shower. This home is designed with a basement foundation.

3,30 X 3,20
11'-0" X 10'-8"

3,30 X 3,20
11'-0" X 10'-8"

3,60 X 3,60
12'-0" X 12'-0"

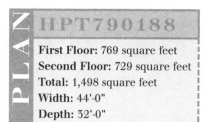

PLAN

HPT790188

First Floor: 769 square feet
Second Floor: 729 square feet
Total: 1,498 square feet
Width: 44'-0"
Depth: 32'-0"

PLAN

HPT790189

First Floor: 1,720 square feet
Second Floor: 724 square feet
Total: 2,444 square feet
Bonus Room: 212 square feet
Width: 58'-0"
Depth: 47'-0"

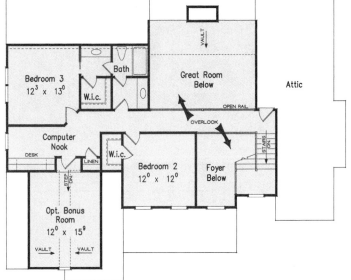

Character and Charm

This traditional two-story home incorporates a side-entrance garage, which adds character and charm to the multi-gabled facade. The entry opens to the dining room and the vaulted great room, where a fireplace is flanked by two radius windows. French doors and a multitude of windows open all of the living spaces to the outdoors. The first-floor master suite features a bath with a whirlpool tub and a walk-in closet. Family bedrooms reside upstairs. Please specify basement or crawlspace foundation when ordering.

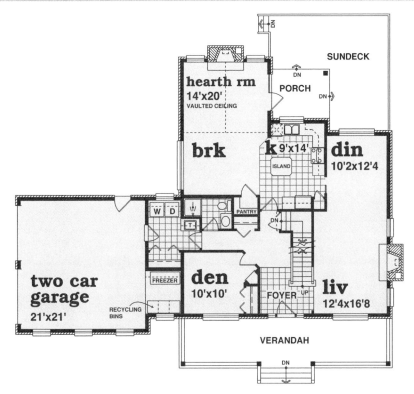

hearth rm
14'x20'
VAULTED CEILING

SUNDECK

PORCH

brk

k 9'x14'
ISLAND

din
10'2x12'4

W D

PANTRY

two car garage
21'x21'

FREEZER

RECYCLING BINS

den
10'x10'

FOYER

liv
12'4x16'8

VERANDAH

PLAN

HPT790190

First Floor: 1,321 square feet
Second Floor: 1,070 square feet
Total: 2,391 square feet
Width: 63'-2"
Depth: 50'-8"

QUOTE ONE®
Cost to build? See page 246
to order complete cost estimate
to build this house in your area!

br2
10'10x10'

66"x36" SOAKER TUB

mbr
12'4x15'

36" HIGH RAILING

DN

W.I.C.

W.I.C.

br3
10'x10'

COMPUTER CENTRE
VAULTED CEILING

br4
12'4x9'4

Touches of Victoriana

Touches of Victoriana add a whisper of grace to this captivating home. Choose brick or wood siding for the exterior finish, as you like. The foyer separates a den from the formal living and dining rooms. The living room offers a cozy fireplace; the den overlooks the rear sun deck. The hearth room and breakfast room form one large gathering area, served by the island kitchen. A door from the hearth room leads out to a covered porch and the sun deck. Four bedrooms occupy the four corners of the second floor.

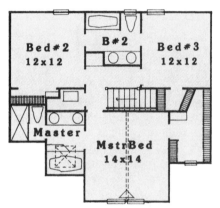

Victorian Farmhouse

Farmhouse-fresh with a touch of Victorian style best describes this charming home. To the right of the entry, a living room features a wet bar and a warming fireplace. At the rear of the plan, an L-shaped kitchen is equipped with an island cooktop. The relaxing master suite with a walk-in closet is located on the second floor with two family bedrooms. The master bath includes a double-bowl vanity, soaking tub and separate shower. The family room, with a fireplace, and the cozy front porch highlight this home.

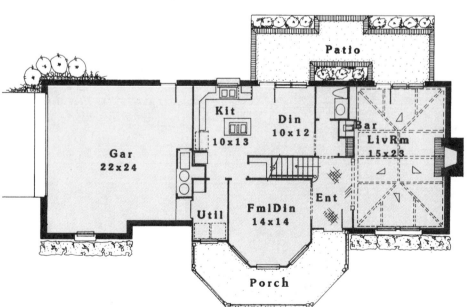

PLAN HPT790191

First Floor: 1,082 square feet
Second Floor: 838 square feet
Total: 1,920 square feet
Width: 66'-10"
Depth: 29'-5"

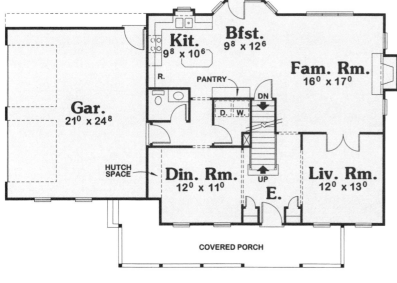

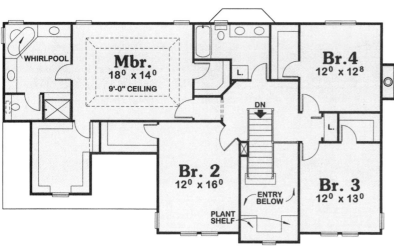

Island Workstation

Victorian detailing lends this four-bedroom home eye-catching charm, with fish-scale shingles, pinnacles and gingerbread decorations on the gables. To the left of the entry, a formal dining room provides space for a hutch. Across the entry, the living room's double doors open to the family room and its warming fireplace. Sharing the open space with the living room are the bay-windowed breakfast nook and the kitchen. This kitchen will please any cook, with an island workstation, a pantry and a window over the sink. Tucked upstairs, away from everyday noises, four bedrooms all include walk-in closets.

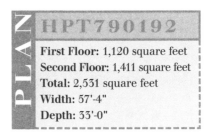

PLAN

HPT790192

First Floor: 1,120 square feet
Second Floor: 1,411 square feet
Total: 2,531 square feet
Width: 57'-4"
Depth: 33'-0"

155

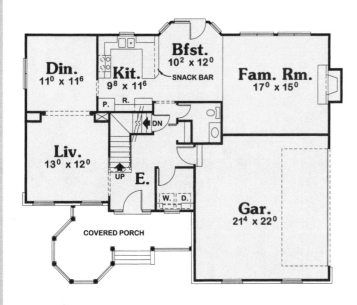

PLAN **HPT790193**

First Floor: 1,091 square feet
Second Floor: 847 square feet
Total: 1,938 square feet
Bonus Room: 166 square feet
Width: 49'-0"
Depth: 40'-0"

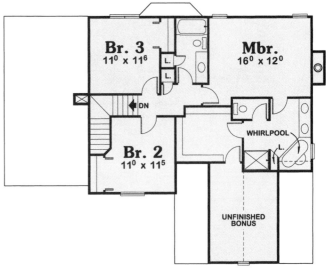

Attached Gazebo

The covered porch with its attached gazebo creates interest as well as offering a delightful area for entertaining outdoors. A view of the living room, with elegant columns, sets the mood for the rest of the home. The dining room, when paired with the living room, shares space for formal occasions. The kitchen and breakfast area open spaciously to the family room and are ideal for family celebrations. Upstairs, the master bedroom offers many options with its unfinished bonus space—great for storage or a private office.

Bayed Turret

The traditional siding and eye-catching bayed turret enhance the graceful exterior textures of this lovely home. The canted bay sitting area in the master suite provides sunny respite and quiet solitude. The vaulted great room makes an excellent gathering spot and spills over into a big, airy kitchen. Guests can make use of the optional study/bedroom. Two additional family bedrooms share a bath upstairs. The bonus room is great for a home office or exercise room. Please specify basement or crawlspace foundation when ordering.

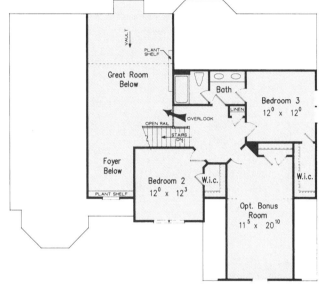

PLAN HPT790194

First Floor: 1,688 square feet
Second Floor: 558 square feet
Total: 2,246 square feet
Bonus Room: 269 square feet
Width: 54'-0"
Depth: 48'-0"

Cozy Traditional

This design's established style coupled with the latest modern amenities make this two-story plan a perfect family home. The foyer is open to the formal dining room, while the vaulted great room features a fireplace. The kitchen overlooks the nearby breakfast room—perfect for casual family meals. Two spacious bedrooms in addition to the first-floor master suite give each family member room to spread out. Please specify basement, crawlspace or slab foundation when ordering.

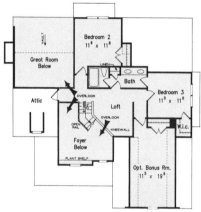

PLAN HPT790195

First Floor: 1,419 square feet
Second Floor: 591 square feet
Total: 2,010 square feet
Bonus Room: 259 square feet
Width: 49'-10"
Depth: 50'-6"

PLAN HPT790196

First Floor: 882 square feet
Second Floor: 793 square feet
Total: 1,675 square feet
Bonus Room: 416 square feet
Width: 49'-6"
Depth: 35'-4"

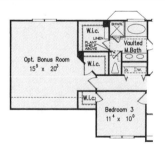

Savvy Style

This fetching country home features a second-floor room-to-grow option that is both savvy and stylish. The first floor places formal living spaces to the front of the design and casual living spaces to the rear of the plan. Upstairs, the master suite is enhanced with a bath that contains a walk-in closet. Please specify basement, crawlspace or slab foundation when ordering.

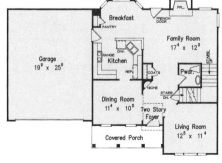

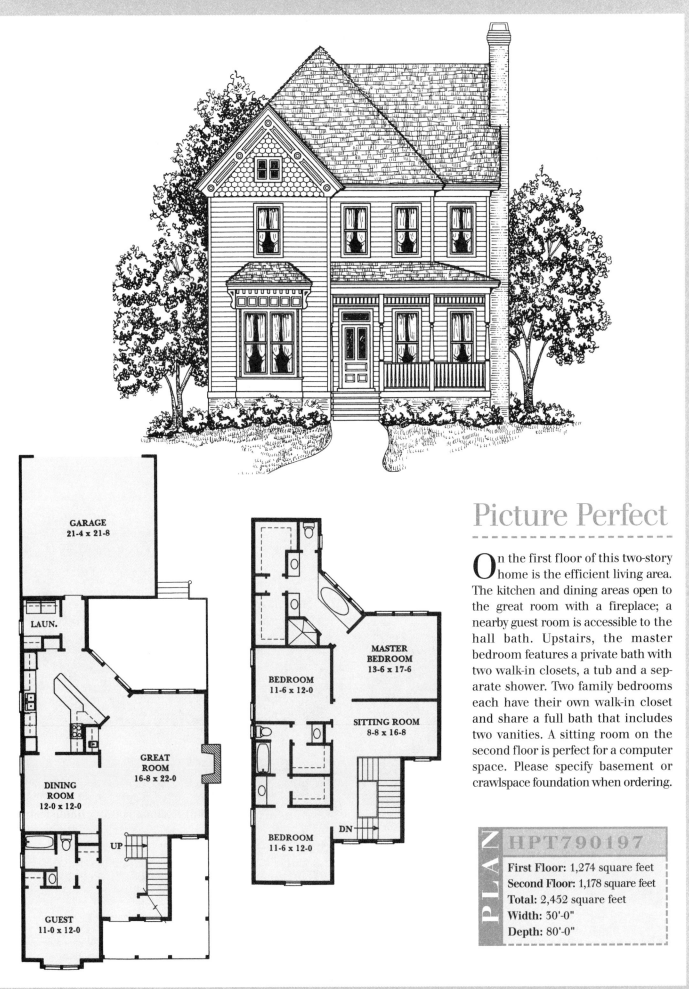

Picture Perfect

On the first floor of this two-story home is the efficient living area. The kitchen and dining areas open to the great room with a fireplace; a nearby guest room is accessible to the hall bath. Upstairs, the master bedroom features a private bath with two walk-in closets, a tub and a separate shower. Two family bedrooms each have their own walk-in closet and share a full bath that includes two vanities. A sitting room on the second floor is perfect for a computer space. Please specify basement or crawlspace foundation when ordering.

PLAN HPT790197

First Floor: 1,274 square feet
Second Floor: 1,178 square feet
Total: 2,452 square feet
Width: 30'-0"
Depth: 80'-0"

GARAGE
21-4 x 21-8

LAUN.

GREAT ROOM
16-8 x 22-0

DINING ROOM
12-0 x 12-0

UP

GUEST
11-0 x 12-0

MASTER BEDROOM
13-6 x 17-6

BEDROOM
11-6 x 12-0

SITTING ROOM
8-8 x 16-8

BEDROOM
11-6 x 12-0

DN

Quaint Country

Traditional and country quaint, this simple two-story home is perfect for the all-American family. A covered front porch welcomes you inside. To the immediate right, the den is a quiet retreat. Straight ahead, the family room is open to the breakfast/kitchen area with a snack bar. Upstairs, the master bedroom features a private bath with a whirlpool tub and a walk-in closet. Two additional family bedrooms share a full hall bath.

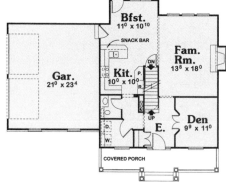

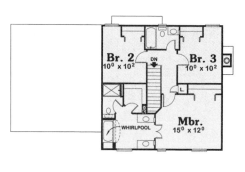

PLAN HPT790199

First Floor: 874 square feet
Second Floor: 754 square feet
Total: 1,628 square feet
Width: 49'-4"
Depth: 33'-4"

Casual Living

A country covered front porch makes a friendly first impression—just perfect for rocking chairs and lemonade in the summer. The entry is flanked by the formal living and dining rooms. The family room with a fireplace, the breakfast area and the island kitchen create the casual living area. A laundry and the garage with storage space complete the first floor. Upstairs, the master bedroom features a pampering private bath with a walk-in closet. Three additional family bedrooms share a full hall bath.

PLAN HPT790198

First Floor: 1,171 square feet
Second Floor: 1,163 square feet
Total: 2,334 square feet
Width: 57'-4"
Depth: 39'-8"

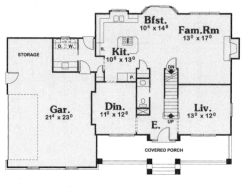

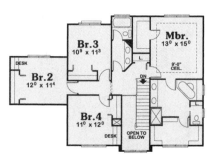

Elegant Simplicity

With a country facade and a covered front porch, this plan boasts elegant simplicity. Front double doors open inside, where straight ahead, the great room is warmed by a fireplace. The kitchen with a snack bar overlooks the breakfast room. The first-floor master suite—secluded for privacy—offers a whirlpool bath and a walk-in closet. Three additional bedrooms reside upstairs and share a full hall bath. A three-car garage connects to the laundry room, conveniently close to the kitchen, and completes the floor plan.

PLAN

HPT790200

First Floor: 1,755 square feet
Second Floor: 693 square feet
Total: 2,448 square feet
Width: 62'-0"
Depth: 44'-4"

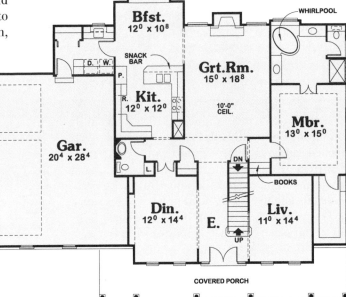

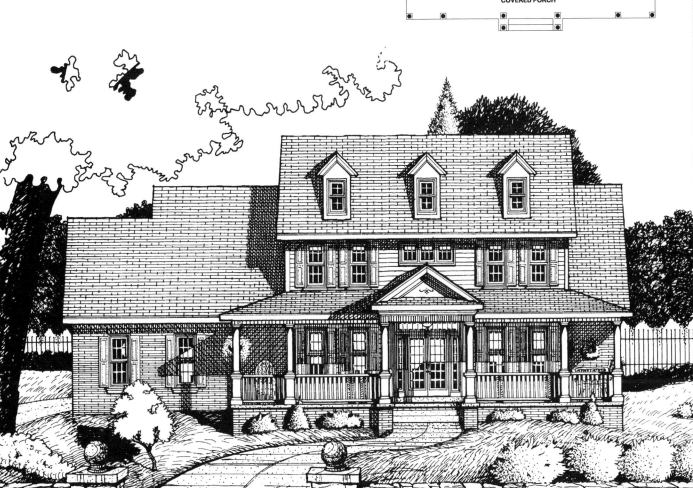

© 1999 Donald A. Gardner, Inc.

Truly Traditional

With its brick facade, hipped roof and elegantly columned entry, this three-bedroom home with a detached garage is a true traditional. A two-story foyer with a tray ceiling precedes the large great room with a fireplace and the adjacent back porch. The spacious kitchen is expanded by a lovely breakfast room. Tray ceilings top each of the upstairs bedrooms as well as the master bath. The master suite includes an oversized walk-in closet and a luxurious bath.
©1999 Donald A. Gardner, Inc.

Early American

Early American design contributes to this home's attractive curb appeal. In the family room, a corner fireplace and built-ins reside along the left wall. The family room and kitchen, with a cooktop island and bayed breakfast area, share access to the backyard through French doors. Four bedrooms and a computer alcove make up the second floor. The master suite features a tray ceiling and a sumptuous private bath. Please specify basement or slab foundation when ordering.

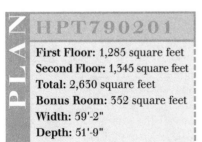

PLAN HPT790201

First Floor: 1,285 square feet
Second Floor: 1,345 square feet
Total: 2,630 square feet
Bonus Room: 352 square feet
Width: 59'-2"
Depth: 51'-9"

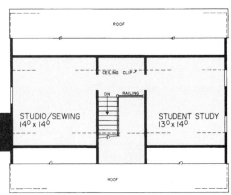

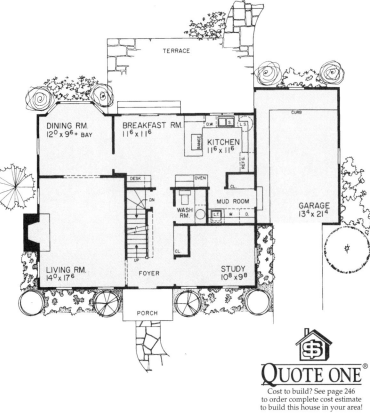

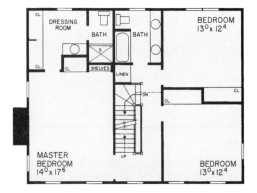

QUOTE ONE®

Cost to build? See page 246
to order complete cost estimate
to build this house in your area!

Third-Floor Studio

The facade of this three-story, pitch-roofed house offers a symmetrical placement of windows and a restrained but elegant central entrance. The central
hall, or foyer, expands midway through the house to a family kitchen. Off the foyer
are two rooms—the living room with a fireplace and the study. Three bedrooms are
housed on the second floor, including a deluxe master suite with a pampering
bath. The windowed third-floor attic can be used as a study and a studio.

Colonial Revival

Double-hung windows and a paneled door framed by pilasters and a pediment announce the Colonial Revival influences of this stately home. Multi-pane windows brighten the living room, which opens to a gourmet kitchen with a walk-in pantry. The great room provides a fireplace flanked by built-in bookshelves and access to a rear deck. A railed staircase off the foyer leads to the second-floor sleeping zone. This home is designed with a basement foundation.

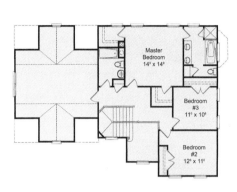

PLAN HPT790205

First Floor: 1,039 square feet
Second Floor: 915 square feet
Total: 1,954 square feet
Bonus Room: 488 square feet
Width: 55'-0"
Depth: 37'-9"

PLAN HPT790204

First Floor: 1,872 square feet
Second Floor: 643 square feet
Total: 2,515 square feet
Bonus Room: 328 square feet
Width: 46'-0"
Depth: 66'-0"

Arts and Crafts

This enchanting design offers a touch of Arts and Crafts with the porch details and accent window. Inside, the formal dining room includes a tray ceiling. The spacious family room is warmed by a massive hearth and accesses the rear porch. The island kitchen is set between the dining and breakfast rooms. The master bedroom features a tray ceiling and private bath. Two additional family bedrooms reside upstairs along with a bonus room. This home is designed with a basement foundation.

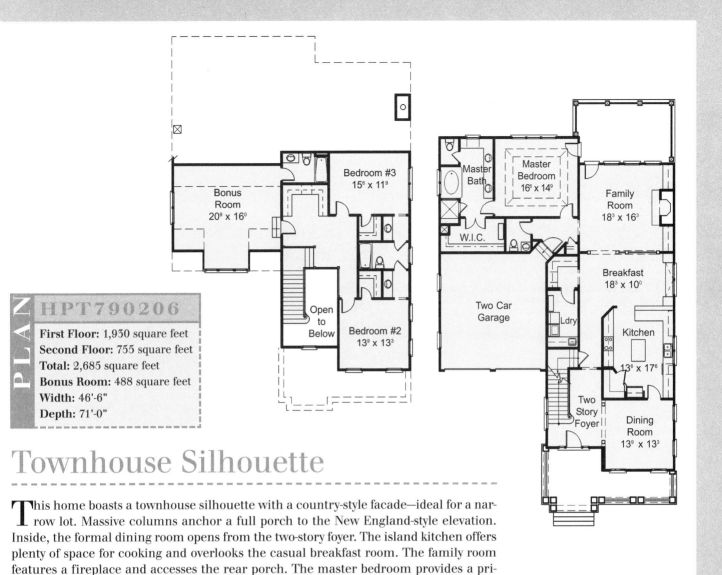

PLAN

HPT790206

First Floor: 1,930 square feet
Second Floor: 755 square feet
Total: 2,685 square feet
Bonus Room: 488 square feet
Width: 46'-6"
Depth: 71'-0"

Townhouse Silhouette

This home boasts a townhouse silhouette with a country-style facade—ideal for a narrow lot. Massive columns anchor a full porch to the New England-style elevation. Inside, the formal dining room opens from the two-story foyer. The island kitchen offers plenty of space for cooking and overlooks the casual breakfast room. The family room features a fireplace and accesses the rear porch. The master bedroom provides a private bath and walk-in closet. Two additional bedrooms upstairs offer walk-in closets and share a bath. This home is designed with a walkout basement foundation.

© Stephen Fuller, Inc.

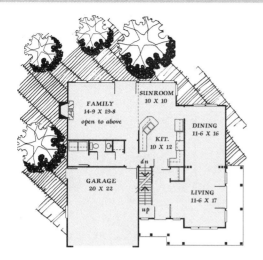

PLAN

HPT790207

First Floor: 1,299 square feet
Second Floor: 937 square feet
Total: 2,236 square feet
Bonus Room: 370 square feet
Width: 49'-0"
Depth: 45'-0"

Classy Farmhouse

This classy three-bedroom farmhouse offers it all. Dormers and Palladian windows welcome visitors to step onto the wraparound porch and come inside for apple pie. French doors open the formal entertainment area to the wraparound porch. A hearth-warmed family room also enjoys access to the great outdoors and opens to the kitchen and sun room. Two family bedrooms, a master suite and a bonus room reside on the second floor.

PLAN

HPT790208

First Floor: 1,104 square feet
Second Floor: 1,144 square feet
Total: 2,248 square feet
Bonus Room: 242 square feet
Width: 62'-6"
Depth: 32'-0"

Colonial Character

This beautiful home features an overhanging second floor with dramatic drop pendants. Inside, the foyer shows gorgeous interior vistas past the staircase to the open great room, which sports a fireplace and plenty of windows for pleasant backyard views. Upstairs, the master suite provides lovely views to the backyard. Two additional bedrooms, a study alcove and a bonus room provide additional space. This home is designed with a basement foundation.

Brick Gables

This traditional Jeffersonian-style home offers brick gables, classic details, horizontal siding, Doric columns and Chippendale railings. From the front porch, French doors open into the dining room. The grand foyer provides a powder room and leads to the family room, which is warmed by a massive hearth. A well-organized kitchen serves the formal dining room through a convenient butler's pantry. Double doors open to the rear porch from the family room. Upstairs, the master suite features a whirlpool bath and walk-in closet. Two additional bedrooms share a bath. This home is designed with a walkout basement foundation.

Family Room 17⁰ x 18⁰

Breakfast 9⁶ x 10⁰

Storage

Ldry

Kitchen 13⁶ x 12⁹

Two Car Garage

Foyer

Dining Room 13⁶ x 15⁶

Master Bedroom 17⁰ x 16⁰

W.I.C.

Master Bath

Bedroom #2 13⁰ x 12⁰

Bonus Room 21⁶ x 14³

Bedroom #3 13⁶ x 13⁰

PLAN HPT790209

First Floor: 1,278 square feet
Second Floor: 1,277 square feet
Total: 2,555 square feet
Bonus Room: 322 square feet
Width: 47'-0"
Depth: 58'-4"

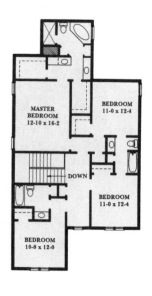

Pavilion Roof

The steeply pitched pavilion roof is a distinctive feature that identifies this house as a classic French design. Inside, a long foyer ushers visitors into a generous great room, which is separated from the kitchen by a wide cased opening. An L-shaped breakfast bar provides a place for a quick snack. A lavish master suite offers separate His and Hers walk-in closets and an oversized shower. Please specify basement or crawlspace foundation when ordering.

PLAN HPT790210

First Floor: 1,326 square feet
Second Floor: 1,257 square feet
Total: 2,583 square feet
Width: 30'-0"
Depth: 78'-0"

PLAN HPT790211

First Floor: 1,247 square feet
Second Floor: 1,221 square feet
Total: 2,468 square feet
Width: 24'-0"
Depth: 86'-0"

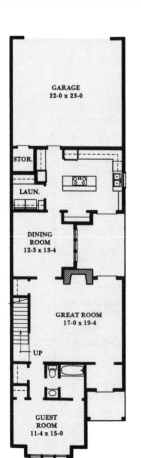

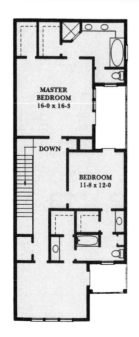

Romantic Character

The romantic character of the hacienda is captured in this appealing residence. The barrel-tile roof, smooth stucco exterior and rope columns are other characteristics of the Spanish Colonial style. The downstairs guest room can double as a study or office. A sunny dining room opens to a spacious kitchen with a large island and breakfast bar. A luxurious master suite privately accesses an upstairs deck. Please specify basement or crawlspace foundation when ordering.

Magnificent Turret

A magnificent turret provides a great accent to the well-crafted look of this historic exterior. Architectural details and timeless materials announce a relaxed interior with comfy niches and grand open spaces. French doors open the living areas to the outside and allow fresh mountain air to waft through unrestrained rooms that own a sense of comfort. Built-in cabinetry frames the massive fireplace, which warms the decor and atmosphere. Window seats invite readers and thinkers to settle down for a while. Arches and columns help define the interior space, lending a sense of privacy to the dining area.

PLAN

HPT790212

First Floor: 874 square feet
Second Floor: 880 square feet
Ground-floor Foyer: 242 square feet
Total: 1,996 square feet
Width: 34'-0"
Depth: 43'-0"

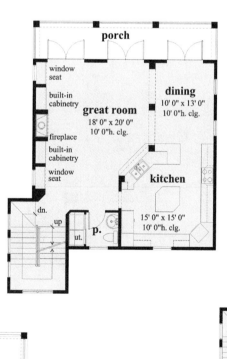

Southern Colonial

This Southern Colonial design boasts decorative two-story columns and large windows which enhance the front porch and balcony. The kitchen opens to a breakfast room, which accesses a side porch. The great room features a warming fireplace and accesses a large rear porch. The master bedroom includes a fireplace as well as a private bath with a whirlpool tub and a walk-in closet. Upstairs, two additional bedrooms share a full hall bath. Please specify crawlspace or slab foundation when ordering.

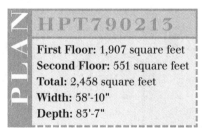

PLAN HPT790213

First Floor: 1,907 square feet
Second Floor: 551 square feet
Total: 2,458 square feet
Width: 58'-10"
Depth: 83'-7"

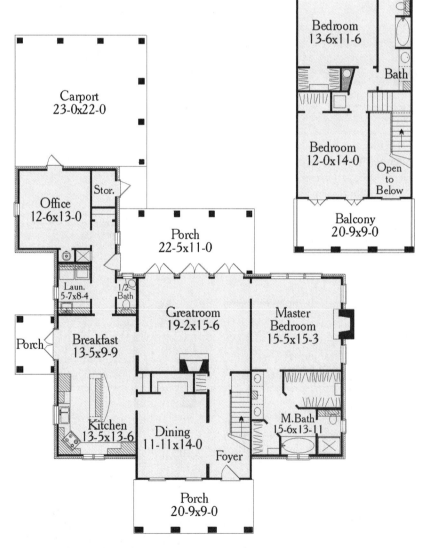

Bedroom 13-6x11-6

Bath

Bedroom 12-0x14-0

Open to Below

Balcony 20-9x9-0

Carport 23-0x22-0

Stor.

Office 12-6x13-0

Porch 22-5x11-0

Laun. 5-7x8-4

1/2 Bath

Porch

Breakfast 13-5x9-9

Greatroom 19-2x15-6

Master Bedroom 15-5x15-3

Kitchen 13-5x13-6

Dining 11-11x14-0

Foyer

M.Bath 15-6x13-11

Porch 20-9x9-0

Two Car Garage
21⁶ x 21⁶

Breakfast
13⁶ x 10⁰

Kitchen
16⁰ x 13⁶

Great Room
20⁶ x 17⁶

Master Bedroom
15⁹ x 16⁶

Bedroom #3
12⁰ x 13³

Dining Room
13³ x 14⁹

Foyer

Bedroom #2
12⁶ x 13³

World-Class Style

With world-class style and spirit, this magnificent design will be a showpiece in any neighborhood. Doric columns and a Monticello-style pediment announce a contemporary interior with a perfect mix of formal and casual space. True to an historic vernacular, the broad foyer serves as a parlor that opens to a completely modern great room with wide-open views. A splendid kitchen offers a walk-in pantry, food-preparation island and wrapping counters. The master suite is truly indulgent with a pampering bath and walk-in closet. This home is designed with a walkout basement foundation.

PLAN HPT790214

Square Footage: 2,697
Width: 64'-4"
Depth: 67'-0"

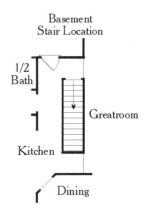

Basement Stair Location

1/2 Bath

Greatroom

Kitchen

Dining

Graceful Appeal

Classical columns give the entrance of this floor plan a graceful appeal. The great room leads through two sets of double doors to the rear porch. This porch can also be accessed by a door connected to the garage and another private door to the master bedroom. The master suite is brilliantly lit by multiple window views to the outdoors. Three additional bedrooms complete the family sleeping quarters. Please specify basement, crawlspace or slab foundation when ordering.

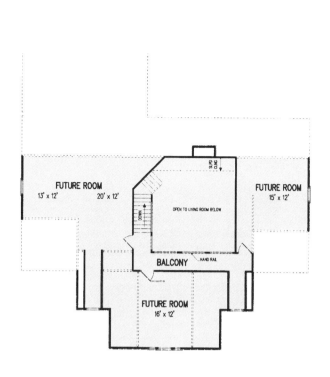

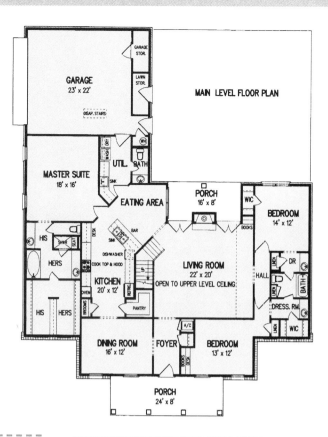

MAIN LEVEL FLOOR PLAN

Central Fireplace

The columned porch of this classic cottage opens to a narrow foyer flanked by the formal dining room and a secondary bedroom. The living room features a two-story ceiling, a central fireplace and a double set of French doors to the rear porch. A spacious kitchen is perfectly located between the dining and breakfast areas. The master suite enjoys an amenity-laden bath and quiet seclusion. Another family bedroom completes this floor. Future space is available on the second floor. Please specify crawlspace or slab foundation when ordering.

PLAN HPT790216

Square Footage: 2,684
Bonus Space: 768 square feet
Width: 62'-0"
Depth: 80'-0"

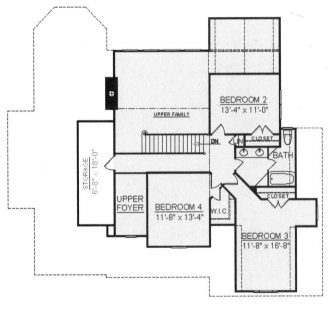

Classic Ambiance

Stucco and gables and a columned front porch add to the timeless appeal of this popular design. Inside, the foyer is flanked by a parlor and formal dining room. The family room with a fireplace and built-ins opens to the rear deck, expanding outdoor living. The kitchen is placed between the garage and breakfast room. The master bedroom features a pampering bath and spacious walk-in closet. Three additional bedrooms share a hall bath upstairs.

PLAN HPT790217

First Floor: 1,803 square feet
Second Floor: 748 square feet
Total: 2,551 square feet
Width: 46'-4"
Depth: 50'-10"

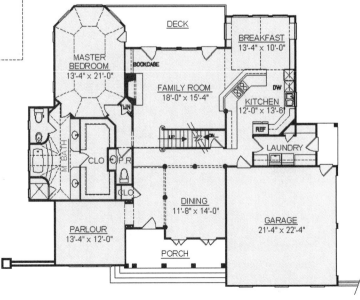

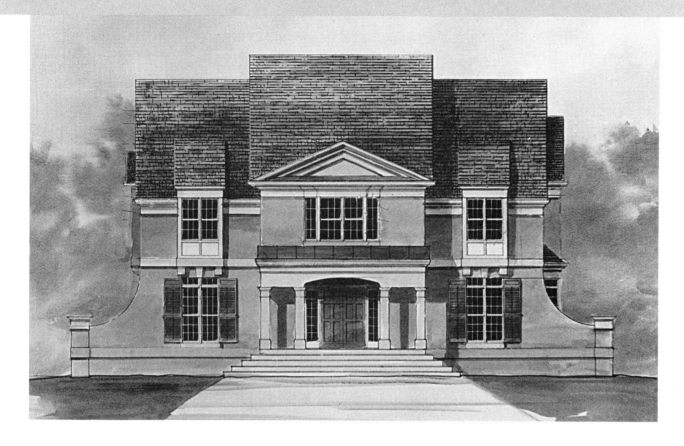

Stately Exterior

This Early American home borrows from a Neoclassic tradition and celebrates elements of the Greek Revival architectural style. While the exterior is symmetrical and stately, the interior boasts luxurious livability. Formal living and dining rooms flank the foyer. A massive fireplace warms the two-story great room. The gourmet island kitchen boasts a pantry and a breakfast room that overlooks the rear porch. Upstairs, the master suite with a romantic fireplace offers a private bath and His and Hers walk-in closets. A loft area overlooks the great room.

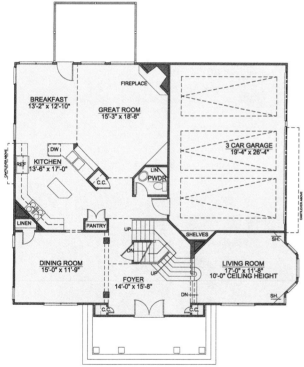

PLAN HPT790218

First Floor: 1,332 square feet
Second Floor: 1,350 square feet
Total: 2,682 square feet
Width: 48'-0"
Depth: 42'-0"

Greek Revival

Four columns announce the grand foyer of this home, which is flanked by a stately library and a formal dining room. The spacious living room boasts a fireplace. The U-shaped kitchen offers plenty of counter space. Nearby, a guest suite or study offers a full bath and opens off the breakfast room. Located on the main floor, the lavish master suite is designed to pamper with a walk-in closet, sumptuous bath and a window bay. Upstairs, two family bedrooms with walk-in closets share a full bath. An optional playroom is at the other end of the hall.

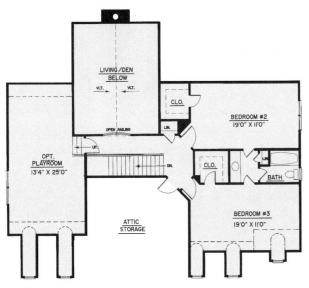

PLAN

HPT790219

First Floor: 1,815 square feet
Second Floor: 699 square feet
Total: 2,514 square feet
Bonus Room: 335 square feet
Width: 55'-0"
Depth: 49'-6"

Master
Bath

Master
Bedroom
15-0x15-9

Courtyard

Garage
21-0x21-0

Garage
21-0x20-9

Bedroom
11-1x11-1

Porch
18-6x6-10

Laun.
6-5x5-1

Storage
7-5x7-8

Bath

Greatroom
18-0x17-6

Kitchen
14-7x10-9

Bedroom
12-7x12-1

Dining
14-7x10-9

Foyer

Porch
23-4x5-6

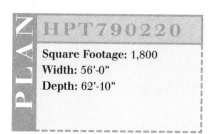

PLAN

HPT790220

Square Footage: 1,800
Width: 56'-0"
Depth: 62'-10"

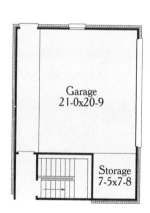

Magnificent
Columns

A classic paneled entry leads to an open foyer, partially defined by magnificent columns. Interior vistas extend to the outdoors through the great room—an airy space that's anchored by a massive fireplace. A convenient arrangement of the formal dining room and gourmet kitchen invites planned events and traditional gatherings as well as casual bashes. The master wing provides a walk-in closet, a garden tub and a view of the courtyard. Clustered secondary bedrooms share a hall that allows access to the outdoors. Plans include an optional detached garage. Please specify basement, crawlspace or slab foundation when ordering.

French Provincial Charmer

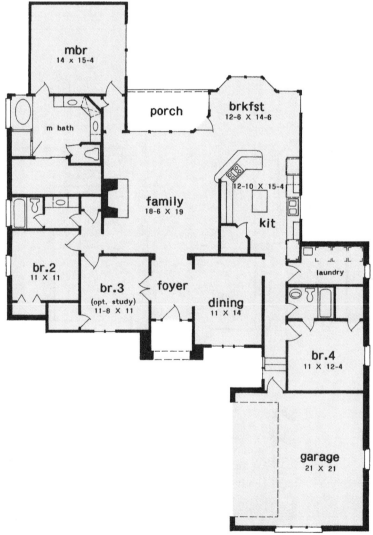

This French Provincial charmer offers a stunning stucco and brick exterior and classic European style. At the heart of the home, the family room provides a fireplace and access to a rear covered porch. The island kitchen serves a breakfast bay that overlooks the backyard. The master suite is tucked away at the back of the plan with a fine bath and walk-in closet. Two family bedrooms—or make one a study—share a full bath and a hall that leads to the family room. An additional suite or guest quarters resides near the service entrance—a perfect arrangement for a live-in relative.

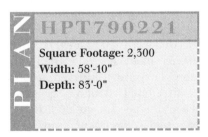

PLAN

HPT790221

Square Footage: 2,300
Width: 58'-10"
Depth: 83'-0"

Old World Ambiance

An Old World ambiance characterizes this European-style home. The elegant stone entrance leads to a two-story foyer. The formal dining room opens through an arch flanked by decorative columns. The great room features a coffered ceiling and a through-fireplace that's also viewed from the kitchen and breakfast room. The master suite includes a luxury bath and a cozy sitting area off the bedroom. A secondary suite offers space for a guest or live-in relative. Upstairs, two secondary bedrooms share a full bath and a balcony hall. Please specify basement, crawlspace or slab foundation when ordering.

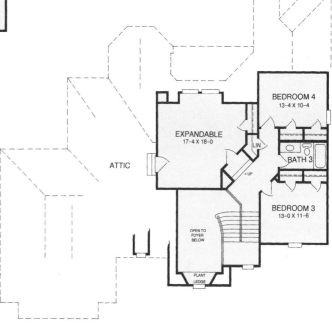

PLAN HPT790222

First Floor: 2,050 square feet
Second Floor: 561 square feet
Total: 2,611 square feet
Bonus Room: 272 square feet
Width: 64'-10"
Depth: 64'-0"

Innovative Amenities

Here's a charming design that has it all! A modern mix of exterior materials announces the innovative amenities of an open interior. A mid-level foyer eases the transition from outdoors to in, and leads up a few steps to a spacious great room that features a corner fireplace. To the left are three bedrooms and a full bath with a whirlpool tub. The efficient kitchen easily serves the formal dining room as well as the sunny breakfast room. Note the grilling porch, offering a place to hook up a gas barbecue. The lavish master suite features built-ins, two walk-in closets and a sumptuous bath. Please specify basement or slab foundation when ordering.

PLAN

HPT790223

Square Footage: 2,249
Finished Basement: 246 square feet
Width: 63'-11"
Depth: 49'-4"

Impressive Facade

Elegant columns mixed with a stone and stucco exterior present an impressive facade that's reminiscent of gentler times. A pair of guardian lions offer a touch of 'tongue and chic' to the upbeat yet Old World exterior. A light-filled interior provides an open arrangement of the formal and casual spaces. The kitchen provides a break-fast area and an overlook to the family room. Three bedrooms, including the spacious master suite with a spa bath and a large walk-in closet, afford both privacy and convenience. The loft offers space for computers and books.

PLAN HPT790224

First Floor: 1,923 square feet
Second Floor: 580 square feet
Total: 2,503 square feet
Width: 49'-0"
Depth: 84'-0"

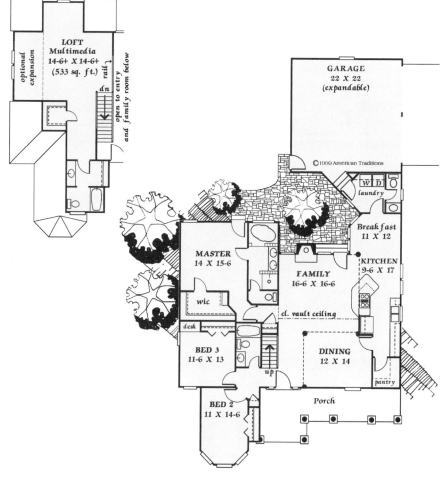

Bright Rooms

Multi-pane windows, shutters and shingle accents adorn the stucco facade of this wonderful French country home. Inside, the foyer introduces the hearth-warmed great room that features access to the rear deck. The dining room, defined from the foyer and great room by columns, enjoys front-yard views. The master suite includes two walk-in closets, rear-deck access and a dual vanity bath. The second floor holds two bedrooms, a study and an unfinished bedroom.

PLAN HPT790225

First Floor: 1,840 square feet
Second Floor: 840 square feet
Total: 2,680 square feet
Bonus Room: 295 square feet
Width: 66'-0"
Depth: 65'-10"

PLAN HPT790300

Square Footage: 2,757
Width: 69'-6"
Depth: 68'-3"

French Elegance

Country French appointments give this home an elegant Old World look. The foyer opens to the well-proportioned dining room, with a twelve-foot ceiling. A stairway is conveniently located in the home to provide access to the optional basement below and the attic above. Double French doors with transoms open to the rear porch. Three additional bedrooms include a flex room that easily converts to a home office or study.

English Country Home

A gentle mix of stucco and stone, a box-bay window and a covered entry make this English country home very inviting. The two-story foyer opens to formal living and dining rooms, bright with natural light. A spacious U-shaped kitchen adjoins a breakfast nook with views of the outdoors. This area flows to the two-story great room, which offers a through-fireplace shared with the media room. Upstairs, a plush retreat awaits the homeowner with a quiet sitting bay. The unfinished bonus room provides further storage space. This home is designed with a walkout basement foundation.

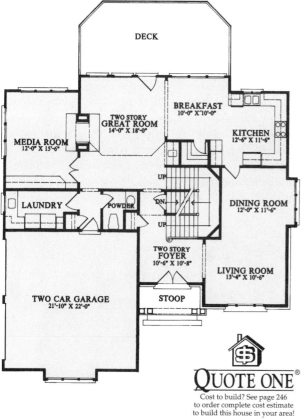

QUOTE ONE®
Cost to build? See page 246
to order complete cost estimate
to build this house in your area!

PLAN

HPT790226

First Floor: 1,395 square feet
Second Floor: 1,210 square feet
Total: 2,605 square feet
Bonus Room: 225 square feet
Width: 47'-0"
Depth: 49'-6"

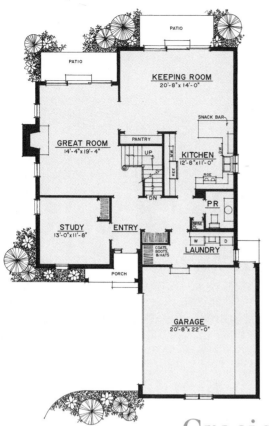

Gracious Rooms

PLAN

HPT790227

First Floor: 1,278 square feet
Second Floor: 1,027 square feet
Total: 2,305 square feet
Width: 42'-6"
Depth: 61'-2"

French Provincial style gives its special touch to this cozy cottage plan. The stucco exterior features shuttered windows and a cupola with a weathervane over the garage. The first floor includes a great room with a fireplace. The keeping room features a snack bar served by the kitchen and provides access to a private patio. A quiet study offers space for computers, books and private conversations. Two patios are accessed through the keeping room and the great room. The second floor includes a generous master suite with dressing space, a knee-space vanity and a walk-in closet.

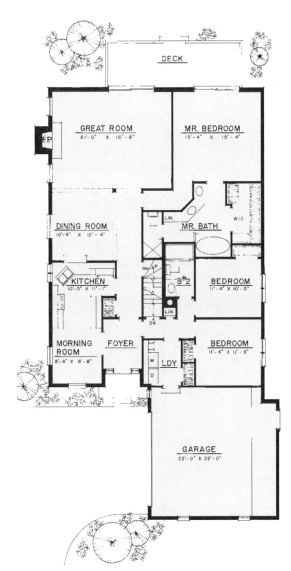

French Countryside

It's easy to imagine this charming one-story home nestled in the picturesque countryside of France. However, this amenity-filled plan—designed to fit handily on a narrow lot—will be at home in any neighborhood. Efficient floor planning places the kitchen and morning room to the left of the foyer, allowing the formal dining room, the great room and the master bedroom to take advantage of rear views. From the garage—cleverly disguised as a barn—there is a laundry room adjoining two secondary bedrooms and a bath. The master bedroom is highlighted by a dressing area with a walk-in closet and a master bath with a whirlpool tub.

PLAN HPT790228

Square Footage: 1,890
Width: 40'-0"
Depth: 73'-4"

Open Interior

This traditional home boasts a large receiving porch and free-flowing interior spaces. The spacious living room is open to the adjacent dining room and has a built-in fireplace and entertainment center. The entry, breakfast area, kitchen, and dining and living areas have twelve-foot ceilings, while other rooms have traditional eight-foot ceilings. The master suite is isolated for privacy and conveniently located only steps away from the kitchen. Please specify crawlspace or slab foundation when ordering.

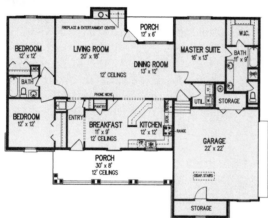

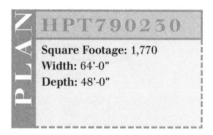

PLAN

HPT790230

Square Footage: 1,770
Width: 64'-0"
Depth: 48'-0"

PLAN

HPT790229

First Floor: 2,024 square feet
Second Floor: 659 square feet
Total: 2,683 square feet
Width: 37'-10"
Depth: 66'-0"

Detailed Transoms

Detailed transoms over four sets of French doors present an interesting facade. Three sets of French doors lead to the family room—where a fireplace and built-ins can be enjoyed. The cooktop island with a snack bar makes gourmet cooking effortless in the L-shaped kitchen. Down a long hallway is a powder room, a study and the master bedroom. A set of double doors in the master bedroom opens to a deluxe private bath with two walk-in closets.

Gracious Charm

A Palladian window set in a stucco facade under a hipped roof lends a gracious charm to this three-bedroom home. The welcoming front porch opens to a living room featuring a corner fireplace. The U-shaped kitchen opens directly to the dining room and its patio access. A utility/storage room connects the two-car garage to the kitchen. This plan splits the master suite from the two family bedrooms on the left for added privacy. Note the dual vanity sinks in the master bath. Please specify crawlspace or slab foundation when ordering.

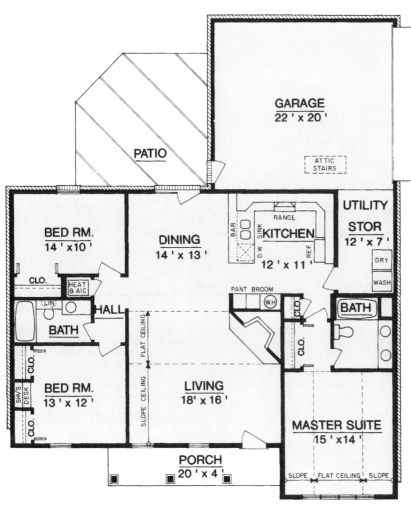

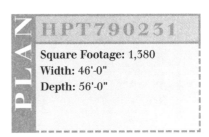

PLAN HPT790231

Square Footage: 1,380
Width: 46'-0"
Depth: 56'-0"

Amenities to Explore

Loads of storage and four bedrooms grace this European design, but there are other amenities to explore. The central family room with a fireplace connects to the breakfast room and island kitchen. The formal living room and dining room flank the foyer. The living room easily converts to a study. The master suite offers a sitting room and a bath with two walk-in closets.

PLAN HPT790233

Square Footage: 2,652
Width: 69'-0"
Depth: 88'-2"

PLAN HPT790232

Square Footage: 2,048
Width: 38'-10"
Depth: 75'-0"

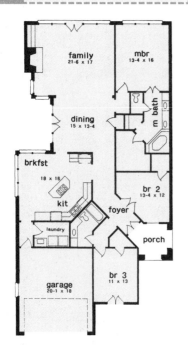

Spacious Rooms

Presenting a narrow frontage, this plan extends back 75 feet and provides spacious rooms for a family. Enter the home through a front corner porch or through a side courtyard that opens to the dining room. A fireplace warms the family room, which accesses the rear yard through French doors. A bright corner breakfast nook highlights the kitchen, which provides a cooktop island and laundry-room access. The master suite features a walk-in closet and separate vanities in the compartmented bath.

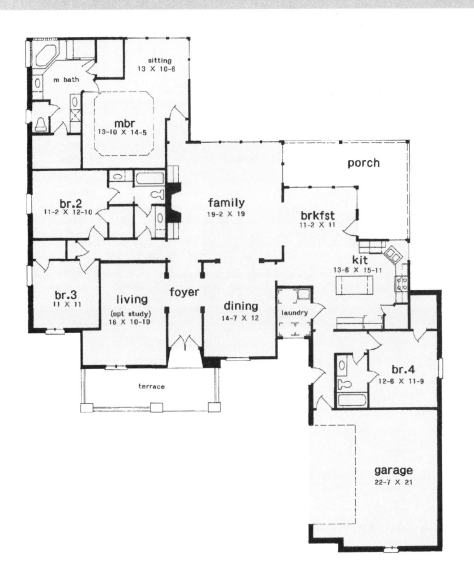

sitting
13 X 10-6

m bath

mbr
13-10 X 14-5

br.2
11-2 X 12-10

porch

family
19-2 X 19

brkfst
11-2 X 11

br.3
11 X 11

living
(opt study)
16 X 10-10

foyer

dining
14-7 X 12

laundry

kit
13-6 X 15-11

terrace

br.4
12-6 X 11-9

garage
22-7 X 21

Fenced Terrace

In true French country style, this home begins with a lovely terrace that announces the double-door entry. The main foyer separates formal living and dining areas and leads back to a large family room with a fireplace and built-ins. The breakfast room overlooks a wrapping porch and opens to the island kitchen. Three bedrooms are found on the left side of the plan—two family bedrooms sharing a full bath and a master suite with a sitting area. A fourth bedroom is tucked behind the two-car garage and features a private bath.

PLAN HPT790234

Square Footage: 2,678
Width: 69'-4"
Depth: 84'-8"

Snack Counter

Formal rooms deck out the front of this plan, which allows great interior vistas from the foyer and entry gallery. The gourmet kitchen boasts a tile floor, a walk-in pantry and a snack counter that's shared with the airy breakfast area. A Pullman ceiling highlights the spacious great room, which provides access to the rear covered patio. The master wing boasts a garden tub, separate lavatories and a door to the patio.

PLAN HPT790236

Square Footage: 2,390
Width: 53'-10"
Depth: 68'-10"

PLAN HPT790235

Square Footage: 1,701
Width: 45'-0"
Depth: 68'-2"

Massive Fireplace

Don't let the bricks and classic columns fool you—this is one home that's fully prepared for the new age. A spacious great room offers an entertainment center, a massive fireplace and, best of all, access to a private side patio. Casual dining space opens to the kitchen, which features a walk-in pantry. Three tall windows and a vaulted ceiling enhance the master suite. Separate lavatories and a garden tub highlight the private bath.

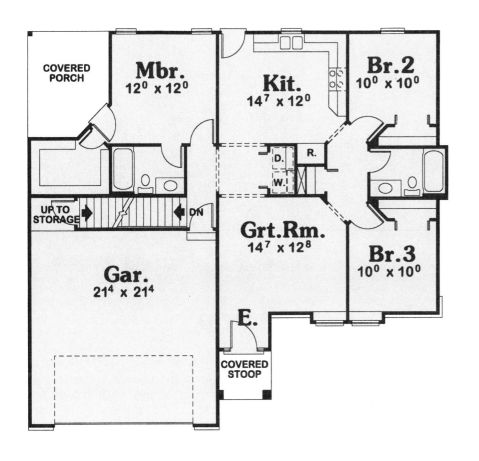

COVERED PORCH

Mbr.
12⁰ x 12⁰

Kit.
14⁷ x 12⁰

Br.2
10⁰ x 10⁰

D.

R.

W.

UP TO STORAGE

DN

Grt.Rm.
14⁷ x 12⁸

Br.3
10⁰ x 10⁰

Gar.
21⁴ x 21⁴

E.

COVERED STOOP

Unique Look

This charming cottage—complete with multi-pane windows and distinguished pediments—has a mixed facade of stucco, brick and siding, giving it a unique and original look. The roomy kitchen boasts double basins, a door to the backyard and a window above the sink to allow extra light for cooking. The master bedroom is enhanced with a private covered porch and a large walk-in closet. Bedrooms 2 and 3, large closets included, share a full bath on the opposite side of the plan, allowing for privacy. Please specify basement or slab foundation when ordering.

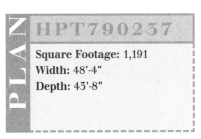

PLAN

HPT790237

Square Footage: 1,191
Width: 48'-4"
Depth: 43'-8"

Inviting Design

An open arrangement of the formal rooms offers many splendid occasions in this inviting design. The right wing of the plan is dedicated to the homeowner's retreat, which offers a walk-in closet, a garden tub and separate lavatories. The casual living space includes an entertainment center. A food-preparation island highlights the gourmet kitchen, which provides a vaulted ceiling and a walk-in pantry. Secondary sleeping quarters cluster around a service hall that includes a laundry.

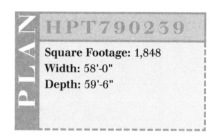

PLAN HPT790239

Square Footage: 1,848
Width: 58'-0"
Depth: 59'-6"

PLAN HPT790238

Square Footage: 2,070
Width: 46'-3"
Depth: 67'-7"

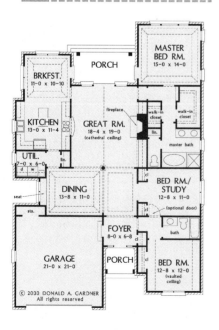

Easy Conversion

Here's a charming Country plan with a heart of gold. The central living space and dining room easily convert from formal to comfortable, inviting any occasion, planned or intimate. An open kitchen features a wrapping peninsular counter with plenty of food-preparation space. Nearby, the breakfast area opens to a covered patio. To the rear of the plan, a spacious family room provides space for retreat and repose. Computers fit easily in this comfort zone.

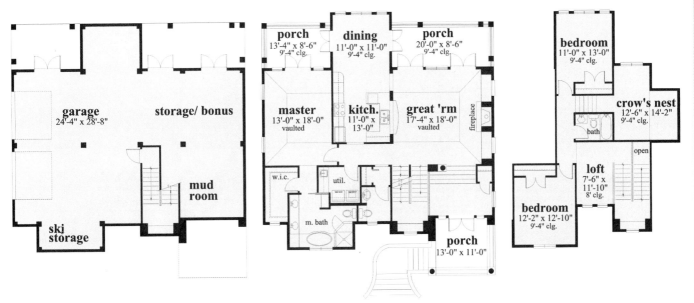

garage
24'-4" x 28'-8"

storage/ bonus

mud room

ski storage

porch
13'-4" x 8'-6"
9'-4" clg.

dining
11'-0" x 11'-0"
9'-4" clg.

porch
20'-0" x 8'-6"
9'-4" clg.

master
13'-0" x 18'-0"
vaulted

kitch.
11'-0" x 13'-0"

great 'rm
17'-4" x 18'-0"
vaulted

fireplace

w.i.c.

util.

m. bath

porch
13'-0" x 11'-0"

bedroom
11'-0" x 13'-0"
9'-4" clg.

crow's nest
12'-6" x 14'-2"
9'-4" clg.

bath

open

loft
7'-6" x 11'-10"
8' clg.

bedroom
12'-2" x 12'-10"
9'-4" clg.

Art of the Country

Dramatic rooflines complement a striking arched-pediment entry and a variety of windows on this refined facade. The entry porch leads to a landing that rises to the main-level living area—an arrangement well suited for unpredictable climates. A fireplace warms the great room, which sports a tray ceiling and opens to the rear porch through lovely French doors. The gourmet kitchen serves a stunning formal dining room, which offers wide views through a wall of windows. Separate sets of French doors let in natural light and fresh air, and permit access to both of the rear porches.

PLAN HPT790240

First Floor: 1,537 square feet
Second Floor: 812 square feet
Total: 2,349 square feet
Width: 45'-4"
Depth: 50'-0"

Charming Haven

With New England charm, this early American Cape Cod is a quaint haven for any family. Enter from the porch to the foyer, which opens to the dining area and great room. The great room is illuminated by a wall of windows and features a fireplace with two built-in niches on either side. An efficient kitchen is brightened by the morning room, which accesses a rear patio. The opposite side of the home is dedicated to the master suite, which includes a vaulted master bath and a spacious walk-in closet. A two-car garage completes this level.

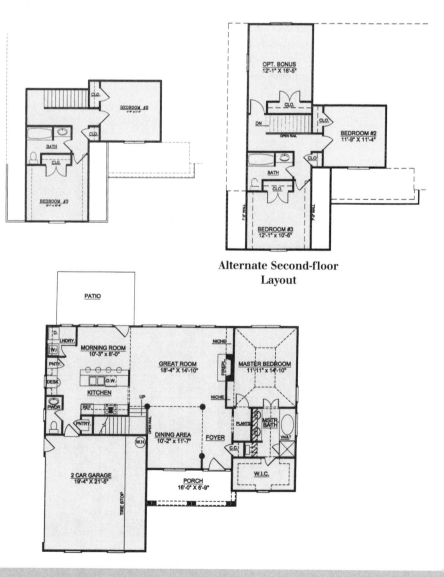

Alternate Second-floor Layout

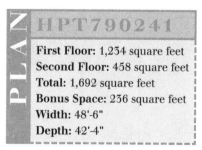

PLAN HPT790241

First Floor: 1,234 square feet
Second Floor: 458 square feet
Total: 1,692 square feet
Bonus Space: 236 square feet
Width: 48'-6"
Depth: 42'-4"

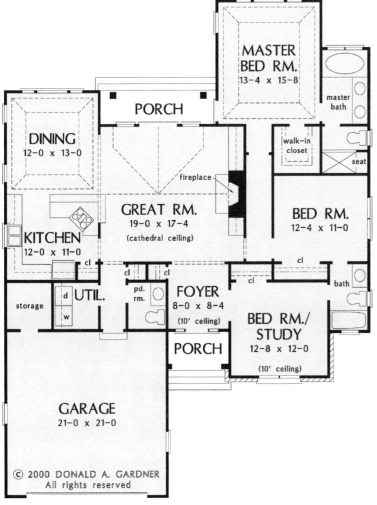

PORCH

MASTER BED RM.
13-4 x 15-8

master bath

DINING
12-0 x 13-0

walk-in closet

seat

fireplace

GREAT RM.
19-0 x 17-4
(cathedral ceiling)

BED RM.
12-4 x 11-0

KITCHEN
12-0 x 11-0

cl

cl

cl

cl

bath

storage

d UTIL.
w

pd. rm.

FOYER
8-0 x 8-4
(10' ceiling)

BED RM./
STUDY
12-8 x 12-0

PORCH

(10' ceiling)

GARAGE
21-0 x 21-0

Comfort and Style

The hipped roof of this three-bedroom home protects a comfortable interior. A study or secondary bedroom opens to the right of the foyer and shares a full bath with an additional bedroom. Adorned with a tray ceiling, the master suite has all the amenities of a luxury home including a walk-in closet, two-sink vanity, soaking tub, separate shower and compartmented toilet. The great room with its beautiful fireplace and built-ins has views of the rear porch. Nearby, the dining room enjoys access to both the kitchen and the great room for easy entertaining.

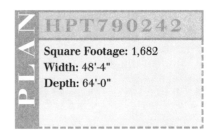

PLAN HPT790242

Square Footage: 1,682
Width: 48'-4"
Depth: 64'-0"

Deck
38'-0" x 12'-0"

Kitchen
10'-0" x 14'-5"

Utility

Dining Rm.
10'-0" x 14'-5"

Pantry

Great Room
20'-0" x 16'-3"
(cathedral clg.)

Master Bedroom
13'-5" x 16'-3"

Porch
22'-8" x 6'-8"

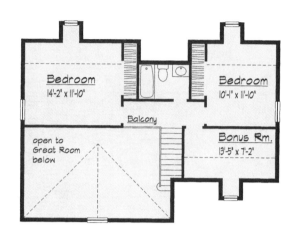

Bedroom
14'-2" x 11'-10"

Bedroom
10'-1" x 11'-10"

Balcony

open to
Great Room
below

Bonus Rm.
13'-5" x 7'-2"

Fine Three-Bedroom Home

PLAN

HPT790243

First Floor: 1,216 square feet
Second Floor: 478 square feet
Total: 1,694 square feet
Bonus Room: 115 square feet
Width: 38'-0"
Depth: 38'-8"

Four pillars support a roof topped by an attractive gable—all covering the front porch of this fine three-bedroom home. Inside, the entrance opens directly to the great room, where a cathedral ceiling and a fireplace are enhancements. A gourmet kitchen offers a work island with a sink and serving counter for the nearby dining room. Located on the main level for privacy, the master bedroom offers two closets. Upstairs, two family bedrooms share a hall bath and access to a bonus room—perfect for a study or computer room. Please specify basement or crawlspace foundation when ordering.

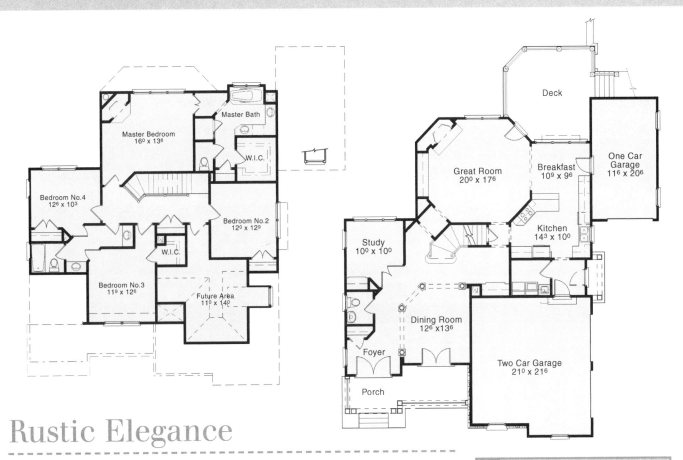

Master Bedroom
16⁰ x 13⁶

Master Bath

W.I.C.

Bedroom No.4
12⁶ x 10³

Bedroom No.2
12⁰ x 12⁹

W.I.C.

Bedroom No.3
11⁹ x 12⁶

Future Area
11⁰ x 14⁰

Deck

Great Room
20⁰ x 17⁶

Breakfast
10⁹ x 9⁶

One Car Garage
11⁶ x 20⁶

Kitchen
14³ x 10⁰

Study
10⁰ x 10⁰

Dining Room
12⁶ x 13⁶

Two Car Garage
21⁰ x 21⁶

Foyer

Porch

Rustic Elegance

This shingle-style home is a rustic yet elegant design that does not reveal itself fully at first glance. Double French doors at the entrance lead to a magnificent gallery hall and winding staircase. Stunning columns define the formal dining room, while French doors open to the front porch. The central hall leads to a quiet study and to the great room, which offers a fireplace and built-in bookshelves. The dramatic staircase outside the great room leads upstairs, where a charming master bedroom includes a fireplace and a walk-in closet. This home is designed with a basement foundation.

PLAN

HPT790244

First Floor: 1,326 square feet
Second Floor: 1,254 square feet
Total: 2,580 square feet
Bonus Room: 230 square feet
Width: 55'-4"
Depth: 57'-6"

Sweet Harmony

Stone, siding, shutters and a covered front porch combine to give this home plenty of curb appeal. Inside, a few steps up will bring you to the main living level. Here, a formal dining room is defined by graceful columns. The great room, kitchen and breakfast room work well to encourage casual get-togethers. Two family bedrooms share a full bath and a hall linen closet. Please specify crawlspace or slab foundation when ordering.

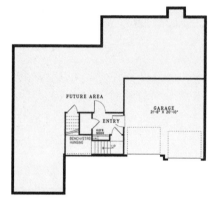

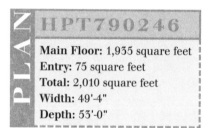

HPT790246

Main Floor: 1,935 square feet
Entry: 75 square feet
Total: 2,010 square feet
Width: 49'-4"
Depth: 53'-0"

HPT790245

Square Footage: 1,142
Width: 46'-0"
Depth: 38'-0"

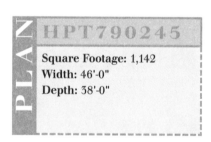

English Manor

Reminiscent of an English Country cottage, this charming plan offers much more than just good looks. The open interior provides space for entertaining as well as cozy places to kick off the shoes and read or reflect. *No boundaries* in the central living and dining area invites a pleasing ambiance, and an arch-top window really brings in the light. A well-organized kitchen provides a casual dining area. This home is designed with a basement foundation.

Bayed Breakfast Nook

Stunning architecture brings out the best on this country facade, with a mix of brick and siding. A fireplace anchors the open living and dining area that serves as the heart of the home. A gourmet kitchen boasts a food-preparation island and an ample pantry. The breakfast nook boasts a bay window. Upstairs, a vaulted ceiling highlights the master suite, which boasts a walk-in closet and a spacious bath. Bedroom 3 features a sitting area with a vaulted ceiling and a plant shelf. Bedroom 2 boasts views of the rear property.

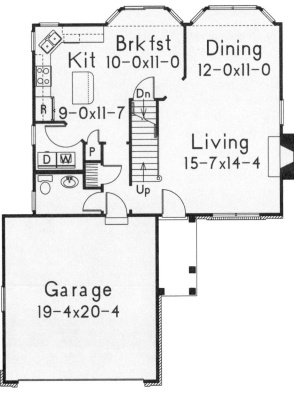

PLAN HPT790247

First Floor: 802 square feet
Second Floor: 773 square feet
Total: 1,575 square feet
Width: 36'-0"
Depth: 46'-8"

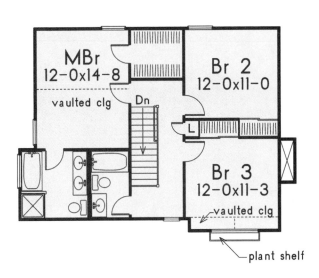

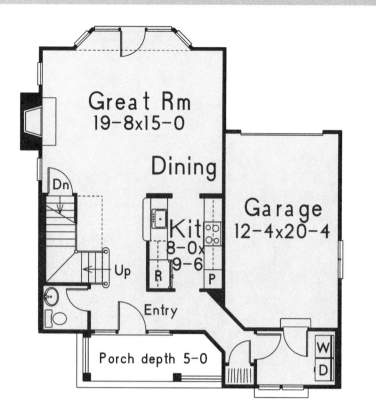

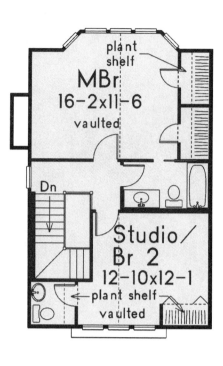

Warming Hearth

PLAN

HPT790248

First Floor: 718 square feet

Second Floor: 576 square feet

Total: 1,294 square feet

Width: 33'-0"

Depth: 35'-8"

This traditional two-story home is delicately distinguished with keystones and lintels above sunburst windows. The entry is well-framed with windows and columns. The covered porch is perfect for relaxing on cool fall evenings. The great room features a warming hearth and shares its space with the dining area. A sitting bay offers entry to the great room from the backyard. The kitchen is complete with plenty of counter space and a pantry. The master bedroom and a family bedroom/studio are located on the second level with a full bath.

Charm Packed

This country cottage has charm packed into every square foot. The front windows offer a simple elegance to this home. A front porch ushers you into a large family room with a fireplace. The kitchen features a cooktop island with an adjoining eating bar, large pantry and built-in desk. The dining room looks out to the patio, providing an outdoor dining area. Three bedrooms with ample closets and two baths create plenty of room for quiet retreats.

GARAGE
22x24

Drive

Patio

Stoop

DINING
10x13

Desk

KITCHEN
10x13

MASTER
16x13

FAMILY ROOM
16x15

10' Clg.

BR.#2
12x10

PORCH

BR.#3
12x10

PLAN HPT790249

Square Footage: 1,393
Width: 42'-0"
Depth: 42'-0"

Nostalgic Bungalow

This nostalgic bungalow's facade is enhanced by a charming gable, twin dormers and a wrapping front porch. Bay windows enlarge both the dining room and the master bedroom, while the vaulted great room receives additional light from a front clerestory window. The kitchen features a practical design and includes a handy pantry and ample cabinets. A nearby utility room boasts a sink and additional cabinet and countertop space. Located downstairs for convenience, the master suite enjoys a private bath and walk-in closet. Upstairs, two more bedrooms and a generous bonus room share a full bath.

PLAN HPT790250

First Floor: 1,293 square feet
Second Floor: 528 square feet
Total: 1,821 square feet
Bonus Room: 355 square feet
Width: 48'-8"
Depth: 50'-0"

Natural Retreat

The grand Palladian window lends plenty of curb appeal to this charming home. The wraparound country porch is perfect for peaceful evenings. The vaulted great room enjoys a large bay window, stone fireplace, pass-through to the kitchen and awesome rear views through the atrium window wall. The master suite features double entry doors, a walk-in closet and a fabulous bath. The optional lower level includes a family room.

PLAN HPT790302

Square Footage: 1,681
Width: 55'-8"
Depth: 46'-0"

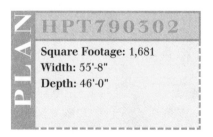

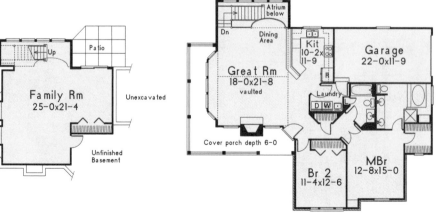

202

House and Garden

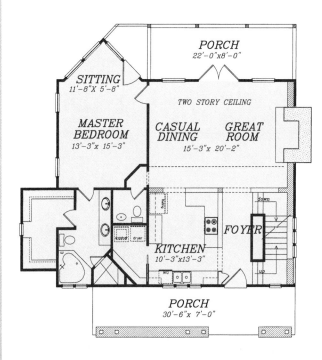

With a combination of shingles and flagstone detailing, this country home is perfect for a rustic setting. The kitchen leads to a laundry area. The two-story casual dining area and great room are combined for a snug atmosphere and share a fireplace. The master bedroom boasts a sitting area, which opens to the rear porch, a walk-in closet, dual basins and a compartmented toilet. The second level is home to two family bedrooms, which share a hall bath. Attic storage is available and a balcony overlook to the great room below is also provided.

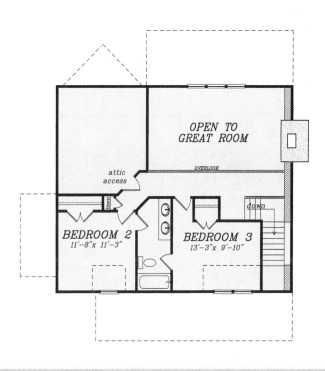

PLAN

HPT790251

First Floor: 1,180 square feet
Second Floor: 528 square feet
Total: 1,708 square feet
Width: 41'-4"
Depth: 45'-0"

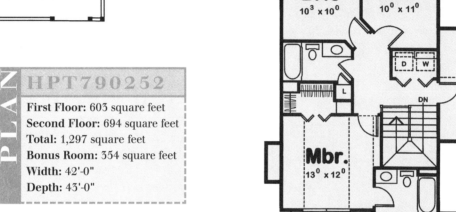

Comfortable Home

Pleasant country style can be found in this comfortable home. A covered porch provides a place for rocking chairs and enjoying the weather. Inside, the tiled foyer has a convenient coat closet. The living room features a bayed window and a fireplace. The dining room and kitchen combination encourages quiet dinners. Upstairs, two family bedrooms share a hall bath while the master suite has its own bath. A convenient laundry can also be found on this floor. Unfinished storage space is available above the garage.

PLAN HPT790252

First Floor: 603 square feet
Second Floor: 694 square feet
Total: 1,297 square feet
Bonus Room: 354 square feet
Width: 42'-0"
Depth: 43'-0"

Traditional Exterior

A traditional exterior with a beautiful Palladian window on the second level gives this home a layer of elegance. A covered porch invites guests into the living room featuring a corner fireplace. Down the hall, the large walk-through kitchen serves the multi-windowed dining area. The master bedroom takes up the entire right wing and enjoys access to the rear porch. Two family bedrooms, a bath and two unfinished storage areas complete the second floor.

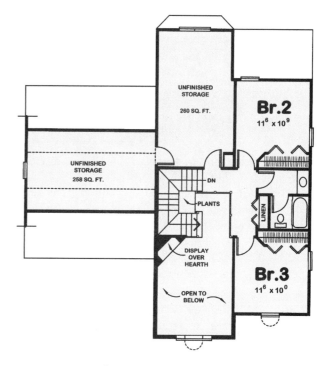

First floor plan:

- **Din.** 11⁸ x 10⁰
- **3 SEASON PORCH**
- **Gar.** 20⁰ x 26⁰
- **Kit.** 11⁸ x 12⁹
- **Mbr.** 12⁰ x 14⁰
- R
- P
- DN
- UP
- D / W / SEAT / DRESSER
- © dbi
- **Liv.Rm.** 12⁰ x 14¹⁰
- 18'-0" CEILING
- COVERED PORCH

Second floor plan:

- **UNFINISHED STORAGE** 260 SQ. FT.
- **UNFINISHED STORAGE** 258 SQ. FT.
- **Br.2** 11⁶ x 10⁹
- DN
- PLANTS
- LINEN
- DISPLAY OVER HEARTH
- **Br.3** 11⁶ x 10⁰
- OPEN TO BELOW

PLAN HPT790255

First Floor: 1,047 square feet
Second Floor: 467 square feet
Total: 1,514 square feet
Bonus Space: 518 square feet
Width: 45'-0"
Depth: 55'-0"

Sophisticated Charm

A wrapping front porch, three gables and a circle-top window lend sophistication and charm to this plan—designed with narrow lots in mind. Columns define the entry to the vaulted great room, which features a fireplace and built-in cabinets. The octagonal dining room showcases a tray ceiling and opens to the side porch through French doors. A master suite, two family bedrooms and a bonus room complete this plan.

PLAN HPT790254

Square Footage: 1,918
Bonus Room: 307 square feet
Width: 48'-8"
Depth: 89'-4"

PLAN HPT790255

Square Footage: 1,481
Bonus Space: 643 square feet
Width: 42'-4"
Depth: 65'-10"

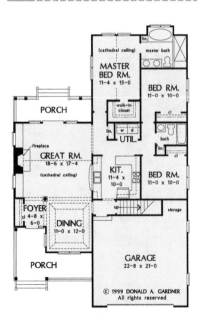

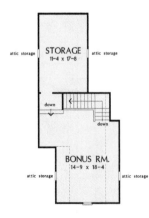

Sweet Modesty

Soaring gables make this narrow-lot design seem larger than its modest square footage, while cathedral and tray ceilings enhance interior spaciousness. A flowing floor plan positions the great room, dining room and kitchen in convenient proximity. The great room features a fireplace with flanking built-in cabinets and bookshelves, access to the back porch and a pass-through to the efficient kitchen.

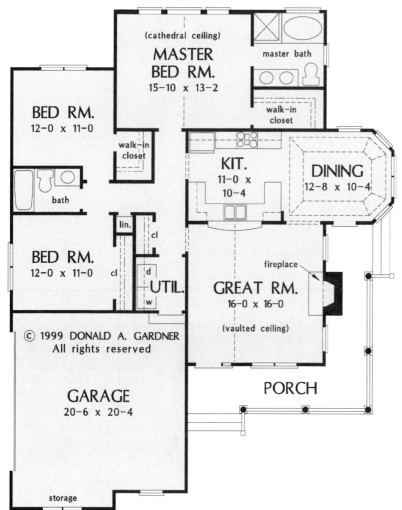

(cathedral ceiling)

MASTER BED RM.
15-10 x 13-2

master bath

walk-in closet

BED RM.
12-0 x 11-0

walk-in closet

bath

KIT.
11-0 x 10-4

DINING
12-8 x 10-4

lin.

cl

BED RM.
12-0 x 11-0

cl

d

w

UTIL.

fireplace

GREAT RM.
16-0 x 16-0

(vaulted ceiling)

GARAGE
20-6 x 20-4

PORCH

storage

Open Floor Plan

Multiple gables, an arched picture win-dow and an L-shaped front porch add size and style to this charming home. An open floor plan enhances spaciousness in the common areas of this compact home, where a vaulted ceiling in the great room and a bay window and tray ceiling in the dining room create volume and ele-gance. A pass-through from the kitchen to the great room adds to the plan's open-ness. The master bedroom boasts a cathe-dral ceiling and a trio of windows. The master bath features a dual-sink vanity and a separate tub and shower.

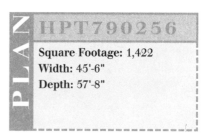

PLAN HPT790256

Square Footage: 1,422
Width: 45'-6"
Depth: 57'-8"

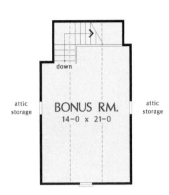

BONUS RM.
14-0 x 21-0

attic storage

down

attic storage

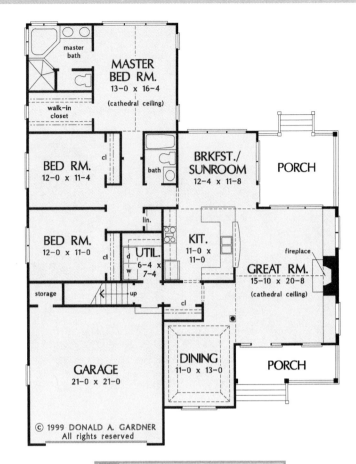

master bath

MASTER BED RM.
13-0 x 16-4
(cathedral ceiling)

walk-in closet

BED RM.
12-0 x 11-4

cl

bath

BRKFST./ SUNROOM
12-4 x 11-8

PORCH

BED RM.
12-0 x 11-0

cl

lin.

UTIL.
6-4 x 7-4

KIT.
11-0 x 11-0

fireplace

GREAT RM.
15-10 x 20-8
(cathedral ceiling)

storage

up

cl

GARAGE
21-0 x 21-0

DINING
11-0 x 13-0

PORCH

Great Gatherings

An entry door surrounded by a sunburst and sidelights enhances this charming porch with its gentle arches between each column. To the left of the entry is a dining room adorned with a tray ceiling and defined from other rooms by a single column. The nearby great room features a warming fireplace and a snack bar served by the kitchen. A breakfast and sun room next to the kitchen enjoys access to the side porch. To the left of the plan are two family bedrooms sharing a bath and a luxurious master suite.

PLAN

HPT790257

Square Footage: 1,845
Bonus Room: 355 square feet
Width: 49'-4"
Depth: 65'-0"

B. NATHAN.

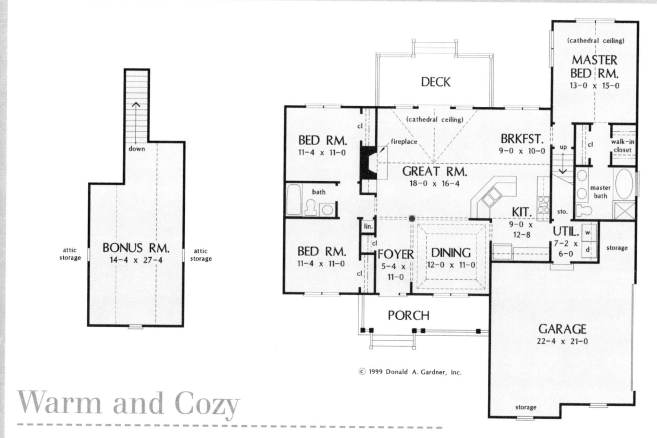

© 1999 Donald A. Gardner, Inc.

Warm and Cozy

A cozy front porch and gables create warmth and style for this economical home with an open floor plan and a sizable bonus room. The openness of the great room, dining room, kitchen and breakfast area increases the feeling of spaciousness. Additional volume is created by a cathedral ceiling that tops the great room and breakfast area, while a tray ceiling adds distinction and elegance to the formal dining room. Living space is extended to the outdoors by way of a rear deck. The master suite is separated from family bedrooms for privacy and features plenty of closet space.

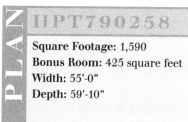

PLAN HPT790258

Square Footage: 1,590
Bonus Room: 425 square feet
Width: 55'-0"
Depth: 59'-10"

© 1999 Donald A. Gardner, Inc

B. NATHAN.

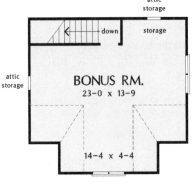

attic
storage

down | storage

attic
storage

BONUS RM.
23-0 x 13-9

14-4 x 4-4

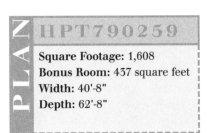

HPT790259

Square Footage: 1,608
Bonus Room: 437 square feet
Width: 40'-8"
Depth: 62'-8"

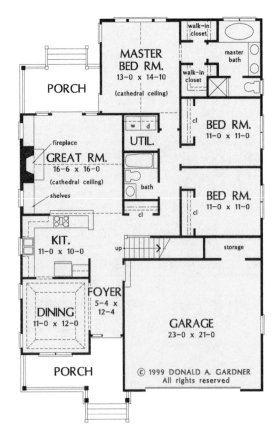

walk-in
closet

**MASTER
BED RM.**
13-0 x 14-10
(cathedral ceiling)

master
bath

PORCH

walk-in
closet

cl | **BED RM.**
11-0 x 11-0

fireplace

w | d

GREAT RM.
16-6 x 16-0
(cathedral ceiling)

UTIL.

bath

shelves

cl

cl | **BED RM.**
11-0 x 11-0

cl

KIT.
11-0 x 10-0

up | storage

FOYER
5-4 x
12-4

DINING
11-0 x 12-0

GARAGE
23-0 x 21-0

PORCH

Rustic Beauty

This rustic beauty provides a practical floor plan as well as delicate details. The great room is warmed by a fireplace and enhanced by cathedral ceilings. Tray ceilings in the dining room create a sophisticated atmosphere. An L-shaped kitchen offers ample counter and preparation space. The master bedroom features many luxuries—a private bath, two walk-in closets and access to a covered porch. Two additional bedrooms own individual closets and share a hall bath. The utility room is conveniently located near all three bedrooms. A bonus room is available for extra storage.

Beautiful Style

P L A N

HPT790260

Square Footage: 1,882
Bonus Room: 363 square feet
Width: 61'-4"
Depth: 55'-0"

An arched window in a center front-facing gable lends style and beauty to the facade of this three-bedroom home. An open common area features a great room with a cathedral ceiling, a formal dining room with a tray ceiling, a functional kitchen and an informal breakfast area. The area separates the master suite from the secondary bedrooms for privacy. The master suite provides a dramatic vaulted ceiling, access to the back porch and abundant closet space. Access to a versatile bonus room is near the master bedroom.

PORCH

(vaulted ceiling)
MASTER
BED RM.
14-8 x 16-8

BED RM.
11-4 x 11-0

(cathedral ceiling)

fireplace

BRKFST.
11-4 x 9-0

pd. rm.

cl

GREAT RM.
16-0 x 18-8

KIT.
11-4 x 11-8

cl

lin.

bath

w

up

d

walk-in closet

master bath

UTIL.
6-0 x 9-0

storage

BED RM.
14-0 x 11-4

FOYER
6-0 x 11-4

cl

cl

DINING
16-4 x 11-4

GARAGE
21-0 x 21-0

PORCH

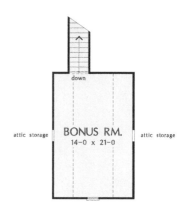

down

attic storage

BONUS RM.
14-0 x 21-0

attic storage

Arts and Crafts

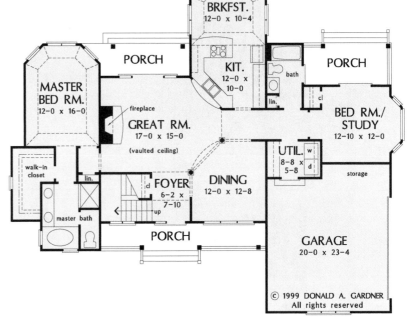

Cedar shakes, siding and stone blend with the Craftsman details of a custom design in this stunning home. The plan's open design and non-linear layout is refreshing and functional. The second-floor loft overlooks a centrally located and vaulted great room, and the breakfast area with a tray ceiling is virtually surrounded by windows to enhance the morning's light. The secluded first-floor master suite features a bay window, tray ceiling, walk-in closet and private bath. The second-floor family bedrooms are illuminated by rear dormers.

PLAN HPT790261

First Floor: 1,580 square feet
Second Floor: 627 square feet
Total: 2,207 square feet
Bonus Room: 214 square feet
Width: 64'-2"
Depth: 53'-4"

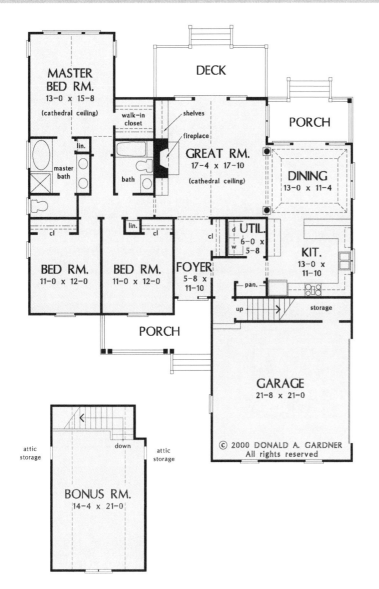

MASTER BED RM.
13-0 x 15-8
(cathedral ceiling)

walk-in closet

DECK

shelves

fireplace

PORCH

GREAT RM.
17-4 x 17-10
(cathedral ceiling)

DINING
13-0 x 11-4

master bath

lin.

bath

lin.

cl

cl

cl

BED RM.
11-0 x 12-0

BED RM.
11-0 x 12-0

FOYER
5-8 x 11-10

UTIL.
6-0 x 5-8

KIT.
13-0 x 11-10

pan.

up

storage

PORCH

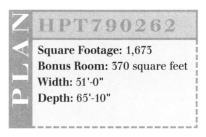

GARAGE
21-8 x 21-0

attic storage

down

attic storage

BONUS RM.
14-4 x 21-0

Stylish Arches

This practical plan features stylish arches on the front porch and cedar shake shingles on the gables for tremendous curb appeal. The foyer features a generous coat closet and access to the great room with its cathedral ceiling, fireplace, built-in shelves and French doors to the rear deck. Columns divide the great room from the dining room, which is enhanced by a lovely tray ceiling. The kitchen boasts a practical design and a sizable pantry. A cathedral ceiling highlights the master suite. Finish the bonus room for extra living space or use it for storage.

PLAN HPT790262

Square Footage: 1,673
Bonus Room: 370 square feet
Width: 51'-0"
Depth: 65'-10"

B. NATHAN

Victorian Flavor

Front and rear porches and bay windows lend this three-bedroom home Victorian flavor. Inside, the entry leads to the living room and the formal dining room, which boasts a bay window. The kitchen adjoins the informal dining area as well as the formal dining room, and overlooks the living room. On the right of the first floor is a bedroom with a walk-in closet and full bath. Upstairs, a family bedroom and a master bedroom share a full bath.

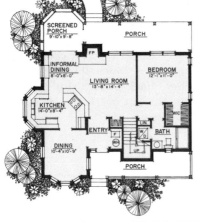

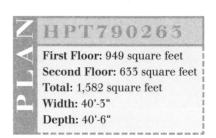

PLAN HPT790263

First Floor: 949 square feet
Second Floor: 633 square feet
Total: 1,582 square feet
Width: 40'-3"
Depth: 40'-6"

On the Waterfront

This narrow design with triple gables, front and back porches and a quartet of bay windows is an optimal home for waterfront property. The great room, dining room and kitchen are open to one another for a spacious, casual atmosphere. Two bedrooms—one with access to a private front porch—share a full bath. The master suite is secluded to the rear of the home and offers back-porch access, dual walk-in closets and a sumptuous bath with a garden tub.

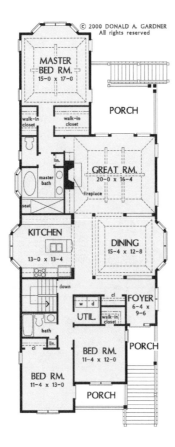

© 2000 Donald A. Gardner
All rights reserved

© 2000 Donald A. Gardner, Inc.

PLAN HPT790264

Square Footage: 1,970
Width: 34'-8"
Depth: 83'-0"

Perfect Charm

Country feelings ring true in this plan with details such as a metal roof, horizontal siding and multi-pane double-hung windows. The recessed front entry leads to a two-story great room, with access to both the front and rear porches. The great room is warmed by a fireplace and features a two-story ceiling. The first-floor master suite has a lavish bath and a walk-in closet. Two family bedrooms are located on the second level.

PLAN HPT790265

First Floor: 1,012 square feet
Second Floor: 556 square feet
Total: 1,568 square feet
Width: 34'-0"
Depth: 48'-0"

Spacious Kitchen

Decorative details complement this home's Country facade. Distinct pedimented arches and a covered porch add sophistication to this plan. The foyer leads to the vaulted great room where a fireplace awaits. Both the master suite and the great room showcase French doors to the rear vaulted porch. The bayed breakfast room sheds light onto the spacious kitchen. Two bedrooms and an equipment room are located on the second level.

PLAN HPT790267

First Floor: 1,710 square feet
Second Floor: 618 square feet
Total: 2,328 square feet
Width: 47'-0"
Depth: 50'-0"

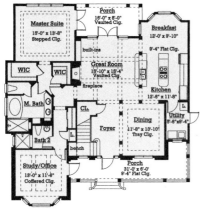

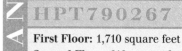

PLAN HPT790266

Square Footage: 2,124
Bonus Room: 296 square feet
Width: 57'-4"
Depth: 68'-8"

©1999 Donald A. Gardner, Inc.

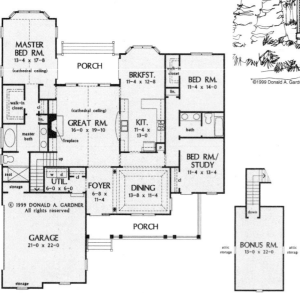

Private Master Suite

A trio of gables and horizontal and vertical siding combine with an inviting L-shaped porch to create this Craftsman-style home. The dining room receives refinement from an elegant tray ceiling. A bay window invites sunlight into the breakfast room and kitchen. Two family bedrooms share a spacious bath that includes double sinks. The master bedroom features back-porch access, ample closet space and a roomy private bath, plus access to the rear step-down porch.

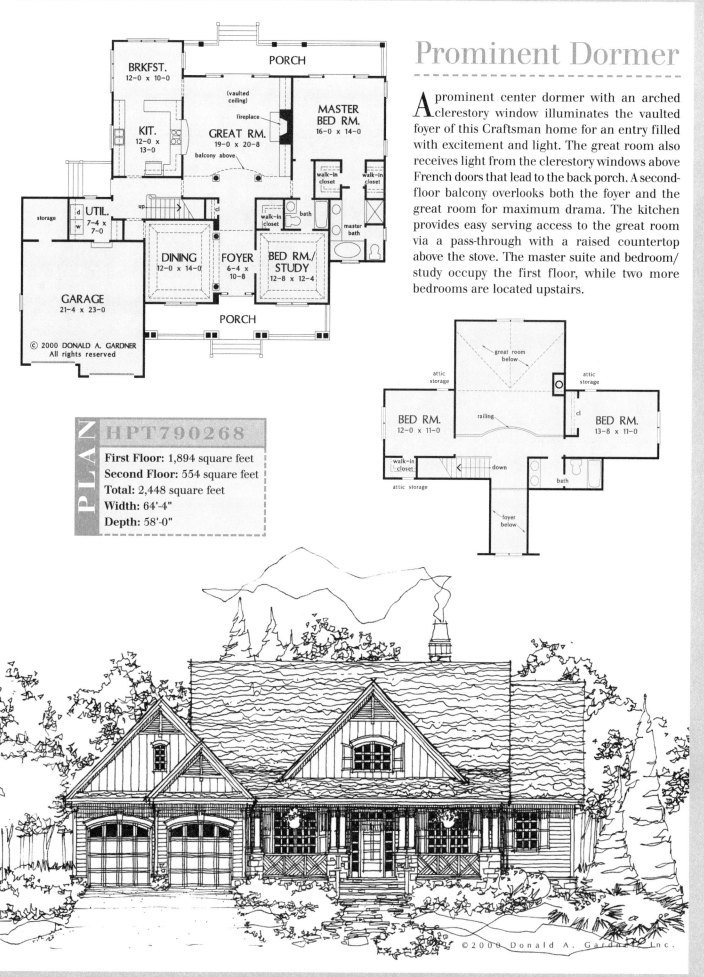

Prominent Dormer

A prominent center dormer with an arched clerestory window illuminates the vaulted foyer of this Craftsman home for an entry filled with excitement and light. The great room also receives light from the clerestory windows above French doors that lead to the back porch. A second-floor balcony overlooks both the foyer and the great room for maximum drama. The kitchen provides easy serving access to the great room via a pass-through with a raised countertop above the stove. The master suite and bedroom/study occupy the first floor, while two more bedrooms are located upstairs.

BRKFST.
12-0 x 10-0

PORCH

(vaulted ceiling)

fireplace

MASTER BED RM.
16-0 x 14-0

KIT.
12-0 x 13-0

GREAT RM.
19-0 x 20-8

balcony above

walk-in closet

walk-in closet

storage

UTIL.
7-4 x 7-0

d
w

up

cl

walk-in closet

bath

master bath

DINING
12-0 x 14-0

FOYER
6-4 x 10-8

BED RM./ STUDY
12-8 x 12-4

GARAGE
21-4 x 23-0

PORCH

PLAN HPT790268

First Floor: 1,894 square feet
Second Floor: 554 square feet
Total: 2,448 square feet
Width: 64'-4"
Depth: 58'-0"

great room below

attic storage

attic storage

BED RM.
12-0 x 11-0

railing

cl

BED RM.
13-8 x 11-0

walk-in closet

down

bath

attic storage

foyer below

Classic Charm

This Southern-raised elevation looks cozy but lives large, with an interior layout and amenities preferred by today's homeowners. Inside, twelve-foot ceilings and graceful columns and arches lend an aura of hospitality throughout the formal rooms and the living space in the great room. Double doors open to the gourmet kitchen, which offers a built-in desk, a snack counter for easy meals and a breakfast room with a picture window. The secluded master suite features His and Hers walk-in closets, a whirlpool tub and a knee-space vanity. Please specify basement, crawlspace or slab foundation when ordering.

PLAN

HPT790269

Square Footage: 2,648
Bonus Room: 266 square feet
Width: 68'-10"
Depth: 77'-10"

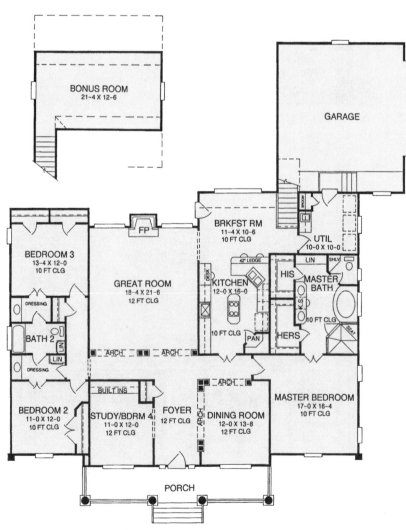

Master
Bedroom

Laundry
6-6x7-0

1/2
Bath   Storage

Basement Stair
Location

Retreat
15-4x8-0

M.Bath
12-3x11-10

Master
Bedroom
15-4x15-8

Porch
20-4x8-0

Breakfast
10-0x13-0

Pantry

Laundry
11-2x7-0

Bedroom
11-9x13-6

Bath

Greatroom
15-9x17-6

Kitchen
12-6x12-3

1/2
Bath

Storage
11-2x3-9

Garage
21-8x21-8

Bedroom
11-6x11-6

Bedroom
11-6x11-6

Foyer

Dining
13-5x11-6

Porch
33-9x8-0

Room to Relax

Aporch full of columns gives a relaxing emphasis to this country home. The dining area resides conveniently near the efficient kitchen. The kitchen island, walk-in pantry and serving bar add plenty of work space to the food-preparation zone. Escape to the relaxing master suite featuring a private sun room/retreat and a luxurious bath set between His and Hers walk-in closets. The great room at the center of this L-shaped plan is complete with a warming fireplace and built-ins. Three family bedrooms enjoy private walk-in closets. Please specify basement, crawlspace or slab foundation when ordering.

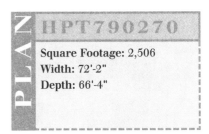

PLAN **HPT790270**

Square Footage: 2,506
Width: 72'-2"
Depth: 66'-4"

PLAN

HPT790271

Square Footage: 2,555
Width: 66'-1"
Depth: 77'-7"

Storage
21-6x11-0

Garage
21-6x25-6

Porch
19-2x12-0

Master
Bedroom/
Sitting
Room
12-9x23-8

M.Bath
10-0x13-6

Laun.
9-0x8-7

1/2
Bath

Greatroom
19-1x17-5

Hv/
Ac

Bath

Bedroom
12-0x13-6

Kitchen
18-0x11-6

Breakfast
14-0x9-0

Dining
11-6x13-6

Foyer

Bedroom
11-6x13-6

Bedroom
12-0x11-7

Porch
31-5x8-0

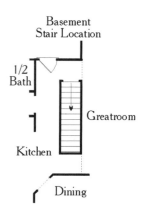

Basement
Stair Location

1/2
Bath

Greatroom

Kitchen

Dining

Skylit Porch

A steeply pitched roof and transoms over multi-pane windows give this house great curb appeal. To the left of the foyer is the formal dining room with through access to the kitchen and breakfast area. A large island/snack bar adds plenty of counter space to the food-preparation area. Double French doors frame the fireplace in the great room, leading to the skylit covered porch at the rear of the home. The master suite has a light-filled sitting room and a luxurious bath with two walk-in closets. Please specify basement, crawlspace or slab foundation when ordering.

Porch
Perfection

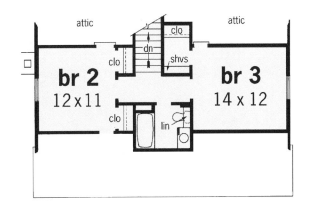

This three-bedroom home is perfect for every family. The entry introduces a large living room with a warming fireplace and views of the front and rear properties. The U-shaped kitchen opens to the dining area. A first-floor master suite features private access to the entry and a luxurious bath with a separate shower and tub. Tucked on the second floor, two family bedrooms share a full bath and attic access. Please specify crawlspace or slab foundation when ordering.

P L A N **HPT790272**

First Floor: 1,136 square feet
Second Floor: 464 square feet
Total: 1,600 square feet
Width: 58'-0"
Depth: 42'-0"

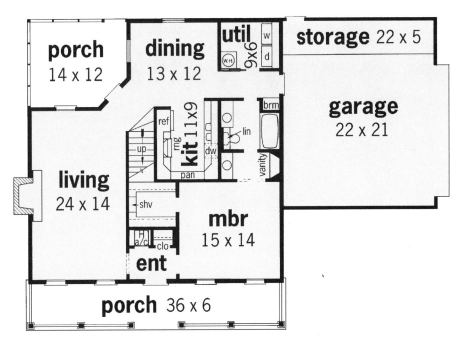

Columned Porch

Two dormers greet visitors above a wonderful porch defined by columns on this three-bedroom home. This unique design features a master bedroom by the foyer. A walk-in closet, dual-sink vanity and whirlpool tub highlight the master bath. The dining area adjoins a kitchen with acres of counter space. Adjacent to the kitchen, the sunny breakfast room opens to the hearth-warmed family room. The second floor includes a bonus room and two family bedrooms, each with a dormer window. Please specify crawlspace or slab foundation when ordering.

PLAN HPT790273

First Floor: 1,395 square feet
Second Floor: 676 square feet
Total: 2,071 square feet
Width: 63'-10"
Depth: 48'-5"

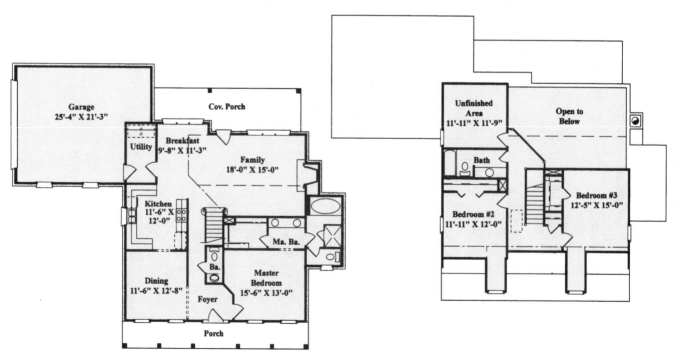

Garage 25'-4" X 21'-3"

Cov. Porch

Utility

Breakfast 9'-8" X 11'-3"

Family 18'-0" X 15'-0"

Kitchen 11'-6" X 12'-0"

Ma. Ba.

Dining 11'-6" X 12'-8"

Ba.

Foyer

Master Bedroom 15'-6" X 13'-0"

Porch

Unfinished Area 11'-11" X 11'-9"

Open to Below

Bath

Bedroom #3 12'-5" X 15'-0"

Bedroom #2 11'-11" X 12'-0"

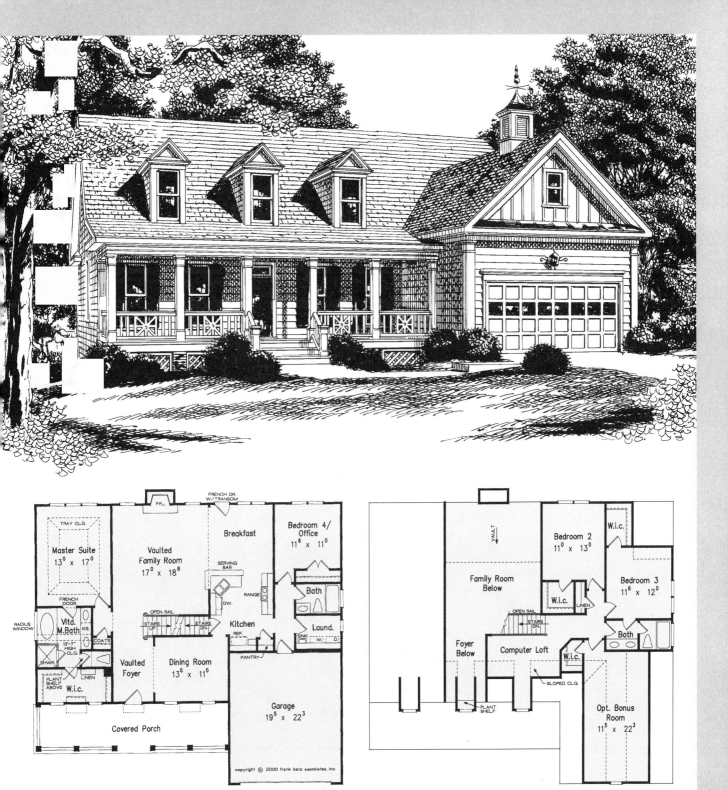

Sumptuous Bath

This home's covered front porch says welcome! Shuttered windows, dormers and a cupola offer a farmhouse look. A vaulted foyer introduces the formal dining room to the right and the vaulted family room with a fireplace directly ahead. The kitchen offers a serving bar and a walk-in pantry. The master suite displays luxury with a tray ceiling and sumptuous bath. A bedroom to the rear is perfect for either a guest suite or home office. Two family bedrooms, a computer loft and an optional bonus room expand the second floor. Please specify basement or crawlspace foundation when ordering.

PLAN HPT790274

First Floor: 1668 square feet
Second Floor: 638 square feet
Total: 2,306 square feet
Bonus Room: 298 square feet
Width: 54'-0"
Depth: 50'-4"

Welcoming Porch

Three dormers and a welcoming porch greet visitors into this four-bedroom home. The foyer—note the charming plant shelf—introduces a dining room to the right with easy access to the pantry and kitchen. This flexible design also offers an optional study with French doors opening left of the foyer. The master suite and breakfast nook enjoy bay windows with French-door access to the backyard. Please specify basement or crawlspace foundation when ordering.

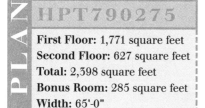

PLAN HPT790275

First Floor: 1,771 square feet
Second Floor: 627 square feet
Total: 2,398 square feet
Bonus Room: 285 square feet
Width: 65'-0"
Depth: 49'-0"

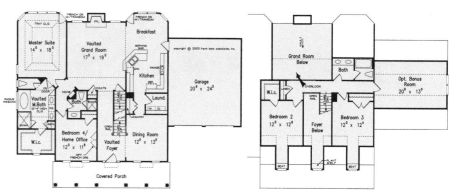

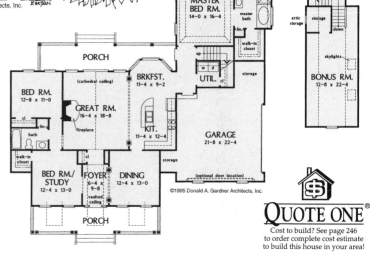

PLAN HPT790303

Square Footage: 1,832
Bonus Space: 425 square feet
Width: 65'-4"
Depth: 62'-0"

© 1995 Donald A. Gardner Architects, Inc.

Charm and Comfort

This plan boasts a cathedral ceiling in the great room. Dormer windows shed light on the foyer, which opens to a front bedroom or study and to the formal dining room. The kitchen is completely open to the great room and features a stylish snack-bar island and a bay window in the breakfast nook. The master suite offers a tray ceiling and a skylit bath. Two secondary bedrooms share a full bath. Bonus space over the garage may be developed in the future.

©1995 Donald A. Gardner Architects, Inc.

Quintessential Country

This roomy country design features two covered porches and an island kitchen with a breakfast area. The long foyer leads to the living room with a fireplace and to the stunning master suite with an oversized tub, glass shower, toilet compartment and His and Hers walk-in closets. The island kitchen is flanked by the formal dining room and a breakfast area with a sunny bay window. Upstairs, a balcony overlooks the living area and leads to three additional bedrooms and two full baths. Please specify crawlspace or slab foundation when ordering.

PLAN HPT790276

First Floor: 1,492 square feet
Second Floor: 865 square feet
Total: 2,357 square feet
Bonus Room: 285 square feet
Width: 66'-10"
Depth: 49'-7"

Open to Below

Bedroom 12'-6" X 10'-6"

Ba.

Balcony

Bedroom 11'-10" X 11'

Ba.

Bedroom 11'-6" X 13'

Gameroom (Unfinished) 17' X 17'-6"

Covered Porch

Living Room 21' X 15'-6"

Breakfast Area 10' X 9'-6"

Utility

Storage

Kitchen 12' X 13'

Two-car Garage 20'-7" X 21'-6"

Bath

Master Bedroom 13' X 17'-8"

1/2 Ba.

Dining Room 12' X 12'-8"

Foyer

Porch

open to
Great Room
below

Balcony

Bonus Rm.
14'-6" x 11'-6"

Bedroom
12'-0" x 11'-0"

open to
Foyer
below

Bedroom
10'-0" x 11'-0"

PLAN

HPT790277

First Floor: 1,870 square feet
Second Floor: 500 square feet
Total: 2,370 square feet
Bonus Room: 222 square feet
Width: 65'-2"
Depth: 51'-9"

Sitting
10'-3" x 7'-7"

Porch
24'-6" x 7'-7"

Sitting
10'-3" x 7'-7"

Kitchen
13'-4" x 13'-7"

Great Room
20'-0" x 16'-10"

Master
Bedroom
14'-6" x 16'-10"

Pantry

Utility

Balcony above

Storage
10'-8" x 4'-4"

Dining Room
11'-0" x 15'-0"

Foyer

Study
11'-0" x 12'-0"

Garage
20'-0" x 21'-8"

Porch
30'-0" x 6'-0"

Gourmet Kitchen

Multiple rooflines and dormers above a relaxing porch invite owners and guests into this three-bedroom farmhouse. The foyer introduces the formal dining room to the left, a study to the right and the great room straight ahead. To the left of the great room sits a kitchen to suit any gourmet cook. A first-floor master suite sits to the right of the plan with a luxurious bath. Upstairs, two family bedrooms share a full bath and a balcony view of the great room. A bonus room is available on this level for future expansion.

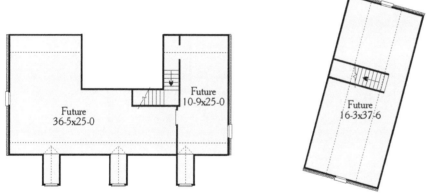

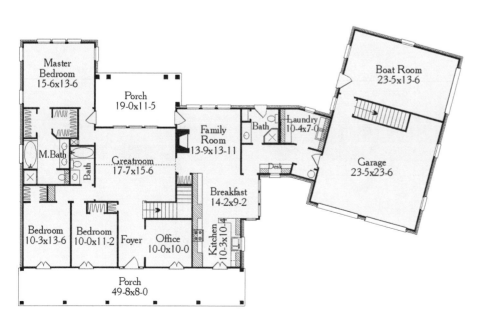

Future
36-5x25-0

Future
10-9x25-0

Future
16-3x37-6

Master
Bedroom
15-6x13-6

Porch
19-0x11-5

Boat Room
23-5x13-6

M.Bath

Bath

Laundry
10-4x7-0

Greatroom
17-7x15-6

Bath

Family
Room
13-9x13-11

Desk

Garage
23-5x23-6

Bedroom
10-3x13-6

Bedroom
10-0x11-2

Foyer

Office
10-0x10-0

Kitchen
10-3x10-4

Breakfast
14-2x9-2

Porch
49-8x8-0

Hyphen Bridging

There is plenty of space to be developed on the second levels of both the house and the garage, making this an ideal country home. An office to the right of the foyer is another bonus. The great room and family room are separated by a warming fireplace, and the family room accesses the rear porch. The breakfast area features a bank of windows, while the kitchen, office and two family bedrooms each have French doors accessing the front porch. Please specify basement, crawlspace or slab foundation when ordering.

PLAN HPT790278

Square Footage: 2,144
Bonus Space: 1,667 square feet
Width: 56'-5"
Depth: 97'-0"

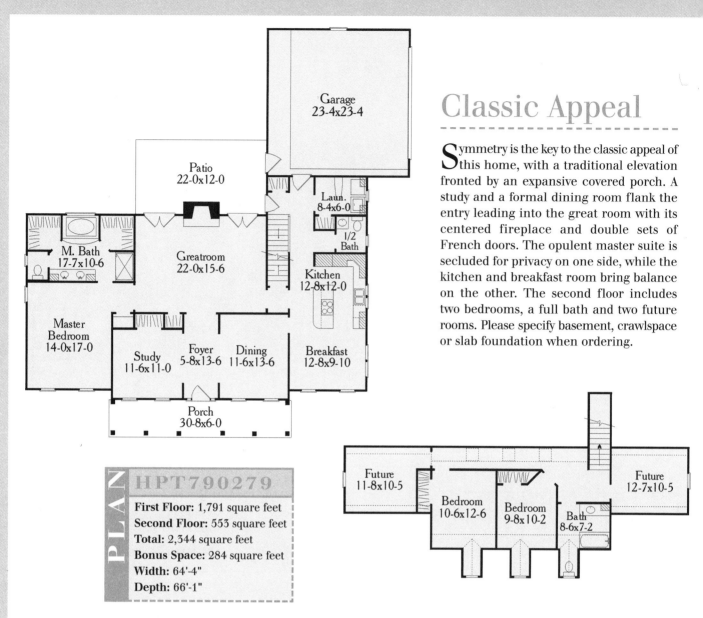

Garage
23-4x23-4

Patio
22-0x12-0

Laun.
8-4x6-0

1/2
Bath

M. Bath
17-7x10-6

Greatroom
22-0x15-6

Kitchen
12-8x12-0

Master
Bedroom
14-0x17-0

Study
11-6x11-0

Foyer
5-8x13-6

Dining
11-6x13-6

Breakfast
12-8x9-10

Porch
30-8x6-0

Classic Appeal

Symmetry is the key to the classic appeal of this home, with a traditional elevation fronted by an expansive covered porch. A study and a formal dining room flank the entry leading into the great room with its centered fireplace and double sets of French doors. The opulent master suite is secluded for privacy on one side, while the kitchen and breakfast room bring balance on the other. The second floor includes two bedrooms, a full bath and two future rooms. Please specify basement, crawlspace or slab foundation when ordering.

PLAN HPT790279

First Floor: 1,791 square feet
Second Floor: 553 square feet
Total: 2,344 square feet
Bonus Space: 284 square feet
Width: 64'-4"
Depth: 66'-1"

Future
11-8x10-5

Future
12-7x10-5

Bedroom
10-6x12-6

Bedroom
9-8x10-2

Bath
8-6x7-2

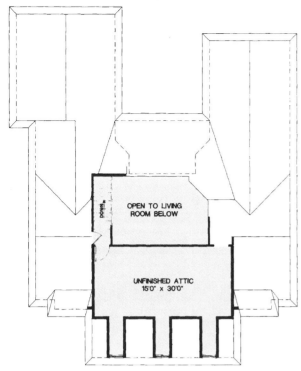

OPEN TO LIVING ROOM BELOW

UNFINISHED ATTIC
15'0" x 30'0"

PLAN HPT790280

Square Footage: 2,123
Bonus Room: 556 square feet
Width: 58'-0"
Depth: 71'-0"

garage
22 x 21

sto
11x7

porch 20 x 11

mbr
20 x 14

entry

skylt   skylt

util
8x8

up

books

living
21 x 15

books

br 2
12 x 12

kit 14 x 11

w   d

dw   ov

mg

bar

r/a

ref

eating
13 x 12

dining
12 x 12

foy

br 3
12 x 12

lin

shr

porch 30 x 8

seat   shr

Sunny Disposition

The heart of this home is its spacious living room with a corner fireplace. The left side of the plan is dedicated to an island kitchen and eating area. The master bedroom features a private entrance to the sun porch, two walk-in closets and a master bath with separate vanities, a compartmented toilet, and a separate shower and a tub. Both family bedrooms include walk-in closets and access to a full bath. Future expansion is possible with the unfinished attic space. Please specify basement, crawlspace or slab foundation when ordering.

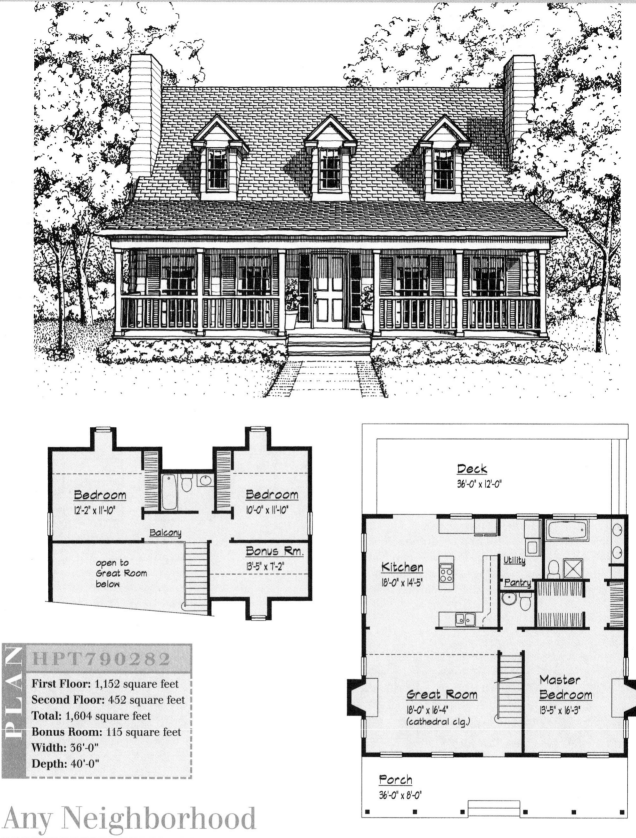

Bedroom
12'-2" x 11'-10"

Bedroom
10'-0" x 11'-10"

Balcony

open to
Great Room
below

Bonus Rm.
13'-5" x 7'-2"

Deck
36'-0" x 12'-0"

Kitchen
18'-0" x 14'-5"

Utility

Pantry

Great Room
18'-0" x 16'-4"
(cathedral clg.)

**Master
Bedroom**
13'-5" x 16'-3"

Porch
36'-0" x 8'-0"

PLAN
HPT790282

First Floor: 1,152 square feet
Second Floor: 452 square feet
Total: 1,604 square feet
Bonus Room: 115 square feet
Width: 36'-0"
Depth: 40'-0"

Any Neighborhood

Three dormers, two chimneys and a covered front porch combine to make this home
attractive in any neighborhood. Inside, a great room greets both family and friends
with a cathedral ceiling and a warming fireplace. An L-shaped kitchen features a cooktop island. The nearby dining area offers rear-porch access. Upstairs, two secondary
bedrooms share a hall bath and access a bonus room—perfect for a study or computer
room. Please specify basement or crawlspace foundation when ordering.

Bedroom
11'-0" x 15'-0"

Bedroom
11'-0" x 15'-0"

Balcony

Deck
14'-0" x 4'-4"

Kitchen
19'-9" x 12'-6"

Utility

Pantry

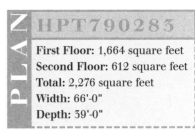

Porch
38'-0" x 7'-0"

Dining Room
13'-6" x 17'-0"
(cathedral clg.)

Living Room
13'-2" x 18'-2"

Foyer
10'-0" x 8'-6"

Master Bedroom
13'-2" x 15'-4"

Sitting Rm.
13'-6" x 13'-0"
(cathedral clg.)

Porch
38'-0" x 7'-0"

Serenity Now

A calming symmetry infuses this wonderful three-bedroom country home. Pillars adorn the exterior and interior of the plan. A balcony overlooks the entry of all guests to the foyer. The hearth-warmed living room opens to the left of the foyer. The sun-filled dining room features a cathedral ceiling and French-door access to the rear deck. The kitchen includes a large island snack bar and a pantry. The master bedroom is a wonderful retreat with a sunny sitting room and private porch. Please specify basement or crawl-space foundation when ordering.

PLAN HPT790283

First Floor: 1,664 square feet
Second Floor: 612 square feet
Total: 2,276 square feet
Width: 66'-0"
Depth: 39'-0"

Smart on Space

This lovely country home provides a powerful combination of well-defined formal rooms, casual living space and flexible areas. A foyer with a convenient coat closet leads to a spacious great room packed with amenities. A cathedral ceiling soars above the heart of this home, made cozy by a massive hearth and views of the outdoors. Decorative columns announce the formal dining room, easily served by a gourmet kitchen, which boasts a breakfast area and bay window. The home-owner's retreat offers a tray ceiling, a lovely triple window and a skylit bath with a garden tub and a walk-in closet. A glass door allows access to a private area of the rear porch—perfect for stargazing and quiet conversation. Bonus space above the garage features its own skylight and additional storage.
©1996 Donald A. Gardner Architects, Inc.

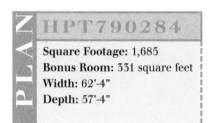

PLAN HPT790284

Square Footage: 1,685
Bonus Room: 331 square feet
Width: 62'-4"
Depth: 57'-4"

© 1996 Donald A. Gardner Architects, Inc.

B. NATHAN

Floor Plan

Second Floor:

bath

walk-in closet | lin.

down

walk-in closet

BED RM. 13-4 x 12-2

BED RM. 13-4 x 12-2

attic storage

BONUS RM. 28-4 x 19-8

attic storage

foyer below (cathedral ceiling)

First Floor:

DECK

DINING 11-4 x 14-0

KIT. 12-0 x 12-0

BRKFST. 10-8 x 11-0

d w | UTIL. 7-0 x 9-0

pan.

pd. rm.

walk-in closet | lin.

master bath

GARAGE 21-0 x 23-8

GREAT RM. 13-4 x 18-4

fireplace

FOYER 7-4 x 5-10

MASTER BED RM. 13-4 x 15-0

PORCH

Happy Days

Astunning Palladian dormer window smartens the exterior of this economical home, while inside, it expands and adds drama to the vaulted foyer. This home features a relaxing front porch, a generous great room with a fireplace, a practical U-shaped kitchen, formal and informal eating areas with bay windows, and a convenient first-floor master suite. A soaking tub, separate shower and dual-sink vanity provide comfort and ease in the master bath. Like the master suite, both upstairs bedrooms include walk-in closets. ©1999 Donald A. Gardner, Inc.

PLAN HPT790285

First Floor: 1,309 square feet
Second Floor: 582 square feet
Total: 1,891 square feet
Bonus Room: 572 square feet
Width: 65'-8"
Depth: 39'-4"

B. NATHAN

233

Cozy Country

With a full wraparound porch, this cozy little plan allows all the comforts of home in a smaller square footage. The great room is open to the kitchen and breakfast nook. A warm fireplace lends its glow to both areas. Family bedrooms on this floor share a full bath and are separated from the master suite on the second floor. With its own private balcony, the master bedroom has a fine bath with a separate shower and tub. A loft or study area that overlooks the great room completes this retreat.

PLAN HPT790286

First Floor: 1,093 square feet
Second Floor: 580 square feet
Total: 1,673 square feet
Width: 52'-0"
Depth: 52'-0"

LD

QUOTE ONE®
Cost to build? See page 246
to order complete cost estimate
to build this house in your area!

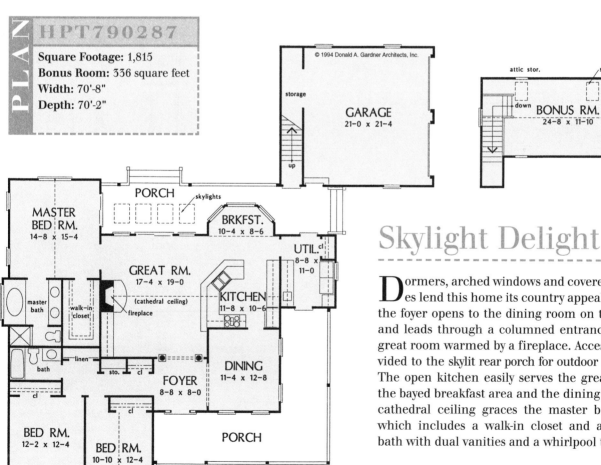

PLAN

HPT790287

Square Footage: 1,815
Bonus Room: 336 square feet
Width: 70'-8"
Depth: 70'-2"

storage

GARAGE
21-0 x 21-4

up

attic stor.

skylights

down

BONUS RM.
24-8 x 11-10

PORCH

skylights

MASTER BED RM.
14-8 x 15-4

BRKFST.
10-4 x 8-6

UTIL.
8-8 x 11-0

cl

GREAT RM.
17-4 x 19-0

(cathedral ceiling)

fireplace

KITCHEN
11-8 x 10-6

master bath

walk-in closet

linen

bath

sto.

cl

FOYER
8-8 x 8-0

DINING
11-4 x 12-8

cl

BED RM.
12-2 x 12-4

BED RM.
10-10 x 12-4

cl

PORCH

Skylight Delight

Dormers, arched windows and covered porch-es lend this home its country appeal. Inside, the foyer opens to the dining room on the right and leads through a columned entrance to the great room warmed by a fireplace. Access is pro-vided to the skylit rear porch for outdoor livability. The open kitchen easily serves the great room, the bayed breakfast area and the dining room. A cathedral ceiling graces the master bedroom, which includes a walk-in closet and a private bath with dual vanities and a whirlpool tub.

QUOTE ONE®

Cost to build? See page 246
to order complete cost estimate
to build this house in your area!

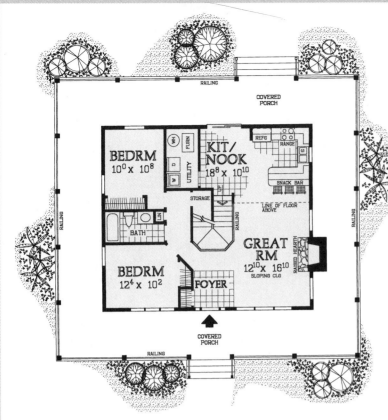

A Love of Nature

Here's a great country farmhouse with a lot of contemporary appeal. The generous use of windows adds exciting visual elements to the exterior as well as plenty of natural light to the interior. An impressive tiled entry opens to a two-story great room with a raised hearth. The kitchen conveniently combines with this area and offers a snack counter in addition to a casual dining nook. The family bedrooms reside on the main level, while an expansive master suite with an adjacent study creates a resplendent retreat upstairs, complete with a private balcony.

PLAN HPT790288

First Floor: 1,093 square feet
Second Floor: 576 square feet
Total: 1,669 square feet
Width: 52'-0"
Depth: 46'-0"

LD

QUOTE ONE®

Cost to build? See page 246
to order complete cost estimate
to build this house in your area!

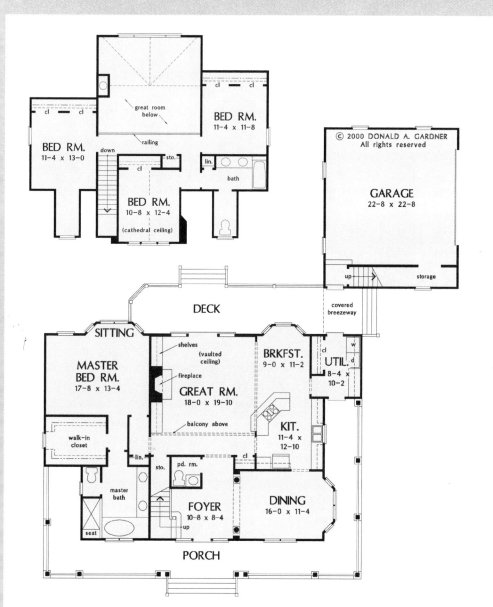

great room below

railing

BED RM.
11-4 x 13-0

cl   cl

down

BED RM.
11-4 x 11-8

cl   cl

sto.

cl

BED RM.
10-8 x 12-4

(cathedral ceiling)

lin.

bath

GARAGE
22-8 x 22-8

up   storage

DECK

covered
breezeway

SITTING

shelves

(vaulted
ceiling)

BRKFST.
9-0 x 11-2

cl

UTIL.
8-4 x
10-2

w
d

MASTER
BED RM.
17-8 x 13-4

fireplace

GREAT RM.
18-0 x 19-10

balcony above

KIT.
11-4 x
12-10

walk-in
closet

lin.

sto.

pd. rm.

cl

master
bath

FOYER
10-8 x 8-4

DINING
16-0 x 11-4

seat

up

PORCH

Friendly Face

The small appearance of this country farmhouse belies the spaciousness that lies within. A large great room lies directly beyond the foyer and boasts a fireplace, shelves, a vaulted ceiling and a door to the rear deck. A bayed breakfast room, located just off the kitchen, looks to a covered breezeway that leads from the house to the garage. The first-floor master bedroom is enhanced with a sitting area, walk-in closet and full bath. The second floor is home to three additional bedrooms, one with a cathedral ceiling, sharing a full bath.

PLAN HPT790289

First Floor: 1,706 square feet
Second Floor: 776 square feet
Total: 2,482 square feet
Bonus Room: 414 square feet
Width: 54'-8"
Depth: 43'-0"

B. NATHAN

Cozy Chalet

This cozy chalet design begins with a railed veranda opening to a living room with a warm fireplace and a dining room with a snack-bar counter through to the kitchen. One bedroom with a roomy wall closet is on the first floor. The second floor holds two additional bedrooms—one a master suite with a private balcony—and a full bath. Additional storage is found on the second floor.

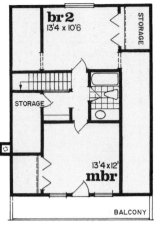

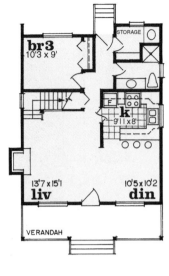

QUOTE ONE®

Cost to build? See page 246
to order complete cost estimate
to build this house in your area!

PLAN

HPT790291

First Floor: 725 square feet
Second Floor: 561 square feet
Total: 1,286 square feet
Width: 25'-0"
Depth: 36'-6"

PLAN

HPT790290

First Floor: 672 square feet
Second Floor: 401 square feet
Total: 1,073 square feet
Width: 24'-0"
Depth: 36'-0"

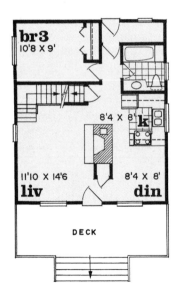

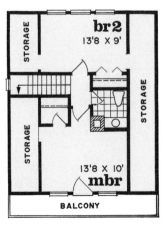

Fun House

This chalet plan is enhanced by a steep gable roof, scalloped fascia boards and fieldstone chimney detail. The front-facing deck and covered balcony add to outdoor living spaces. The fireplace is the main focus in the living room, separating the living room from the dining room. One bedroom is found on the first floor, while two additional bedrooms and a full bath are upstairs. Three large storage areas are also found on the second floor.

PLAN

HPT790292

First Floor: 871 square feet
Second Floor: 1,047 square feet
Total: 1,918 square feet
Width: 32'-0"
Depth: 47'-0"

GARAGE
22'-8" x 20'-8"

COVERED PORCH

P.

KITCHEN
11'-6" x 11'-10"

BREAKFAST
11'-6" x 10'-4"

SCREENED PORCH

DINING ROOM
11'-6" x 11'-10"

PDR.

OPT. SHELVES

GATHERING ROOM
19'-8" x 14'-0"

UP

PORCH

SUITE 2
11'-6" x 11'-10"

SUITE 3
11'-6" x 13'-0"

BATH

LIN.

STOR.

BALCONY

MASTER BATH

DN

LAUNDRY

MASTER SUITE
16'-2" x 14'-0"

W.I.C.

Primal Screen

With its shingle and siding exterior, this home has an air of oceanfront living. A large covered porch accesses a spacious gathering room, complete with a fireplace and optional shelving units. An archway leads from the gathering room to the dining room, which is highlighted with a wall of windows and boasts a doorway to the kitchen. The breakfast area overlooks a screened porch and flows smoothly into a U-shaped kitchen. The sleeping quarters reside upstairs and include two family suites, two full baths, a master suite with a tray ceiling, and a convenient laundry room.

Short Story

This symmetrical design offers single-story convenience with an optional bonus room over the garage—great for a home office! A formal living room could also be used as a fourth bedroom. The columned dining room opens into a spacious family room with a fireplace and built-in shelves, plus a nice view of the rear porch through a series of French doors. The master suite also accesses the porch. Two family bedrooms share a full hall bath.

PLAN HPT790293

Square Footage: 1,363
Width: 30'-0"
Depth: 60'-0"

Personal Space

With a master bedroom and living area that open to the rear, this is a home that begs for a terrific backyard. It offers great privacy while creating a sense of spaciousness with its open design. The living room has a corner fireplace and French doors that lead to the covered rear porch. The master bath has an oversized tub/shower and a double-sink vanity area. In addition to the master suite, this home has two family bedrooms.

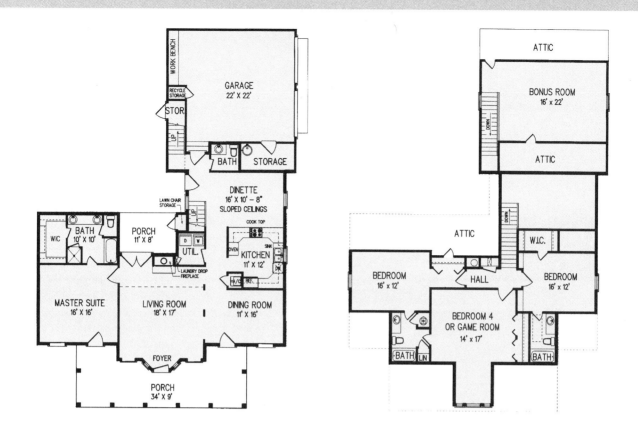

WORK BENCH

GARAGE
22' X 22'

RECYCLE STORAGE

STOR

BATH | STORAGE

DINETTE
16' X 10'– 8"
SLOPED CEILINGS

LAWN CHAIR STORAGE

COOK TOP

UP

UTIL.

OVEN | KITCHEN
11' X 12'

SINK

WIC

BATH
10' X 10'

PORCH
11' X 8'

LAUNDRY DROP
FIREPLACE

HVAC RET.

MASTER SUITE
16' X 16'

LIVING ROOM
18' X 17'

DINING ROOM
11' X 16'

FOYER

PORCH
34' X 9'

ATTIC

BONUS ROOM
16' x 22'

ATTIC

DOWN

ATTIC

DOWN

W.I.C.

BEDROOM
16' x 12'

HALL

BEDROOM
16' x 12'

BATH | LN

BEDROOM 4
OR GAME ROOM
14' x 17'

BATH

Country Appeal

A cross gable above a roomy porch lends country appeal to this four-bedroom home. The master suite boasts a private bath and a walk-in closet. The U-shaped kitchen features a dinette with sloped ceilings. Three bedrooms reside on the second level. Two of these bedrooms share a hall bath that includes a dressing area while the third bedroom contains its own bath and walk-in closet—perfect for guests. Please specify basement, crawlspace or slab foundation when ordering.

PLAN HPT790295

First Floor: 1,510 square feet
Second Floor: 1,032 square feet
Total: 2,542 square feet
Bonus Room: 394 square feet
Width: 52'-0"
Depth: 74'-0"

A new Web site, **www.eplans.com**, *provides a way for you to*

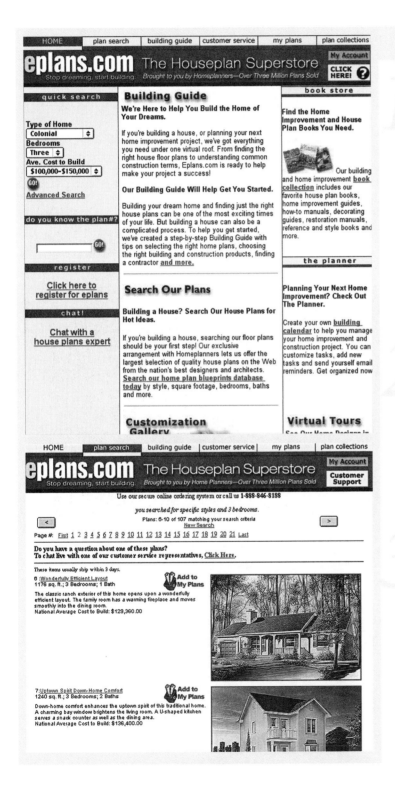

THE EPLANS SITE

SEARCH FOR PLANS

The heart of the site is the Plan Search feature that offers an extensive database of plans for your consideration. Do a simplified search by style, number of bedrooms and approximate cost to build in order to find appropriate homes in your range. Or, choose a more advanced search that includes choices for square footage, number of floors, number of bedrooms and baths, width and depth, style, amenities, garage size and, if you prefer, a specified designer.

Either way, you gain access to a selection of homes that meets your specifications, allowing you to easily make comparisons. The site shows front perspectives as well as detailed floor plans for each of your choices. You can even look at enlarged versions of the drawings to make more serious analyses.

SAVE FAVORITE PLANS

As you're doing your searches, you can save favorite plans to a personal portfolio called My Plans so that you can easily recall them for future reference and review. This feature stores summary information for each of the plans you select and allows you to review details of the plan quickly without having to re-search or re-browse. You can even compare plans, deleting those that don't measure up and keeping those that appeal, so you can narrow down your search more quickly.

PURCHASE PLANS

Once you've made your final choice, you can proceed to purchase your plan, either by checking out through our secure online ordering process or by calling the toll-free number offered in the site. If you choose to check out online, you'll receive information about foundation options for your chosen plan, plus other helpful products such as a building cost estimator to help you gauge costs to build the plan in your zip code area, a materials list specific to your plan, color and line renderings of the plan, and mirror and full reverses. Information relating to all of these products can also be reviewed with a customer service representative if you choose to order by phone.

search for home plans that is as simple as pointing and clicking.

also on the EPLANS site...

VIRTUAL TOURS

In order to help you more completely visualize the homes as built, eplans offers virtual tours of a select group of homes. Showing both interior and exterior features of the homes, the virtual tour gives you a complete vision of how the floor plans for the home will look when completed. All you have to do is choose a home in the Virtual Tour gallery, then click on an exterior or interior view. The view pops up and immediately begins a slow 360° rotation to give you the complete picture. Special buttons allow you to stop the rotation anywhere you like, reverse the action, or move it up or down, and zoom in on a particular element. There's even a large-screen version to allow you to review the home in greater detail.

CUSTOMIZATION GALLERY

For a special group of plans, a customization option allows you to try out building product selections to see which looks the best and to compare styles, colors, and textures. You'll start with an eplans design rendering and then be given options for such elements as roofing, columns, siding, and trim, among others. A diverse grouping of materials and color options is available in each product category. As you choose each option, it will appear on the rendering, allowing you to mix and match options and try out various design ideas. When you're satisfied with your choices, you can enlarge the view, print it out or save it in your personalized Home Project Folder for future reference.

The eplans site is convenient and contains not only the best home plans in the business, but also a host of other features and services. Like Home Planners handy books and magazines, it speaks your language in user-friendly fashion.

In fact, if you want or need more help, there is a Live Person, real-time chat opportunity available with one of our customer service representatives right on the site to answer questions and help you make plans selections.

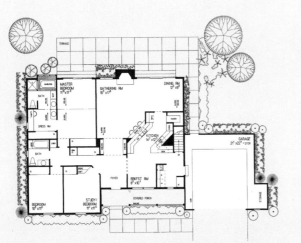

SELECT A PRODUCT

Select a color range   All

Select a style   All

Find by name/number   [go]

Click on a product to apply it to the image.

Alexandria   Annapolis   Antique Quaker   Antique Rose

Ashbury   Autumn Rose   BH200 232   Ballatyne

Remove Product

Products 1 - 8 of 20

Image Quality: ○ Normal ● High

FINAL SELECTIONS

Save Your Finished Design to Your Home Project Folder

[PRINT] [ENLARGE] [VIEW LIST OF APPLIED PRODUCTS] [SELECT NEW HOME]

Customize your plan—without spending a penny or hammering a nail! The Customization Gallery lets you "try on" various material colors and styles before you make decisions.

The eplans.com Advantage

also on the EPLANS site...

BUILDING GUIDE AND TASK PLANNER

Because building a home is a complicated process, eplans gets you started with a step-by-step Building Guide. Covering everything from choosing a lot to settling into your new home, the Building Guide gives tips and valuable information to help you understand the entire process of constructing your new home. Learn about the steps in framing your home, different foundation types and which might work best for your building situation, financing your project, home products such as appliances, and much, much more. A handy glossary is available in each section that helps define terms that relate to the information in that section.

Within the Building Guide is a unique Task Planner outlining each of the various tasks involved in residential construction over the entire 16-week (average) life of the project. Simply tell Task Planner when you plan to start construction or when you plan to move into the finished home, and it will create a calendar that shows each of the many steps involved in building your home. You can customize tasks, add new tasks, and send yourself email reminders that help you manage the building project. In addition, each task in the calendar is linked to a tip or information piece in the Building Guide to help make the process easier to follow and understand. Choose the Calendar View, which shows a month-by-month progression of construction, or the Task View, which lists each task by category and shows its due date.

While there are hundreds of home plans sites on the Web, only eplans.com offers the variety, quality, and ease of use you want when doing a search for the perfect home. From expert advice to online ordering of plans, eplans gives you a full complement of services, information, home plans, and planning tools to make your building experience easy and enjoyable. Log on to www.eplans.com to begin your search for the home you've always wanted.

LET US SHOW YOU
OUR HOME BLUEPRINT PACKAGE!

BUILDING A HOME? PLANNING A HOME?
OUR BLUEPRINT PACKAGE HAS NEARLY EVERYTHING YOU NEED TO GET THE JOB DONE RIGHT,

whether you're working on your own or with help from an architect, designer, builder or subcontractors. Each Blueprint Package is the result of many hours of work by licensed architects or professional designers.

QUALITY

Hundreds of hours of painstaking effort have gone into the development of your blueprint plan. Each home has been quality-checked by professionals to insure accuracy and buildability.

VALUE

Because we sell in volume, you can buy professional quality blueprints at a fraction of their development cost. With our plans, your dream home design costs substantially less than the fees charged by architects.

SERVICE

Once you've chosen your favorite home plan, you'll receive fast, efficient service whether you choose to mail or fax your order to us or call us toll free at 1-800-521-6797. After you have received your order, call for customer service toll free 1-888-690-1116.

SATISFACTION

Over 50 years of service to satisfied home plan buyers provide us unparalleled experience and knowledge in producing quality blueprints.

ORDER TOLL FREE 1-800-521-6797

After you've looked over our Blueprint Package and Important Extras, call toll free on our Blueprint Hotline: 1-800-521-6797, for current pricing and availability prior to mailing the order form on page 253. We're ready and eager to serve you. After you have received your order, call for customer service toll free 1-888-690-1116.

Each set of blueprints is an interrelated collection of detail sheets which includes components such as floor plans, interior and exterior elevations, dimensions, cross-sections, diagrams and notations. These sheets show exactly how your house is to be built.

SETS MAY INCLUDE:

FRONTAL SHEET
This artist's sketch of the exterior of the house gives you an idea of how the house will look when built and landscaped. Large floor plans show all levels of the house and provide an overview of your new home's livability, as well as a handy reference for deciding on furniture placement.

FOUNDATION PLANS
This sheet shows the foundation layout including support walls, excavated and unexcavated areas, if any, and foundation notes. If slab construction rather than basement, the plan shows footings and details for a monolithic slab. This page, or another in the set, may include a sample plot plan for locating your house on a building site.

DETAILED FLOOR PLANS
These plans show the layout of each floor of the house. Rooms and interior spaces are carefully dimensioned and keys are given for cross-section details provided later in the plans. The positions of electrical outlets and switches are shown.

HOUSE CROSS-SECTIONS
Large-scale views show sections or cut-aways of the foundation, interior walls, exterior walls, floors, stairways and roof details. Additional cross-sections may show important changes in floor, ceiling or roof heights or the relationship of one level to another. Extremely valuable for construction, these sections show exactly how the various parts of the house fit together.

INTERIOR ELEVATIONS
Many of our drawings show the design and placement of kitchen and bathroom cabinets, laundry areas, fireplaces, bookcases and other built-ins. Little "extras," such as mantelpiece and wainscoting drawings, plus molding sections, provide details that give your home that custom touch.

EXTERIOR ELEVATIONS
These drawings show the front, rear and sides of your house and give necessary notes on exterior materials and finishes. Particular attention is given to cornice detail, brick and stone accents or other finish items that make your home unique.

INTRODUCING EIGHT IMPORTANT
PLANNING AND CONSTRUCTION AIDS DEVELOPED BY
OUR PROFESSIONALS TO HELP YOU SUCCEED IN YOUR HOME-BUILDING PROJECT

MATERIALS LIST

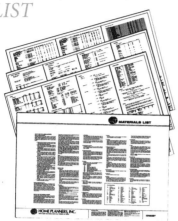

(Note: Because of the diversity of local building codes, our Materials List does not include mechanical materials.)

For many of the designs in our portfolio, we offer a customized materials take-off that is invaluable in planning and estimating the cost of your new home. This Materials List outlines the quantity, type and size of materials needed to build your house (with the exception of mechanical system items). Included are framing lumber, windows and doors, kitchen and bath cabinetry, rough and finish hardware, and much more. This handy list helps you or your builder cost out materials and serves as a reference sheet when you're compiling bids. Some Materials Lists may be ordered before blueprints are ordered, call for information.

SPECIFICATION OUTLINE

This valuable 16-page document is critical to building your house correctly. Designed to be filled in by you or your builder, this book lists 166 stages or items crucial to the building process. It provides a comprehensive review of the construction process and helps in choosing materials. When combined with the blueprints, a signed contract, and a schedule, it becomes a legal document and record for the building of your home.

QUOTE ONE®

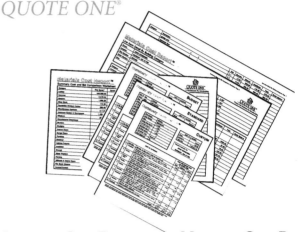

SUMMARY COST REPORT   **MATERIAL COST REPORT**

A product for estimating the cost of building select designs, the Quote One® system is available in two separate stages: The Summary Cost Report and the Material Cost Report.

The **Summary Cost Report** is the first stage in the package and shows the total cost per square foot for your chosen home in your zip-code area and then breaks that cost down into various categories showing the costs for building materials, labor and installation. The report includes three grades: Budget, Standard and Custom. These reports allow you to evaluate your building budget and compare the costs of building a variety of homes in your area.

Make even more informed decisions about your home-building project with the second phase of our package, our **Material Cost Report.** This tool is invaluable in planning and estimating the cost of your new home. The material and installation (labor and equipment) cost is shown for each of over 1,000 line items provided in the Materials List (Standard grade), which is included when you purchase this estimating tool. It allows you to determine building costs for your specific zip-code area and for your chosen home design. Space is allowed for additional estimates from contractors and subcontractors, such as for mechanical materials, which are not included in our packages. This invaluable tool includes a Materials List. A Material Cost Report cannot be ordered before blueprints are ordered. Call for details. In addition, ask about our Home Planners Estimating Package.

If you are interested in a plan that is not indicated as Quote One®, please call and ask our sales reps. They will be happy to verify the status for you. To order these invaluable reports, use the order form.

CONSTRUCTION INFORMATION

*IF YOU WANT TO KNOW MORE ABOUT TECHNIQUES—
and deal more confidently with subcontractors —
we offer these useful sheets. Each set is an excellent
tool that will add to your understanding of these
technical subjects. These helpful details provide
general construction information and
are not specific to any single plan.*

PLUMBING

The Blueprint Package includes locations for all the plumbing fixtures, including sinks, lavatories, tubs, showers, toilets, laundry trays and water heaters. However, if you want to know more about the complete plumbing system, these Plumbing Details will prove very useful. Prepared to meet requirements of the National Plumbing Code, these fact-filled sheets give general information on pipe schedules, fittings, sump-pump details, water-softener hookups, septic system details and much more. Sheets also include a glossary of terms.

ELECTRICAL

The locations for every electrical switch, plug and outlet are shown in your Blueprint Package. However, these Electrical Details go further to take the mystery out of household electrical systems. Prepared to meet requirements of the National Electrical Code, these comprehensive drawings come packed with helpful information, including wire sizing, switch-installation schematics, cable-routing details, appliance wattage, doorbell hook-ups, typical service panel circuitry and much more. A glossary of terms is also included.

CONSTRUCTION

The Blueprint Package contains information an experienced builder needs to construct a particular house. However, it doesn't show all the ways that houses can be built, nor does it explain alternate construction methods. To help you understand how your house will be built—and offer additional techniques—this set of Construction Details depicts the materials and methods used to build foundations, fireplaces, walls, floors and roofs. Where appropriate, the drawings show acceptable alternatives.

MECHANICAL

These Mechanical Details contain fundamental principles and useful data that will help you make informed decisions and communicate with subcontractors about heating and cooling systems. Drawings contain instructions and samples that allow you to make simple load calculations, and preliminary sizing and costing analysis. Covered are the most commonly used systems from heat pumps to solar fuel systems. The package is filled with illustrations and diagrams to help you visualize components and how they relate to one another.

THE HANDS-ON HOME FURNITURE PLANNER

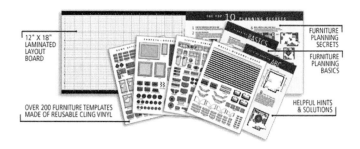

Effectively plan the space in your home using The **Hands-On Home Furniture Planner**. It's fun and easy—no more moving heavy pieces of furniture to see how the room will go together. And you can try different layouts, moving furniture at a whim.

The kit includes reusable peel and stick furniture templates that fit onto a 12" x 18" laminated layout board—space enough to layout every room in your home.

Also included in the package are a number of helpful planning tools. You'll receive:

- ✓ Helpful hints and solutions for difficult situations.
- ✓ Furniture planning basics to get you started.
- ✓ Furniture planning secrets that let you in on some of the tricks of professional designers.

The **Hands-On Home Furniture Planner** is the one tool that no new homeowner or home remodeler should be without. It's also a perfect housewarming gift!

*To Order, Call Toll Free
1-800-521-6797*

After you've looked over our Blueprint Package and Important Extras on these pages, call for current pricing and availability prior to mailing the order form. We're ready and eager to serve you. After you have received your order, call for customer service toll free 1-888-690-1116.

THE DECK BLUEPRINT PACKAGE

Many of the homes in this book can be enhanced with a professionally designed Home Planners Deck Plan. Those homes marked with a **D** have a complementary Deck Plan, sold separately, which includes a Deck Plan Frontal Sheet, Deck Framing and Floor Plans, Deck Elevations and a Deck Materials List. A Standard Deck Details Package, also available, provides all the how-to information necessary for building *any* deck. Our Complete Deck Building Package contains one set of Custom Deck Plans of your choice, plus one set of Standard Deck Building Details, all for one low price. Our plans and details are carefully prepared in an easy-to-understand format that will guide you through every stage of your deck-building project. This page shows a sample Deck layout to match your favorite house. See Blueprint Price Schedule for ordering information.

THE LANDSCAPE BLUEPRINT PACKAGE

For the homes marked with an **L** in this book, Home Planners has created a front-yard Landscape Plan that is complementary in design to the house plan. These comprehensive blueprint packages include a Frontal Sheet, Plan View, Regionalized Plant & Materials List, a sheet on Planting and Maintaining Your Landscape, Zone Maps and Plant Size and Description Guide. These plans will help you achieve professional results, adding value and enjoyment to your property for years to come. Each set of blueprints is a full 18" x 24" in size with clear, complete instructions and easy-to-read type. A sample Landscape Plan is shown below. See Blueprint Price Schedule for ordering information.

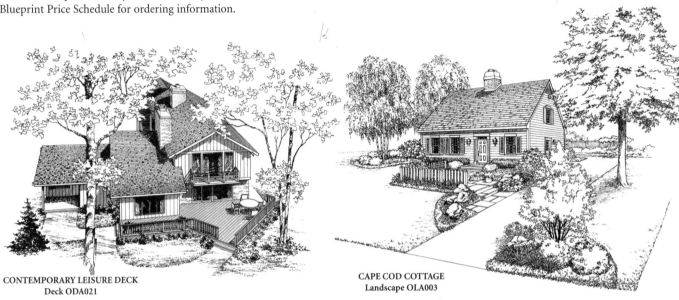

CONTEMPORARY LEISURE DECK
Deck ODA021

CAPE COD COTTAGE
Landscape OLA003

REGIONAL ORDER MAP

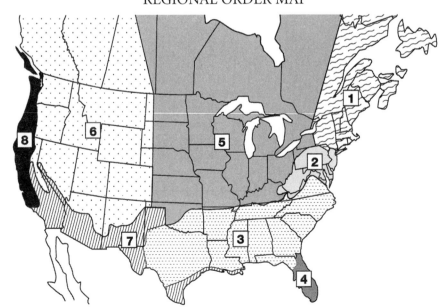

Most Landscape Plans are available with a Plant & Materials List adapted by horticultural experts to 8 different regions of the country. Please specify the Geographic Region when ordering your plan. See Blueprint Price Schedule for ordering information and regional availability.

Region	1	Northeast
Region	2	Mid-Atlantic
Region	3	Deep South
Region	4	Florida & Gulf Coast
Region	5	Midwest
Region	6	Rocky Mountains
Region	7	Southern California & Desert Southwest
Region	8	Northern California & Pacific Northwest

BLUEPRINT PRICE SCHEDULE

Prices guaranteed through December 31, 2002

TIERS	1-SET STUDY PACKAGE	4-SET BUILDING PACKAGE	8-SET BUILDING PACKAGE	1-SET REPRODUCIBLE*
P1	$20	$50	$90	$140
P2	$40	$70	$110	$160
P3	$70	$100	$140	$190
P4	$100	$130	$170	$220
P5	$140	$170	$210	$270
P6	$180	$210	$250	$310
A1	$440	$480	$520	$660
A2	$480	$520	$560	$720
A3	$520	$560	$600	$780
A4	$565	$605	$645	$850
C1	$610	$655	$700	$915
C2	$655	$700	$745	$980
C3	$700	$745	$790	$1050
C4	$750	$795	$840	$1125
L1	$825	$875	$925	$1240
L2	$900	$950	$1000	$1350
L3	$1000	$1050	$1100	$1500
L4	$1100	$1150	$1200	$1650

* Requires a fax number

OPTIONS FOR PLANS IN TIERS A1–L4

Additional Identical Blueprints
In same order for "A1–L4" price plans ....**$50 per set**
Reverse Blueprints (mirror image)
with 4- or 8-set order for "A1–L4" plans..**$50 fee per order**
Specification Outlines..**$10 each**
Materials Lists for "A1–C3" plans ....**$60 each**
Materials Lists for "C4–L4" plans..**$70 each**

OPTIONS FOR PLANS IN TIERS P1–P6

Additional Identical Blueprints
In same order for "P1–P6" price plans...**$10 per set**
Reverse Blueprints (mirror image) for "P1–P6" price plans ....**$10 fee per order**
1 Set of Deck Construction Details ....**$14.95 each**
Deck Construction Package ....**add $10 to Building Package price**
(includes 1 set of "P1–P6" plans, plus 1 set Standard Deck Construction Details)
1 Set of Gazebo Construction Details ....**$14.95 each**
Gazebo Construction Package ....**add $10 to Building Package price**
(includes 1 set of "P1–P6" plans, plus 1 set Standard Gazebo Construction Details)

IMPORTANT NOTES

The 1-set study package is marked "not for construction."
Prices for 4- or 8-set Building Packages honored only at time of original order.
Some foundations carry a $225 surcharge.
Right-reading reverse blueprints, if available, will incur a $165 surcharge.
Additional identical blueprints may be purchased within 60 days of original order.

To use the Index, refer to the design number listed in numerical order (a helpful page reference is also given). Note the price tier and refer to the House Blueprint Price Schedule above for the cost of one, four or eight sets of blueprints or the cost of a reproducible drawing. Additional prices are shown for identical and reverse blueprint sets, as well as a very useful Materials List for some of the plans. Also note in the Plan Index those plans that have Deck Plans or Landscape Plans. Refer to the schedules above for prices of these plans. The letter "Y" identifies plans that are part of our Quote One® estimating service and those that offer Materials Lists.

To order, Call toll free 1-800-521-6797 for current pricing and availability prior to mailing the order form. FAX: 1-800-224-6699 or 520-544-3086.

PLAN INDEX

DESIGN	PRICE	PAGE	MATERIALS LIST	QUOTE ONE®	DECK	DECK PRICE	LANDSCAPE	LANDSCAPE PRICE	REGIONS
HPT790001	C2	4	Y						
HPT790002	C1	5	Y	Y					
HPT790003	C2	6	Y	Y					
HPT790004	C2	7	Y						
HPT790005	A4	8							
HPT790006	A4	9							
HPT790007	C2	10							
HPT790008	C1	11							
HPT790009	C2	12							
HPT790010	A4	13							
HPT790011	A3	14	Y						
HPT790012	A4	15	Y	Y					
HPT790013	A4	16	Y	Y			OLA024	P4	123568
HPT790014	C1	17	Y	Y			OLA010	P3	1234568
HPT790015	A4	18							
HPT790016	A4	19	Y	Y			OLA024	P4	123568
HPT790017	A4	20	Y	Y	ODA017	P2			
HPT790018	C2	21	Y	Y	ODA004	P2	OLA020	P4	123568
HPT790019	A4	22							
HPT790020	A4	23	Y						
HPT790021	C1	24	Y		ODA018	P3	OLA021	P3	123568
HPT790022	A4	25	Y						
HPT790023	A4	26							
HPT790024	A3	34	Y						
HPT790025	A4	35	Y	Y	ODA003	P2			
HPT790026	A4	31	Y	Y					
HPT790027	A4	27	Y						
HPT790028	A4	29	Y						
HPT790029	A4	28	Y						
HPT790030	A3	30							
HPT790031	A4	32	Y						
HPT790032	A3	33	Y						
HPT790033	A3	36							
HPT790034	C2	36							
HPT790035	C2	37							
HPT790036	C3	38							
HPT790037	A3	38							
HPT790038	C1	39							
HPT790039	A3	40							
HPT790040	A2	40							
HPT790041	A2	41	Y						
HPT790042	A2	42							
HPT790043	C1	42							
HPT790044	A2	43							
HPT790045	A2	44							
HPT790046	A3	44	Y						
HPT790047	A4	45							
HPT790048	A4	46							
HPT790049	A1	46							
HPT790050	A1	47	Y						
HPT790051	A2	48	Y						
HPT790052	A1	48	Y	Y					
HPT790053	A3	49	Y						
HPT790054	C2	50	Y	Y			OLA001	P3	123568
HPT790055	A3	50	Y	Y					
HPT790056	A3	51	Y	Y	ODA011	P2	OLA008	P4	1234568
HPT790057	C1	52	Y	Y	ODA006	P2	OLA021	P3	123568
HPT790058	C1	52	Y						
HPT790059	A2	53	Y	Y	ODA018	P3	OLA021	P3	123568
HPT790060	A1	54	Y						

BEFORE FILLING OUT THE ORDER FORM, PLEASE CALL US ON OUR TOLL-FREE BLUEPRINT HOTLINE 1-800-521-6797. YOU MAY WANT TO LEARN MORE ABOUT OUR SERVICES AND PRODUCTS. HERE'S SOME INFORMATION YOU WILL FIND HELPFUL.

OUR EXCHANGE POLICY

With the exception of reproducible plan orders, we will exchange your entire first order for an equal or greater number of blueprints within our plan collection within 90 days of the original order. The entire content of your original order must be returned before an exchange will be processed. Please call our customer service department for your return authorization number and shipping instructions. If the returned blueprints look used, redlined or copied, we will not honor your exchange. Fees for exchanging your blueprints are as follows: 20% of the amount of the original order...plus the difference in cost if exchanging for a design in a higher price bracket or less the difference in cost if exchanging for a design in a lower price bracket. **(Reproducible blueprints are not exchangeable or refundable.)** Please call for current postage and handling prices. Shipping and handling charges are not refundable.

ABOUT REPRODUCIBLES

When purchasing a reproducible you may be required to furnish a fax number. The designer will fax documents that you must sign and return to them before shipping will take place.

ABOUT REVERSE BLUEPRINTS

Although lettering and dimensions will appear backward, reverses will be a useful aid if you decide to flop the plan. See Price Schedule and Plans Index for pricing.

REVISING, MODIFYING AND CUSTOMIZING PLANS

Like many homeowners who buy these plans, you and your builder, architect or engineer may want to make changes to them. We recommend purchase of a reproducible plan for any changes made by your builder, licensed architect or engineer. As set forth below, we cannot assume any responsibility for blueprints which have been changed, whether by you, your builder or by professionals selected by you or referred to you by us, because such individuals are outside our supervision and control.

ARCHITECTURAL AND ENGINEERING SEALS

Some cities and states are now requiring that a licensed architect or engineer review and "seal" a blueprint, or officially approve it, prior to construction due to concerns over energy costs, safety and other factors. Prior to application for a building permit or the start of actual construction, we strongly advise that you consult your local building official who can tell you if such a review is required.

ABOUT THE DESIGNS

The architects and designers whose work appears in this publication are among America's leading residential designers. Each plan was designed to meet the requirements of a nationally recognized model building code in effect at the time and place the plan was drawn. Because national building codes change from time to time, plans may not comply with any such code at the time they are sold to a customer. In addition, building officials may not accept these plans as final construction documents of record as the plans may need to be modified and additional drawings and details added to suit local conditions and requirements. We strongly advise that purchasers consult a licensed architect or engineer, and their local building official, before starting any construction related to these plans.

LOCAL BUILDING CODES AND ZONING REQUIREMENTS

At the time of creation, our plans are drawn to specifications published by the Building Officials and Code Administrators (BOCA) International, Inc.; the Southern Building Code Congress (SBCCI) International, Inc.; the International Conference of Building Officials (ICBO); or the Council of American Building Officials (CABO). Our plans are designed to meet or exceed national building standards. Because of the great differences in geography and climate throughout the United States and Canada, each state, county and municipality has its own building codes, zone requirements, ordinances and building regulations. Your plan may need to be modified to comply with local requirements regarding snow loads, energy codes, soil and seismic conditions and a wide range of other matters. In addition, you may need to obtain permits or inspections from local governments before and in the course of construction. Prior to using blueprints ordered from us, we strongly advise that you consult a licensed architect or engineer—and speak with your local building official—before applying for any permit or beginning construction. We authorize the use of our blueprints on the express condition that you strictly comply with all local building codes, zoning requirements and other applicable laws, regulations, ordinances and requirements. Notice: Plans for homes to be built in Nevada must be re-drawn by a Nevada-registered professional. Consult your building official for more information on this subject.

TOLL FREE 1-800-521-6797

REGULAR OFFICE HOURS:
8:00 a.m.-10:00 p.m. EST, Monday-Friday,
10:00 a.m.-7:00 p.m. EST Sat & Sun.

If we receive your order by 3:00 p.m. EST, Monday-Friday, we'll process it and ship within **two business days**. When ordering by phone, please have your credit card or check information ready. We'll also ask you for the Order Form Key Number at the bottom of the order form.

By FAX: Copy the Order Form on the next page and send it on our FAX line: 1-800-224-6699 or 520-544-3086.

Canadian Customers Order Toll Free 1-877-223-6389

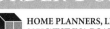

ORDER FORM

DISCLAIMER

The designers we work with have put substantial care and effort into the creation of their blueprints. However, because they cannot provide on-site consultation, supervision and control over actual construction, and because of the great variance in local building requirements, building practices and soil, seismic, weather and other conditions, WE CANNOT MAKE ANY WARRANTY, EXPRESS OR IMPLIED, WITH RESPECT TO THE CONTENT OR USE OF THE BLUEPRINTS, INCLUDING BUT NOT LIMITED TO ANY WARRANTY OF MERCHANTABILITY OR OF FITNESS FOR A PARTICULAR PURPOSE. **ITEMS, PRICES, TERMS AND CONDITIONS ARE SUBJECT TO CHANGE WITHOUT NOTICE. REPRODUCIBLE PLAN ORDERS MAY REQUIRE A CUSTOMER'S SIGNED RELEASE BEFORE SHIPPING.**

TERMS AND CONDITIONS

These designs are protected under the terms of United States Copyright Law and may not be copied or reproduced in any way, by any means, unless you have purchased Reproducibles which clearly indicate your right to copy or reproduce. We authorize the use of your chosen design as an aid in the construction of one single family home only. You may not use this design to build a second or multiple dwellings without purchasing another blueprint or blueprints or paying additional design fees.

HOW MANY BLUEPRINTS DO YOU NEED?

Although a standard building package may satisfy many states, cities and counties, some plans may require certain changes. For your convenience, we have developed a Reproducible plan which allows a local professional to modify and make up to 10 copies of your revised plan. As our plans are all copyright protected, with your purchase of the Reproducible, we will supply you with a Copyright release letter. The number of copies you may need: 1 for owner; 3 for builder; 2 for local building department and 1-3 sets for your mortgage lender.

ORDER TOLL FREE!

**For information about any of our services or to order call
1-800-521-6797**

**Browse our website:
www.eplans.com**

BLUEPRINTS ARE NOT REFUNDABLE EXCHANGES ONLY

**For Customer Service, call toll free
1-888-690-1116.**

HOME PLANNERS, LLC wholly owned by Hanley-Wood, LLC
3275 WEST INA ROAD, SUITE 110 • TUCSON, ARIZONA • 85741

THE BASIC BLUEPRINT PACKAGE
Rush me the following (please refer to the Plans Index and Price Schedule in this section):
___Set(s) of reproducibles*, plan number(s) _____ $_____
    indicate foundation type _____ surcharge (if applicable): $_____
___Set(s) of blueprints, plan number(s) _____ $_____
    indicate foundation type _____ surcharge (if applicable): $_____
___Additional identical blueprints (standard or reverse) in same order @ $50 per set $_____
___Reverse blueprints @ $50 fee per order. Right-reading reverse @ $165 surcharge $_____

IMPORTANT EXTRAS
Rush me the following:
___Materials List: $60 (Must be purchased with Blueprint set.) Add $10 for Schedule C4–L4 plans $_____
___**Quote One**® Summary Cost Report @ $29.95 for one, $14.95 for each additional,
    for plans _____ $_____
    Building location: City _____ Zip Code _____
___**Quote One**® Material Cost Report @ $120 Schedules P1–C3; $130 Schedules C4–L4,
    for plan_____(Must be purchased with Blueprints set.) $_____
    Building location: City _____ Zip Code _____
___Specification Outlines @ $10 each $_____
___Detail Sets @ $14.95 each; any two $22.95; any three $29.95; all four for $39.95 (save $19.85) $_____
    ❑ Plumbing ❑ Electrical ❑ Construction ❑ Mechanical
___Home Furniture Planner @ $15.95 each $_____

DECK BLUEPRINTS
(Please refer to the Plans Index and Price Schedule in this section)
___Set(s) of Deck Plan _____.
___Additional identical blueprints in same order @ $10 per set. $_____
___Reverse blueprints @ $10 fee per order. $_____
___Set of Standard Deck Details @ $14.95 per set. $_____
___Set of Complete Deck Construction Package (Best Buy!) Add $10 to Building Package.
    Includes Custom Deck Plan _____ Plus Standard Deck Details

LANDSCAPE BLUEPRINTS
(Please refer to the Plans Index and Price Schedule in this section.)
___Set(s) of Landscape Plan _____ $_____
___Additional identical blueprints in same order @ $10 per set $_____
___Reverse blueprints @ $10 fee per order $_____
Please indicate appropriate region of the country for Plant & Material List. Region _____

POSTAGE AND HANDLING SIGNATURE IS REQUIRED FOR ALL DELIVERIES.	1–3 sets	4+ sets
DELIVERY No CODs (Requires street address—No P.O. Boxes)		
•Regular Service (Allow 7–10 business days delivery)	❑ $20.00	❑ $25.00
•Priority (Allow 4–5 business days delivery)	❑ $25.00	❑ $35.00
•Express (Allow 3 business days delivery)	❑ $35.00	❑ $45.00
OVERSEAS DELIVERY	fax, phone or mail for quote	

Note: All delivery times are from date Blueprint Package is shipped.

POSTAGE (From box above) $_____
SUBTOTAL $_____
SALES TAX (AZ & MI residents, please add appropriate state and local sales tax.) $_____
TOTAL (Subtotal and tax) $_____

YOUR ADDRESS (please print legibly)
Name _____
Street_____
City _____State_____Zip _____
Daytime telephone number (required) (_____) _____
* Fax number (required for reproducible orders) _____
TeleCheck® Checks By Phone℠ available
FOR CREDIT CARD ORDERS ONLY
Credit card number _____ Exp. Date: (M/Y) _____
Check one ❑ Visa ❑ MasterCard ❑ Discover Card ❑ American Express

Order Form Key

HPT792

Signature (required) _____
Please check appropriate box: ❑ Licensed Builder-Contractor ❑ Homeowner

ORDER TOLL FREE!
1-800-521-6797

BY FAX: Copy the order form above and send it on our FAXLINE: 1-800-224-6699 OR 520-544-3086

HELPFUL BOOKS FROM HOME PLANNERS

TO ORDER BY PHONE **1-800-322-6797**

1 BIGGEST & BEST

1001 of our best-selling plans in one volume. 1,074 to 7,275 square feet. 704 pgs $12.95 1K1

2 ONE-STORY

450 designs for all lifestyles. 800 to 4,900 square feet. 384 pgs $9.95 OS

3 MORE ONE-STORY

475 superb one-level plans from 800 to 5,000 square feet. 448 pgs $9.95 MO2

4 TWO-STORY

443 designs for one-and-a-half and two stories. 1,500 to 6,000 square feet. 448 pgs $9.95 TS

5 VACATION

430 designs for recreation, retirement and leisure. 448 pgs $9.95 VS3

6 HILLSIDE

208 designs for split-levels, bi-levels, multi-levels and walkouts. 224 pgs $9.95 HH

7 FARMHOUSE

300 Fresh Designs from Classic to Modern. 320 pgs. $10.95 FCP

8 COUNTRY HOUSES

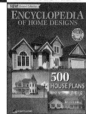

208 unique home plans that combine traditional style and modern livability. 224 pgs $9.95 CN

9 BUDGET-SMART

200 efficient plans from 7 top designers, that you can really afford to build! 224 pgs $8.95 BS

10 BARRIER-FREE

Over 1,700 products and 51 plans for accessible living. 128 pgs $15.95 UH

11 ENCYCLOPEDIA

500 exceptional plans for all styles and budgets—the best book of its kind! 528 pgs $9.95 ENC

12 ENCYCLOPEDIA II

500 completely new plans. Spacious and stylish designs for every budget and taste. 352 pgs $9.95 E2

13 AFFORDABLE

300 Modest plans for savvy homebuyers.256 pgs. $9.95 AH2

14 VICTORIAN

210 striking Victorian and Farmhouse designs from today's top designers. 224 pgs $15.95 VDH2

15 ESTATE

Dream big! Eighteen designers showcase their biggest and best plans. 224 pgs $16.95 EDH3

16 LUXURY

170 lavish designs, over 50% brand-new plans added to a most elegant collection. 192 pgs $12.95 LD3

17 EUROPEAN STYLES

200 homes with a unique flair of the Old World. 224 pgs $15.95 EURO

18 COUNTRY CLASSICS

Donald Gardner's 101 best Country and Traditional home plans. 192 pgs $17.95 DAG

19 COUNTRY

85 Charming Designs from American Home Gallery. 160 pgs. $17.95 CTY

20 TRADITIONAL

85 timeless designs from the Design Traditions Library. 160 pgs. $17.95 TRA

21 COTTAGES

245 Delightful retreats from 825 to 3,500 square feet. 256 pgs. $10.95 COOL

22 CABINS TO VILLAS

Enchanting Homes for Mountain Sea or Sun, from the Sater collection. 144 pgs $19.95 CCV

23 CONTEMPORARY

The most complete and imaginative collection of contemporary designs available anywhere. 256 pgs. $10.95 CM2

24 FRENCH COUNTRY

Live every day in the French countryside using these plans, landscapes and interiors. 192 pgs. $14.95 PN

25 SOUTHERN

207 homes rich in Southern styling and comfort. 240 pgs $8.95 SH

26 SOUTHWESTERN

138 designs that capture the spirit of the Southwest. 144 pgs $10.95 SW

27 SHINGLE-STYLE

155 Home plans from Classic Colonials to Breezy Bungalows. 192 pgs. $12.95 SNG

28 NEIGHBORHOOD

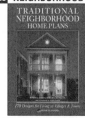

170 designs with the feel of main street America. 192 pgs $12.95 TND

29 CRAFTSMAN

170 Home plans in the Craftsman and Bungalow style. 192 pgs $12.95 CC

30 GRAND VISTAS

200 Homes with a View. 224 pgs $10.95 GV

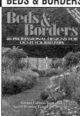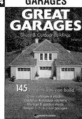

FOR FASTER SERVICE ORDER ONLINE AT
www.hwspecials.com

HEAT-N-GLO
1-888-427-3973
WWW.HEATNGLO.COM

Heat-N-Glo offers quality gas, woodburning and electric fireplaces, including gas log sets, stoves, and inserts for preexisting fireplaces. Now available gas grills and outdoor fireplaces. Send for a free brochure.

Ideas for your next project. Beautiful, durable, elegant low-maintenance millwork, mouldings, balustrade systems and much more. For your free catalog please call us at 1-800-446-3040 or visit www.stylesolutionsinc.com.

ARISTOKRAFT
ONE MASTERBRAND CABINETS DRIVE
JASPER, IN 47546
(812) 482-2527
WWW.ARISTOKRAFT.COM

Aristokraft offers you superb value, outstanding quality and great style that fit your budget. Transform your great ideas into reality with popular styles and features that reflect your taste and lifestyle. $5.00

THERMA-TRU DOORS
1687 WOODLANDS DRIVE
MAUMEE, OH 43537
1-800-THERMA-TRU
WWW.THERMATRU.COM

The undisputed brand leader, Therma-Tru specializes in fiberglass and steel entry doors for every budget. Excellent craftsmanship, energy efficiency and variety make Therma-Tru the perfect choice for all your entry door needs.

---

225 GARDEN, LANDSCAPE
AND PROJECT PLANS
TO ORDER, CALL
1-800-322-6797

225 Do-It-Yourself designs that help transform boring yards into exciting outdoor entertainment spaces. Gorgeous gardens, luxurious landscapes, dazzling decks and other outdoor amenities. Complete construction blueprints available for every project. Only $19.95 (plus $4 shipping/handling).

HAVE WE GOT PLANS FOR YOU!

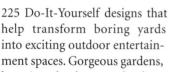

Your online source for home designs and ideas. Find thousands of plans from the nation's top designers...all in one place. Plus, links to the best known names in building supplies and services.